THE UFO CONSPIRACY

THE
UFO
CONSPIRACY

The First Forty Years

JENNY RANDLES

JAVELIN BOOKS
LONDON · NEW YORK · SYDNEY

First published in the UK 1987 by Blandford Press
This Javelin Books edition first published 1988
Artillery House, Artillery Row, London SW1P 1RT

Distributed in the United States by
Sterling Publishing Co., Inc.,
2 Park Avenue, New York, NY 10016

Distributed in Australia by
Capricorn Link (Australia) Pty Ltd,
PO Box 665, Lane Cove, NSW 2066

British Library Cataloguing in Publication Data

Randles, Jenny
 The UFO conspiracy : the first forty years.
 1. Unidentified flying objects—History
 I. Title
 001.9'42'09   TL789

ISBN 0 7137 1867 6

Typeset by Word Perfect 99 Ltd
Printed in Great Britain by The Guernsey Press Ltd.,
Guernsey, C.I.

CONTENTS

PART FOUR: THE UFO COVER-UP

AUTHOR'S NOTE

On 24 June 1947 an American pilot saw a group of strange objects in the sky. He described them as moving 'like saucers skipping across water'. From this an anonymous journalist invented the term 'flying saucer', later adapted by Captain Ed Ruppelt, the USAF intelligence officer responsible for such matters, to the more familiar UFO (Unidentified Flying Object). Four decades have elapsed since such events. In that time the UFO mystery has gone through many phases – but now we have all the facts, accumulations of evidence and major revelations through the official study projects operated by the world's leading nations. It is time to set these things before you and assess the situation forty years on.

Let us keep in mind that the UFO phenomenon may represent an even greater reality. It is our choice to treat it as a threat or an opportunity for human knowledge.

(Part of the address given to the United Nations on 27 November 1978 by Dr Jacques Vallée, now the world's principal UFO scientist.)

This book is dedicated to Dr J. Allen Hynek, who left the earth with Halley's Comet during 1986. We shall continue the fight for truth in his honour.

INTRODUCTION

Both 'UFO' and 'Conspiracy' are emotive words. Put them together in a single phrase, as I have done, and you produce what some will call sensationalism. But I am not about to offer cheap thrills as a substitute for truth. I do mean all that I write and believe that what I say can be simply demonstrated. This book is a catalogue of facts, not of dreams.

It is popular, especially in the USA, to say that a 'cover-up' of UFO reality by official sources is responsible for all the problems that beset this subject. That is a rather naive statement. Many of the difficulties stem from the basic inadequacies of amateur investigators, who have turned to the sky in search of a fairy tale rather than the truth. However, the suggestion that an attitude of disinformation prevails on some vast scale – so vast it is often called 'the Cosmic Watergate' – is surprisingly justified if you look deep enough.

This recognition provokes countless questions. *Why* should the existence of this phenomenon be hidden? After all, UFOs are seen by hundreds of thousands of people and can not very easily be denied. *How* could any significant breakthroughs be withheld from public gaze for more than a very short while? Surely *somebody* would want to blow wide open the story of the century?

I have no intention of running away from such matters. However, before we begin there are a few overriding points to consider.

UFOs exist. The evidence that will confront you in the pages that follow makes that conclusion inescapable if you accept that science is about learning *new* things. We know more in 1987 than we did in 1937. There will be wonders in 2037 we have not the slightest inkling of right now. Anyone who says UFOs are impossible, because scientists have not 'discovered' them, has no understanding of what scientists do.

UFOs have also been investigated by every major government on earth, and are *still* being studied at an official level in China, France, Spain, the USSR, the USA, *and* the United Kingdom – to name but six leading nations. If UFOs were 'bunk', or of no great importance, do you really think every leading power and super power would make the same crass error and submit to this absurdity?

Yet, and here lies the rub, these nations (except one or two who are refreshingly open) play a dangerous game of double bluff. Their records and their actions speak for themselves. I have not conjured up some imaginative scenario, but have based this story on official documents and statements by people from the heart of the matter. These demonstrate a total concern about the UFO mystery. However, in strange contradiction of this, the public statements of these people mislead and sometimes lie. They downplay importance, denounce witnesses, refute investigations, and cast around a smokescreen of apathy that would be extremely worrying − if we could think for more than a moment that it was not a charade. To disregard the awesome facts staring blankly at us all would be a demonstration of ineptitude and incompetence so enormous that none of us could sleep soundly in our beds. For we trust our very lives to these people, who now hold in their hands many ways to destroy our planet − not the least of which is an electronic arsenal of deadly weapons.

It has to be inconceivable that inexplicable objects dancing across our skies would get the categorical brush-off after four decades of study. They do not. These official investigations continue; which, any application of logic will tell you, means we *have* made some discoveries of apparent importance. No government in these economy-conscious days throws money down the drain after a non-existent phenomenon.

That said, ask yourself one question. Why are you being *told* that the phenomenon is non-existent?

If the major powers consort to deny something they are all taking very seriously, we are left to speculate. Of course, we might be wrong in such speculation, but it seems appropriate to assume that they have good reasons for the perpetuation of the myth of UFO nonsense. Reasons that may also be potentially disturbing.

Put these facts together in a bowl and stir. Whatever combination of the truth emerges is up to your own credibility threshold. I am not about to try to force any option onto you. I contend very simply that one thing is clear: the public is being deceived on a colossal scale. Ordinary citizens are being labelled 'fools' for honestly describing what they saw. The media is being manipulated by force-fed information that directs it towards required goals. Science is being hoodwinked by the powers-that-be, who may well want to preserve the monopoly they hold for research within the secret services.

I submit that this *does* meet the requirements to be called a conspiracy.

Jenny Randles,
September 1986

Part One:

THE
UFO
INVASION

1 THE UFOs ARRIVE – JUNE 1947

The magnificent peaks of the Cascade Mountains glistened in the sunshine. Through the thin air the snow-capped summit of Mount Rainier rose to a height of 4392 m (14,400 ft). Further in the distance stood the brooding volcano of Mount St Helens, dormant and forgotten but awaiting its moment of destiny. In 1980 it would blister with alarming speed as steam and lava built within. Then it would explode into one, final, cataclysmic act of devastation.

Kenneth Arnold, 32, from Boise, Idaho, had more on his mind than the breathtaking scenery. It was Tuesday, 24 June 1947 – an ordinary, summer's day. At least it should have been. In fact, it was a date that changed history.

Arnold, like many post-war Americans, enjoyed a small degree of affluence. This allowed him to fly his own light aircraft around the five states that formed his domain. As a reasonably successful businessman the new Callair model gave him freedom to roam the north-western territories and land in rough fields and pastures.

That day he had left Chehalis in Washington State to head south-east on the long voyage home. He was due to stop at Yakima *en route,* but first he was taking an hour-long detour to search for a missing aircraft. It was a US Marine Curtiss C—46 Commando transport plane that had gone down somewhere in the mountains. As a search and rescue flyer and deputy federal marshal it was his duty to keep a lookout for signs of the accident. He was always quite willing to go out of his way to help fellow aeronauts who might be in trouble.

Besides, this was such a beautiful day to be at one with the elements.

Sadly, Kenneth Arnold never found that missing craft, but he did find the greatest puzzle of the twentieth century.

It was approaching 3 pm as the pilot cruised through the crystal-clear skies at just over 2800 m (9000 ft). Suddenly, a bright flash glinted on his canopy. The strong sunlight was reflecting off something far in the distance, which was heading very rapidly south. He guessed that it had to be at least 30 km (18½ miles) away.

Concentrating now on the thing in the sky, it was obvious that this was not one single object but a line of flattened, crescent-shaped discs. There seemed to be nine of them, in an echelon formation, not unlike that of a flock of flying geese. They were linked almost in a magical fashion, yet ducked and bobbed and then rose as they moved. It was this sudden dipping which made them catch the sun and flash very brightly.

Later, Arnold said of these objects that 'they were flat like a pie-can, and so shiny that they reflected the sun's rays like a mirror'. He was naturally very surprised. In an interview with the famous American radio journalist, Ed Murrow, on 7 April 1950, Arnold added, 'I was baffled by the fact that they did not have any tails . . . I judged their wing-span to be at least 100 ft (30 m) across. Their sighting did not particularly disturb me at the time, except that I had never seen planes of that type.'

It was certainly a mystery to this experienced pilot. He told Murrow, 'I never could understand why the world got so upset about 9 discs, as these things didn't seem to be a menace. I believed that they had something to do with our Army and Air Force.' Even so, they had no tails, and no wings. They were totally unlike anything he had ever witnessed before.

Using his skills at navigation he timed their flight against two peaks, whose distance apart he could later measure. Gauging the speed from his cockpit clock, he worked out something utterly incredible. They were moving well in excess of 1600 km (1000 miles) per hour. In 1947 that outdid everything a man-made plane could achieve. He began to wonder not only if these were secret weapons, but also if they were of this earth.

When he landed at Yakima he told some friends about what had happened. Later he flew on to Pendleton, a small airfield just over the border into Oregon. Upon arrival he was greeted by a posse of journalists eager to learn more. Arnold had no idea of the monster he had just unleashed onto the world.

Of course, free publicity would not harm his business potential. Selling fire-fighting equipment was a lucrative field and a few cynics did question his motives. Indeed it did seem curious that other pilots from Boise began to see UFOs too – and Arnold himself claimed other sightings. Nevertheless he insisted that his observations over Mount Rainier were not a stunt and he retained his passionate interest in the subject until his death in 1984. It seems highly unlikely that such lasting concern would result from a figment of his imagination.

Quite why the story spread as it did nobody fully understands. Perhaps the world needed an antidote after the horrors of war. Arnold did tell his adventure in graphic detail and used words that were tailor-made for posterity. In fact there was a minor misunderstanding that created the name by which we now know the phenomenon. He had explained to newsmen that the objects he saw had skipped through the atmosphere in the same way as you might cast a saucer across a pool of calm water and make it bounce as many times as you can. He had *not* claimed that the craft were saucer-shaped, but the name 'flying saucers' was immediately invented. It was a priceless tag-line for this wonderful tale. The media used it well and encouraged other observers to come forward.

A great new mystery was before the world. Most people said it would not last the summer and like all nine-day wonders would quickly disappear; but most people were very wrong.

The UFOs had arrived, and forty years later they seem determined to stay.

This flying saucer situation is not all imaginary or seeing too much in some natural phenomenon. Something is really flying around.

(Conclusion to a July 1947 FBI/Army intelligence study report, based on a detailed analysis of the Arnold case, and fifteen other UFO encounters reported during the first month of the 'flying saucer' mystery. Declassified in 1976 by the American 'Freedom of Information' Act.)

Oddly enough the Kenneth Arnold sighting was *not* the first. Today we recognise that a growing 'wave' of reports began that same month in the USA, although very few were made public. Even the intelligence analysis just quoted carries the Mount Rainier case as number four in its list. The first seems to have been at fifteen minutes after noon on 19 May 1947 when three railway employees at Manitou Springs in Colorado observed some small silvery objects through binoculars.

However, there can be no denying that the Washington State encounter brought the mystery to life. It made everybody talk about these aerial visions. What were they? Where did they come from? Were they American or Russian? If neither, could they be visitors from another world? Within a few weeks almost everyone knew what a 'flying saucer' was, and many were out looking for them. A deluge of cases flooded into the newspapers and military bases. The pressure on the authorities to do something about the matter became irresistible.

Nobody seemed very keen to shoulder the responsibility. If these things *were* secret weapons, the Americans knew that they could not be 'friendly'. They had to be either Soviet or alien. For the Communist bloc to test such powerful craft in such a brazen way over enemy territory was a thought too awful to contemplate, but it had to be considered. This explains why the FBI (to check out witnesses for communist sympathies) and the Army-Air Force (to study the flight characteristics of these 'weapons') both had to get in on the act very quickly.

It also explains why there was almost paranoid secrecy.

Of course, from the point of view of the government, it might well have been preferable if the objects did prove to be spaceships. It was the least disturbing alternative!

In fact, the Kenneth Arnold sighting was rather untypical. Many that have followed it are far more strange and worrying. Multiple objects in formation are not at all common, and are often suggestive of an explanation. However, the encounter over Mount Rainier began man's forty-year love affair with these mysterious visitors.

Reasonable suggestions were quickly put forward. Did Arnold see an unusual mirage of the mountain peaks, produced by the very clear air and warm weather? This is not such a strange idea. Most of us are familiar with mirages in the summer, where pools of water appear to form on a roadway ahead, and when you drive towards them they disappear. This is because nothing was there in the first place. They are images of the sky transposed onto the ground by the way light rays bend through hot and cold air masses. Something similar *might* have happened over the Cascade Mountains that day in 1947.

Dr J. Allen Hynek, called in as a scientific consultant by the authorities a few months later, pointed out that Arnold's estimate of distance and object size did not agree. If they were 30 km away, in order for Arnold to see them as 'recognisable' objects the craft would have had to be enormous, the size of mountains. If they were far smaller, as the witness believed, then they could not have been more than a few km away. This in turn reduces their speed to one *not* impossible for moving aircraft. Of course, if a mirage was involved this itself would be stationary, and it would be the motion of Arnold's plane that would create the illusion of movement.

Hynek concluded, in the government's (then secret) files: 'In view of the above (the objects) were travelling at subsonic speeds and may, therefore, have been some sort of known aircraft.' However, the intelligence men had checked this out. No aircraft were around. The possibility could not apply. Instead the case was recorded as a 'mirage' in the final list of statistics, when all 13,000 cases which the US Air Force ultimately compiled were declassified in 1976.

Arnold himself never bought the 'official' verdict. As an experienced pilot who had flown the Cascades many times we must respect his opinion. He was there and we were not. In stating his reasons why it could not be a mirage (declassified statement which was written on 12 July 1947) Arnold points out; 'I observed these objects not only through the glass of my airplane but turned my airplane sideways where I could open my window and observe them with a completely unobstructed view [without sunglasses].' This certainly would make a mirage explanation rather unlikely.

Not for the last time we see two major problems of the official UFO records. Explanations used to dismiss them from all further consideration often fail to correspond with the facts at hand. We are left with a very difficult choice. An apparently sober, sincere and honest witness − whose background usually checks out as near to impeccable – has reported something which goes against all our expectations. It is easy to escape by claiming that the witness *must* be wrong; but what if that witness were yourself? How would you feel to be told that what you *know* you saw with your own two eyes *cannot* have been there, because scientists (who have probably never met you and were certainly not with you at the time of the events) have decreed that what you claim is impossible.

This is the outcome now faced by hundreds of thousands of witnesses throughout the world. Can they all be wrong?

It would not be surprising if the Arnold sighting *were* explained. Most serious UFO investigators (inside and outside the government authorities!) recognise that between 80 and 90 per cent of cases can be reduced to misperceptions of one form or another. The 24 June 1947 case remains in abeyance, but its importance is not lessened. It was the first. It set the mould. From that day on the world could never be the same.

As the American military wrestled with the headaches that each new day and its dozens of sightings brought to them, there was an exciting question before mankind.

For years we had dreamt of life on other worlds. Science-fiction writers and *Flash Gordon* movies had used this to enthrall us. Now the reality stared our planet in the face.

The universe is a big place, and we might not live here alone.

2   DID WE CATCH ONE? – JULY 1947

Roswell, New Mexico, 1500 miles south-east of the Cascade Mountains lies amidst a land of hot deserts scarred in two quite different ways. The sun beats down relentlessly, baking the earth into weird rock formations; but an invisible power also cooks the dust. For it was here, in the research and test grounds of White Sands, Los Alamos and Alamogordo, that atomic weapons were developed and exploded: a cry to the universe that man had come of age – or that we could now destroy ourselves.

Is it mere coincidence that this special place became the centre of the first true conspiracy of the UFO era, or that it became the focus for many baffling encounters?

On 2 July 1947, at about 9.50 pm, a large glowing object appeared in the sky above New Mexico. It was seen to head north-west for the desert near Corona. Hardware-dealer Dan Wilmot and his wife reported it. Just one more UFO in the fast-mounting pile. If you bear in mind what local farmer William Brazel has to say, however, then it may have been far more than that.

A thunderstorm was raging, with fierce lightning cracking the sky in countless jagged beams. Amidst the tumult Brazel heard a mysterious explosion. It did not sound like thunder, but he assumed that it had to be. Next day, in the hot sun, the desert was scattered with debris – peculiar, light-coloured metal fragments. Something had evidently blown apart above the ground, dropping pieces onto the desert before continuing its interrupted flight. Had a plane been struck by lightning and lost part of its fuselage? The rancher thought little more about it at the time.

That same day a man called Barnett was working out at Magdalene, about 150 miles away (on the course the Wilmots' UFO had been heading). He found something shiny reflecting in the sand. Going to investigate, he discovered wreckage of what seemed to be a disc, 9 metres (30 feet) across. Later a military truck arrived and supervised the investigation of the crash site. Perhaps this was some experimental aircraft that had suffered unexpected calamity. Although he did not know about the Roswell sighting, or Brazel's curious find by his ranch, Barnett did not believe that this was so. He had very good reason. He had seen bodies – apparently

18

dead and thrown from the wreck. They were not wearing army uniforms. In fact they did not look human. From a distance it was hard to see detail, but they seemed to be wearing silvery suits, and they were only 1 metre (3 feet) tall!

That *something* happened near Roswell in July 1947 is undeniable. For we now have reams of first-hand testimony and documents obtained under the American Freedom of Information Act. They confirm what the witnesses are saying.

Of course, if this incident *was* a UFO crash, confusion would have reigned. Nobody would have known what to do. Eventually decisions would have been swift and incisive, and if it ever happened again the authorities would be prepared. On this first occasion, however, mistakes might be expected. That is exactly what the facts seem to tell us.

On 6 July 1947, three days after Brazel first found the debris, he drove into the nearest town and learned of the stories about flying saucers. Was this what had crashed, he wondered? He told the local sheriff, who in turn called Roswell Air Force Base. Responding to the call, the officer in charge of intelligence, Major (later Lt. Col.) Jesse Marcel, made the trek out to the Brazel ranch. It was so out of the way that an overnight stop was necessary. When he saw the extraordinary crash material he determined to collect it all and notify his commanding officer right away. There was no doubt in his mind this was a significant discovery.

Meanwhile an information officer back at the base had jumped the gun and leaked the story, believing it to be something of public concern. He was severely chastised later, but the most important thing at that time was to stifle the 'rumour'. This occurred very swiftly, but not before many people had heard it.

One of these was a certain RCAF officer, then driving across the American mid-west. He distinctly recalls following the story on the local news bulletins until the items on the 'UFO crash' suddenly ceased. When he reached his destination on the eastern seaboard a couple of days later he expected the story to be world headlines. In fact nobody outside New Mexico seemed to have known about it. This officer went on to become a TV celebrity in Britain, hosting quiz shows like *Double Your Money* and the talent programme *Opportunity Knocks*. His name was Hughie Green.

With the debris back at the Roswell base Brigadier General Roger Ramey came onto the scene to supervise matters. He was extremely concerned about the premature release of information which is evidenced by an FBI memo (now released by Freedom of Information, sometimes abbreviated to FoI). This was from Dallas, Texas, to the FBI headquarters, and was dated 6.17 pm on 8 July 1947 – twenty-four hours after the wreckage had been ferried back by Major Marcel. The memo is labelled 'Urgent' and headed 'Flying Disc – Information Concerning'. It says, in part, 'Major Curtan,

HQ eighth air force, telephonically advised this office that an object purporting to be a flying disc was recovered near Roswell, New Mexico, this date . . . Information provided this office because of national interest in case and fact that [certain media sources] attempting to break story of location of disc today.'

An official release (watered down somewhat) had been issued by the base a few hours before this notice to the FBI, but General Ramey was still worried enough to require a complete dismissal of the case. He ordered that a 'cover story' be set up. Major Marcel was sent with the wreckage (it filled an entire bomber plane!) to Wright Field (later Wright Patterson Air Force Base, Dayton, Ohio). Situated there was the Foreign Technology Division of the Army/Air Force. It was also there that the official government UFO project was set into motion a few weeks later.

At the same time as this move, a statement was being publicly released that explained the whole affair as a mistake. The debris was just the remains of one of their own weather balloons, which none of the officers at Roswell had seemingly been able to identify. Because of this it would *not* be flown to Wright Field.

Despite that, the FBI memo says it *was* 'being transported to Wright Field by special plane for examination . . . Major Curtan advised would request Wright Field to advise (FBI) results of examination.' If they did, then these results have never been made available under FoI.

Researchers William Moore and Stanton Friedman have provided outstanding evidence (of which this summary is but a fraction) that supports the reality of these events. We do not know anything about the supposed disc and aliens discovered at Magdalene (if we are to believe Barnett). As for the debris at Corona, it was remarkably light; yet exceptionally tough, metallic in appearance but different from any known metal and covered partially by pictorial markings not unlike hieroglyphics! The same description has come independently from many people who saw it, including the (now retired) Lt. Col. Jesse Marcel himself.

Something crashed. It is almost impossible to believe that it was just a balloon. The evidence that this was a deliberate invention to buy time and put the public off the scent seems overwhelming. If it was not a balloon then what was it, and why do the authorities continue to lie?

It was definitely not a weather or tracking device, nor was it any sort of plane or missile . . . It was something I had never seen before, or since . . . it certainly wasn't anything built by us.

(Extract from an interview about the Roswell crash given in 1979 by the intelligence officer who was first on the scene in 1947, then Major Jesse Marcel.)

These stories are typical of those collected by Moore and others. In his careful papers (published between 1980 and 1985) he has discovered a staggering array of witnesses. Their testimony is consistent and very hard to refute. Yet its consequences are astonishing.

Within little more than a week of the Kenneth Arnold sighting, one of his 'flying saucers' seems to have *crashed* in New Mexico. If the evidence is correct then the answer to at least part of the UFO mystery was in the hands of the authorities forty years ago, but remains hidden as the biggest secret on earth. If the evidence is false, then an awful lot of people (ordinary citizens, military officers, scientists and government officials) are liars.

Historian Dr David Jacobs points out the difficulties of such a cover-up. 'A recovered UFO would constitute arguably the most important scientific event in the history of mankind.' Hundreds of scientists would have to be involved. Thousands of photographs, sample reports and documents would exist. Because of this, 'Over the years secrecy would be increasingly more difficult to maintain. More and more people would have to know about the UFO.' Including, one imagines, all the Presidents since Truman. Unless, of course, nobody told them! This raises all manner of ethical questions. To keep from society the existence of an alien artefact would be a crime against science. It does seem inconceivable that such a conspiracy could be maintained without leaks.

Nevertheless there *have* been leaks. As Dr Richard Hall challenges, there is 'a small but growing body of credible reports, along with some supplementary data and documentation . . . The information is of a calibre that cannot be offhandedly dismissed.' It involves sworn affidavits and first-person testimony, sometimes obtained freely, but often with great reluctance from the person concerned. These people have been tracked down by researchers like William Moore or his colleague Leonard Stringfield (whose data files on this topic argue a strong case that at least *two* crashes have happened).

Two crashes? Indeed. Aside from the Roswell affair in 1947, there appears to be independent corroboration of a second incident at Kingman, Arizona. This comes from a Naval Intelligence officer who spoke of bodies he had seen being offloaded at Wright Patterson Air Force Base, allegedly flown there from Kingman. An engineer involved in Atomic Energy Commission work with the US Air Force claims that he was taken with other specialists in blacked-out buses to a desert site near Kingman on 21 May 1953. At the location he saw a 9 metre (30 foot) diameter disc embedded in the sand and a humanoid figure almost 1 metre (3 feet) tall, inside a tent and under guard. It appeared to be dead. He has sworn a legal document to this effect and his diaries from the time (although cryptic) certainly confirm he was on a 'special mission' at the stated period.

There are even medical men who say they have studied these bodies. All their accounts generally agree with one another. Taken together they form either the greatest fairytale of all time or the biggest untold secret.

One can perhaps imagine a blanket of secrecy to protect early disclosure of this discovery. The West may well have wanted to learn the UFO technology first. Why, though, after all this time, does it remain a secret? If this *is* true there seem to be limited possibilities. Perhaps the technology is still beyond us. It may be like a Stone Age man trying to figure out the workings of an atomic reactor. Perhaps an agreement was reached with whoever (or whatever) pilots these craft. In exchange for their friendliness, their presence would be hidden. If such a bargain has been struck, did we have any choice in the matter? In a war between pea-shooters and atom bombs there can only be one victor. If there *are* aliens who have craft that can cross the galaxy, it is a fair bet they have weapons that could devastate the earth.

Between 1947 and 1952 (whilst the atomic tests were at their peak) the number of UFO sightings around New Mexico reached an extraordinary level. Often they involved green balls of light that behaved exceedingly strangely and moved exceptionally fast. Noted scientist Dr Lincoln La Paz masterminded Project Twinkle, an ultra-secret study to attempt to understand them. These things had succeeded in penetrating one of the most intensive security nets in the USA, and they had done so as if it did not exist.

We still do not know what these 'green fireballs' were. As soon as sophisticated monitor stations were set up to examine them, the fireballs moved. When the stations were moved the fireballs vanished! They were not meteors – La Paz (a meteor expert) was adamant on that. They were examined in top-secret meetings by many worried scientists, with security clearances that went through the roof. These included Dr Edward Teller, the 'father' of the H-bomb.

The New Mexico UFOs certainly were real. Many scientists (including La Paz) saw them, as did Intelligence officers. The only question the meetings had before them was what on earth (or off it) these things might be! Whilst they continued to zip through the heart of atomic weapons research it is hardly surprising that the UFO subject was considered to be of the utmost secrecy.

Had it been otherwise the authorities would have been derelict in their duty.

. . . the Air Force knew by the middle of July 1947 that saucers were real and not man-made . . . the technology represented by the [recovered] *disc . . . was so far beyond our own that it could not be understood immediately . . . Therefore it would be necessary to treat the disc as a military secret. This would mean containing all information about it within some small group.*

(Part of paper by US Navy Physicist, Dr Bruce Maccabee.)

---

3 OPERATION INTERCEPT – 1948

With the Soviets practically eliminated as a UFO source the idea of interplanetary spaceships was becoming more popular.
(Captain Edward J. Ruppelt, USAF Intelligence, head of UFO investigation study.)

By early 1948 the US Air Force had already established UFO reality to their own satisfaction. Lt. General Nathan F. Twining, Chief of Staff of what was then still the US Army, had called for a security coding to be granted to what was being colloquially named 'Project Saucer'. He said, 'The phenomenon reported is something real and not visionary or fictitious.' Advising his boss, Brigadier General George Shulgen, produced a rapid response. On 30 December 1947 the order (with a '2A' classification security) initiated 'Project Sign'. Wright Patterson Air Force Base in Dayton, Ohio, was given responsibility for the project.

Eight days later Wright Patterson were having a nightmare.

On 7 January 1948, at 1.15 pm, several people at Maysville, Kentucky, called the local highway patrol to report seeing an unidentified object high in the sky. The police contacted the tower at Godman Field, an air base 80 miles west of the town. They had no aircraft in the vicinity but agreed to check with Wright Patterson. The situation board here showed no traffic either.

At about 1.35 pm the police phoned Godman again. This time they had received calls from more towns much further to the west. If the same object was involved in both these sightings it was either exceptionally high (to be visible over a vast area) or moving exceedingly fast. The locations of the 1.15 and 1.35 calls were 140 miles apart.

The suggestion was that this had been a fast-moving object, because witnesses at the second location (Owensboro) had described a similar large, round thing moving to the west at what was termed 'a pretty good clip'. Godman were forced to check again, but there was still no aircraft that ought to be there. They also realised that if this was a genuine 'intruder' it had whizzed past them just to the north of the base, assuming its course had been steady.

At 1.45 pm T. Sergeant Quinton Blackwell, assistant tower operator at Godman, scanned the skies to the *south* of the base (presumably having seen nothing in the north or west). Here he picked out a dim light in the hazy sky. It seemed to be static and so he called his superior, Lt. Orner, who in turn brought out the operations officer, Captain Carter, and eventually the base commander, Colonel Guy Hix. Hix did not arrive until 2.20 pm, and the object was still more or less in the same position, looking like 'an ice-cream cone' through binoculars. Other descriptions tell of a 'parachute canopy' or 'an umbrella'.

The original reports from Maysville and Owensboro seem extremely hard to relate with this stationary thing south of the base. It is more than possible that the officers, alerted by the supposed presence of a UFO, had scoured the heavens until they found a light which they *assumed* was the object. In reality it was not what had traversed 140 miles on an east-to-west course in just twenty minutes.

Whilst the military personnel at Godman were trying to puzzle out their dim light in the sky, four North American F—51 Mustang trainer aircraft of the National Guard flew fatefully into their traffic zone. Captain Thomas Mantell, bound for a rendezvous with destiny, was in charge of what was actually a ferrying mission bound from Georgia to Standiford Field, just to the north in Kentucky. At about 2.40 pm they passed overhead, having arrived from more or less the point in the sky where the UFO was hovering. They had seen nothing. Nevertheless, the baffled officers suggested that Mantell and his men might go and take a look.

One plane, low on fuel, went straight to Standiford. The other three, led by Mantell, turned around and set after the object. Those on the ground vectored him towards it and Mantell, perhaps bravely, perhaps recklessly, made a spiralling climb. It is alleged that none of the F—51s were fitted with oxygen masks and to ascend anywhere much over 15,000 feet would be extremely foolish. Pilots have it drummed into them during the training that above such an ascent the air is so thin that they risk losing consciousness with almost certainly fatal consequences. Yet this risk is precisely the one which Thomas Mantell decided to take.

At 2.45 pm his F—51 was well ahead of his two wingmen, who were desperately trying to tell Mantell that they could go no higher, and that he ought to give up the chase. One of them is reported to have got to 20,000 feet before descending. Mantell was last seen at 22,500 feet, still climbing and saying that he would level off at 25,000 feet for just a few minutes.

In a recent evaluation of this case T. Scott Crain has suggested that the pilot *did* have oxygen. It is true that this has always been presumed not to be the case, but it is also known that Mantell's home base was not the same as his fellows, and all we know for sure is that *they* did not have any oxygen. Crain asks why an experienced flyer would behave in this manner *unless* he felt secure. A long-term friend of the man, having told the Air Force enquiry into the matter that it was inconceivable that Mantell would disregard safety rules, added 'unless he was after something that he believed to be more important than his life or his family'.

The last (garbled) messages from Mantell as he rose out of communication were picked up on the ground, but not recorded. There was agreement and disagreement amongst Godman tower operators who heard them. They accept that he *had* seen the object 'above and ahead of me', and some thought he said it was 'metallic and tremendous in size'. At about 3.15 pm he was still trying to close in but apparently getting no nearer. One of the wingmen, who also caught a brief glimpse of the object, says that it looked like a 'teardrop' and 'seemed fluid'. These are similar descriptions to those offered by the ground observers.

A more interesting, yet dubious, claim comes second-hand via someone who was a friend of this wingman. He supposedly was informed 'confidentially' that the airman had seen the UFO more clearly. As explained to investigator Leonard Stringfield, it had seemed to release a beam that had struck Mantell's F—51! The reality status of this uncorroborated account must remain in doubt, although Stringfield regards it as sincere.

One of the F—51s landed, refuelled and took off after the now missing pilot. He did not find Mantell's aircraft or the UFO. At 3.45 pm, after two hours, during which it had merely drifted a little to the west, Godman finally lost sight of the UFO from the ground. About one hour later came the news that Mantell's F—51 had crashed, destroying the plane and killing its pilot. His watch had stopped at 3.18 pm. A ground witness had seen the F—51, but *not* the UFO, reporting that it had plunged in an almost vertical dive and broken up in mid-air.

The final link in this disturbing case came from an anonymous caller who (at about 3.50 pm) telephoned Godman field to say that he had seen an object in the sky south of Madisonville (even further west of the base than Owensboro and over 200 miles from the first sighting location at Maysville). He had been foxed by the light until he studied it through a telescope, then he had identified it as a balloon. Quite why he then bothered to report it to the Air Force remains unknown.

The official accident investigation was handled with urgency and in silence, although the fact of the crash was impossible to hide, as were the civilian UFO sightings that seemed (to many) to have an obvious bearing. The Air Force knew that the cry would easily emerge that Mantell had been shot from the skies by dastardly aliens, if they gave even a hint that they too were taking such a view quite seriously! This 'ray gun' theory for Mantell's death has been a popular myth of the past forty years, but has almost no substance. Not even the most biased UFO researcher has disputed the basic Air Force stance on the *reason* for the crash, that the pilot blacked out due to lack of oxygen, lost control of his aircraft and did not regain consciousness before it hit the ground. He had certainly made no attempt to eject.

Of course, what does remain in considerable doubt is exactly what Mantell was chasing when he met his terrible fate.

According to Captain Ed Ruppelt, when he later became head of the Air Force UFO investigation project, he had to reconstruct the details from a half-destroyed micro-film record. Crucial facts (e.g. the names of Mantell's wingmen) were missing from the reports he took over in 1952, less than five years after the crash. However, he says that the files demonstrated that the intelligence officers who were involved quickly formed the impression that Mantell had died in pursuit of a UFO, and that the UFO was probably a spaceship! Of course, no such explanation could be offered to the public. It would provoke enormous panic and pressure for information the Air Force could not then give, because they had no idea what was going on themselves. So an answer – any answer – was necessary.

Fortunately, they had just taken on a professional astronomer, Dr J. Allen Hynek from the Ohio University, and Wright Patterson used him as a scientific consultant to try to resolve the puzzling cases. Hynek had calculated that the planet Venus (brightest 'star' in the heavens) was in more or less the exact point south of Godman where the UFO had been observed. Planets, just like the sun, do drift slowly west as the day drags on, exactly as the object witnessed had apparently done.

This make-do solution was accepted by most folk, willing to put the UFO business down to a fad or delusion in any event. Those who had seen something themselves, or who had spoken to the growing number of witnesses, or simply had more faith in the intelligence of Air Force pilots, became very suspicious of the motives behind this dismal excuse for an explanation.

In their written accounts the Air Force team were far more cautious and more interested in the possibility of a balloon being to blame. Sadly for them, they could find no shred of evidence that a balloon ought to have been where the UFO was. So their report concluded, 'it might have been Venus or it could have been a balloon. Maybe two balloons. It probably was Venus except that this is doubtful because Venus was too dim to be seen in the afternoon'. This masterpiece of gobbledegook was not made public in 1948. It takes little skill at translation to realise that it really means the Air Force did not have a clue, but desperately wanted to create the illusion that they had solved the case.

In 1952 Hynek went public when demolishing the Venus answer. The planet *is* bright (at night) but can only be seen as a tiny speck of light on exceptionally clear days and if you know precisely where to look for it. 7

January 1948 was *not* a clear day and something much more substantial than a speck of light had been reported. It is just about possible that the observers from the Godman tower had found Venus by scanning the horizon with binoculars. It is very improbable this is what Mantell saw. Venus, of course, was not the object that moved from Maysville to Owensboro in twenty minutes.

Looking back with the benefit of hindsight Captain Ruppelt was under no external pressure to solve the case quickly. He also knew that a classified navy project had launched 'sky hook' balloons from southern Ohio in the late 1940s. Such objects could climb very high, were metallic in appearance, would be readily described as 'teardrop' or 'umbrella' shaped and might well have drifted into the area given the weather conditions and wind directions on that January day. Because the 'sky hook' project was classified in 1948, neither the staff at Godman nor the original Air Force investigators would be likely to know about it.

All of this is fine in theory. The only problem was that Ruppelt could find no evidence that a 'sky hook' project release had occurred on that day, or any relevant day. Indeed, psychologist Dr David Saunders, writing twenty years later after Colorado University had studied UFOs under a half-million dollar grant from the US government, says most definitely that the records they were given access to (supposedly absolutely complete) showed no release from Ohio on 7 January 1948.

Ruppelt concluded that Mantell *could* have seen a balloon; but for such a balloon to have been seen from all the scattered locations of the other sightings it would have had to travel far beyond the maximum possible wind speed or at a height way above that achievable by even the sophisticated 'sky hook'. Perhaps the original UFO was just that – a UFO; then, by tragic coincidence, Mantell was vectored onto a balloon that chanced to be visible from Godman at the same time.

We will sadly never know for certain, but the case remains one of the major mysteries in the UFO story.

When credible reportings of sightings are received the Air Force is attempting to send up jet interceptor planes in order to obtain a better view of these objects.

(From one of the documents released in 1976 under the US Freedom of Information Act. Part of an FBI status report on UFOs.)

The Mantell death was a vital turning point in UFO history. In the light of posterity we can see a solution that might be feasible. Explanation or no explanation, however, the newly-created Project Sign saw the pilot as earth's first casualty in a 'war of the worlds'. Although most hoped the death was not an indication of overt alien hostility, it was assumed amongst many intelligence officers that the UFO subject had now become very serious and potentially deadly.

Matters were not helped when 1948 continued to bring more aerial encounters. Military aircraft, following the operation intercept order, were told to observe but *not* to provoke an attack.

On 24 July an Eastern Airlines DC—3 flying out of Houston bound for Atlanta nearly collided with a UFO over Montgomery, Alabama. The two civilian pilots (Clarence Chiles and John Whitted) saw the cigar-shaped object very clearly as it flashed by with a turbulent wake. They had to make an emergency evasion. Some sceptics proposed it was a meteor, with which the air crew never agreed. Meteors do not create turbulence and should be seen by hundreds on the ground. This one was not. The Project Sign evaluation was 'unknown', but years later this was altered to 'meteor' when nobody was looking.

Again on 1 October at Fargo, North Dakota, another F—51 met a UFO. Lt. George Gorman was coming in to land when he saw a light ahead of him. He started an intercept. For several minutes a game of 'cat and mouse' ensued before the light rose up and disappeared. He told Sign, 'I had the distinct impression that its manoeuvres were controlled by thought or reason.' Several people on the ground, the pilot of a light plane flying nearby, and his passenger, all saw the UFO. The official explanation is that it was a lighted balloon.

Then, on 18 November, a North American T—6 Texan lining up to land at Andrews Air Force Base near Washington DC saw another UFO. The pilot once more obeyed instructions and even switched his lights on and off but brought no response from the UFO. As he tried to close in the light accelerated over him and squirmed away like a slippery eel as he circled back round. After ten minutes the UFO veered east and headed towards the Atlantic. The pilot got a good look. It was 'a dark grey oval-shaped object smaller than my T—6'.

On the ground at the base officers and flight crew saw the whole thing. They had no explanation, and neither did Project Sign this time.

The memory of Mantell must have haunted these brave attempts to find out what lay behind the UFO mystery, but the intelligence staff at Wright Patterson needed no more convincing. Based on these accumulating cases from trained observers they concluded that UFOs were real and probably extra-terrestrial. They put this into an 'Estimate of the Situation' report and sent it to the very top.

Chief of Staff, General Hoyt Vandenberg, threw the report back. Sign fought this by direct petition. Look at the facts, they told the Pentagon. It is obvious that neither we nor the Russians have anything that can perform like this. Vandenberg was unmoved. He ordered Project Sign to destroy all copies of their report.

A few weeks later Sign was asked to produce their final analysis. It showed one-fifth of cases unexplained and called for a more detailed study. Shortly afterwards Project Sign was closed down and its team members transferred elsewhere.

4 A BREACH IN OUR DEFENCES – 1950

This matter is considered top secret by intelligence officers of both the army and the Air Forces.

(Secret brief on 'Protection of Vital Installations': Subject UFOs: 31 Jan 1949.)

The cold frozen wastes of Alaska are an outpost of the western military defences. Only the narrow Bering Strait separates this desolate glacier-locked landscape from the USSR. An accident of geography has turned the otherwise depopulated zone into one where surveillance and security are at their highest levels.

During the first three years of UFO reports there had been many instances of a security breach. Unknown to almost everyone (even those who had sufficient clearance to know something about official UFO study) one secret group – Project Twinkle – was endeavouring to find out what kept flying over atomic weapons research centres and rocketry development bases with terrifying ease. No suggestion that they ever *did* find out has been made public. UFOs had also buzzed sensitive airfields and power and communication systems, but nobody knew what to do about it. Top-secret evaluations and discussions (such as the one quoted above) had struggled to find ways to cope with the problem. None had succeeded.

At the same time as these things the public had been informed of the closure of UFO interest and that there was really nothing going on.

On 22 January 1950 Lt. Smith, a US Navy patrol plane pilot, was conducting a routine security flight over Alaska. It was 2.40 am. He was from Kodiak, an island base to the south of the Bering Sea, well into American territory and presumed safe. Suddenly his radar detected an object 20 miles north. It vanished quickly, without being seen by the pilot.

Now on alert, Smith continued to monitor his scope. At 2.48 am either the same or a different object turned up south of Kodiak. If it had moved on a steady path since the last radar reading its speed would be about 225 mph, by no means unreasonable for an aircraft.

Smith radioed Kodiak, but was advised that there was no known traffic where his blip was. As they debated this, the radar officer, A.L.C. Gaskey, was reporting that his screen was being scrambled in a way he had never experienced before. It was as if some high-powered electronics were interfering with the radar beam, making it difficult to follow the course of the UFO.

Meanwhile, moored south of Kodiak was the USS *Tillamock*. Quarter Master Morgan was standing guard on the deck as 3 am approached. Suddenly, 'a very fast moving red glow light, which appeared to be of exhaust nature, seemed to come from the south-east, moved clockwise in a large circle in the direction of, and around, Kodiak, and returned out in a generally south-east direction.'

Morgan called MMC Carver, the other watch officer. He also saw the object, which proved equally inexplicable to him. He described it as like a large ball of orange fire. It was in view an estimated 30 seconds. Despite its change in direction (flying both into and with a fairly blustery wind) and the utter silence of the location, no sound whatsoever was heard from the object. Had it been a jet aircraft it surely would have made a noise.

Lt. Smith was continuing his airborne patrols with the radar interference now gone. Suddenly the scope detected a new target five miles from him and moving exceptionally fast. The time was now 4.40 am, almost two hours after the events described above. The blip was actually leaving a trail on the radar screen, so rapid was its motion. Immediately the pilot called all his crew and told them to look out for the UFO. They saw it almost right away, closing the five-mile gap in just ten seconds, suggesting a then quite fantastic speed of 1800 mph!

Smith now turned to pursue the object, which was ahead of them and shooting off. He did try to get closer, but the object was too manoeuvrable. Witness descriptions speak of 'two orange lights – rotating about a common centre like two jet aircraft making slow rolls in tight formation'. Then, suddenly, the thing made a sharp turn and was heading straight for Smith's aircraft! In his words, he 'considered this to be a highly threatening gesture' and switched off all his lights to make the plane less of a target in the inky sky. The UFO flew by and moved off south-east, disappearing inside four minutes.

Nobody at Kodiak had an answer for this case, which was one of the earliest of a type called the 'radar-visual'. When a strange target is seen behaving unusually on a radar screen, then it is possible to opt for some sort of distortion of the system or a weather-induced radar mirage; but if the object is also visually spotted by witnesses on the ground, in the air, or even both, then this interpretation becomes less credible. As in this example, it presents prime scientific evidence for a genuine unknown.

The US Navy evaluated the case highly. No fewer than 36 copies of the detailed report were distributed to various security agencies. Of these, *none* were ever released or published. The FBI copy (from which this summary is written) came to light a quarter of a century later, missing much crucial

31

data. These include eight appendices containing signed statements and scientific analysis of the peculiar radar interference.

The six-page report we *do* have categorically rules out most possible answers and concludes, 'the objects must be regarded as phenomena . . . the exact nature of which could not be determined'.

After less than thirty months of the UFO mystery the US government's filing cabinets were fast choking beneath the weight of cases of this calibre.

If there is an extraterrestrial civilisation which can make objects as are reported, then it is most probable that its development is far in advance of ours . . . such a civilisation might observe that on earth we now have atomic bombs and are fast developing rockets. In view of the past history of mankind, they would be alarmed. We should, therefore, expect at this time above all to behold such visitations.

(Part of the final report of Project Sign, written by Professor George Valley, of MIT, one of the chief scientific advisers to the US President. Dated: February 1949.)

The rejection of the 'Estimate of Situation' report about alien UFOs, the abrupt closure of Project Sign and the remarkably rapid creation and dissolution of a sequel venture (Project Grudge) all seem very hard to comprehend, particularly when seen against the background of inflowing cases and secret reports such as that by Professor Valley. Grudge was initiated in the same month as the above analysis but published its final verdict inside a few weeks. This argued that cases should be vigorously 'debunked', that ways be found to defuse interest in UFOs and that the subject be demoted to a routine level within the Air Force.

It is understandable why some see in these actions the likelihood that the government of the world's then most powerful nation did *not* reject the 'Estimate' but *accepted* it. Given this, Grudge would be seen as an exercise to try to divert the problem from public attention, its study having passed into the hands of top security cleared scientists deep below the surface.

There are persistent stories that such a team of people did (does?) exist. The code name MJ-12 (or Majestic Twelve) is said to apply. We will see some of the evidence later in the book. Bear in mind, though, that *if* MJ-12 was created around this time its security classification would at least have been equal to that granted the 'Manhattan Project' (the building of the atom bomb) during the recently concluded war. Its existence would almost certainly be unknown to everyone publicly associated with UFOs (meaning journalists, intelligence officers, press spokesmen and scientists such as Dr J. Allen Hynek, then involved with the Air Force's open study of the field).

Not to have created a team such as MJ-12 would have to be seen as an act of great folly. Considering the evidence as it stood in 1948 or 1949, the very least that was necessary was a continued monitor. You must make your own mind up about whether the President of the USA made a reckless error of judgement or took a sensible security precaution.

The aftertaste of these political moves was the creeping suspicion about an official 'cover-up'. Reporters, in particular, had studied dozens of cases and knew better than anyone the strength of the evidence. Negative pronouncements in the face of this and the absurd explanations (e.g. the Venus answer to the Mantell death) implied that something devious was afoot to almost everyone who had bothered to check the subject out.

In fact, the chances are that the authorities were simply baffled. There is little doubt that the prospect of extraterrestrial spacecraft was taken seriously, but, unless something had indeed been captured at Roswell in July 1947, the cover-up was more likely a product of ignorance than of secret knowledge. The dire need was to find out what was going on: where the UFOs came from, what they were doing here, and so on. It may well have seemed sensible to manufacture the impression that UFOs were considered explained as a method of distracting private scientific enterprise from probing the subject and possibly going public with its discoveries. If discoveries were to be made it could well have been deemed important that security-cleared scientists got to them first (preferably *western* security-cleared scientists).

We might anticipate some sort of allied plan at this stage to prevent other NATO countries giving the game away. Alternatively, perhaps those in Europe merely looked to the USA for a lead, saw it publicly decrying UFOs and followed the same path.

Of course, journalists had no access to secret reports (not even the ones we have now thanks to the Freedom of Information Act, let alone the ones we do *not* have now!). This gave them no perspective on the issues involved. They only saw the arrogant dismissals of mounting evidence and interpreted these as the masking of guilty knowledge. The usual reason cited by those who considered the problem at this time was that the authorities wanted to prevent panic and society collapsing under the discovery of a 'threat' from 'Mars'. The famous radio broadcast by Orson Welles (where a modern dramatisation of the H.G. Wells story *War of the Worlds* had been so realistic that thousands had believed it was actually happening!) was often quoted.

So, the amateur UFO hunters began to accuse those co-ordinating US Air Force public relations groups of huge conspiracies. The latter, who in all probability had no awareness of any such thing, not surprisingly, treated this with great aversion and assumed the sleuths to be sensationalist cranks. This drove a wedge between the two sides, creating a battlefront situation which was doomed to perpetual stalemate. This may even have been part of the secret plan, since it bought the American government invaluable time.

Of all the proponents of the conspiracy theory it was a retired US Marine, Donald Keyhoe, who was to have the most impact. He had interviewed several military witnesses and had enough friends in the services to give him an insight into what was going on. His perceptions of the early years were blinkered and can now be seen as somewhat distorted, but he was undoubtedly better informed than almost anyone not constrained to total silence.

Keyhoe spent most of 1949 putting together an explosive article entitled 'The Flying Saucers are Real', which was published by *True* magazine the same month as the Kodiak, Alaska, events unfolded outside the gaze of everyone without an 'A' security clearance.

The article evaluated the best cases then made public, including Mantell, the Eastern Airlines DC-3 sighting, and George Gorman. It concluded that the Air Force was hiding the alien reality of UFOs.

True Magazine for January 1950 is reputed to have been one of the most widely read publications of all time. It provoked a sensation. Within weeks Keyhoe had expanded his work into a book, using the same title. This was the first in what has now became a deluge of literary efforts, although English author Gerald Heard was only weeks behind with his study of the same cases, entitled *Riddle of the Flying Saucers*.

These steps (according to security papers now released) turned Keyhoe into a security risk. He was put under FBI and CIA scrutiny, as indeed have been other leading UFO researchers in the years since.

If we were forced to accept the official view on UFOs we might well ask why a 'myth-making' writer about a 'non-existent' phenomenon would be of such concern to the intelligence services!

5 INVASION WASHINGTON DC – 1952

The reports of incidents convince us that there is something going on that must have immediate attention.

(H. Marshall Chadwell, Assistant Director of Scientific Intelligence, CIA, 2 Dec 1952.)

In those early years of the UFO phenomenon one cry was often heard. If UFOs are real, why don't they show themselves to everyone and land on the White House lawn? Indeed, that theme was woven into several science-fiction movies in the first half of the 1950s. In the summer of 1952, science-fiction almost became a reality.

With Project Grudge on hold, the Air Force was officially no longer interested in the subject. Yet behind the scenes there was frantic activity. Intelligence Officer Captain Edward J. Ruppelt had been assigned to reshape the study and field the mounting concern within the Pentagon. That was October 1951. By March 1952 his recommendations for a new project were accepted and the code name Project Blue Book was assigned to it. Ruppelt, who quickly became convinced of UFO reality and often investigated cases on his own initiative and even at his own expense, says the title was based on a college exam paper filled with tough questions.

Sightings had not exactly brimmed over during the period of transition. December 1951 brought only ten reports to the USAF files, whilst May 1952 gave them a more promising 79. Of course, the media were recording many others, since the average witness was unlikely to call his nearest air base to alert an official project which (so far as he knew) might or might not exist, and might or might not care about the sighting anyway!

However, this was the calm before the storm. June produced 149 cases, and the next two months over 700 between them! This was now the greatest wave the USA had ever experienced, or indeed was to experience.

During this time the USAF 'Operation Intercept' programme was in full swing. Naturally, it was not publicised, but in his 1956 'memoirs' (having left the Air Force utterly frustrated by their failure to support his calls for better effort) Ruppelt recorded several of them. For instance, he tells how two North American F—86 Sabre fighters were vectored onto a target in the thick of this summer 1952 wave. The pilots had a broad-daylight view of the UFO, fired tracer rounds at the unknown and watched it accelerate away out of range. Upon landing, the officer who had fired was debriefed by his Colonel, who accepted the pilot's explanation and sympathised with his actions. They were contrary to all official policy, however, so the base commander simply informed Ruppelt, who then destroyed the report before giving it to Washington.

The overture may have been insignificant, but the main performance that followed caught the full imagination of the public.

At 11.40 pm on the night of 19 July 1952, the long-range 'overfly' radar at Washington DC civilian airport picked up a formation of seven 'blips' that were 15 miles south and not far from Andrews Air Force Base. A controller on duty, Ed Nugent, presumed them to be military traffic as they moved at between 100 and 130 mph. He was puzzled, as none were supposed to be there, but his bafflement gave way to great concern when two of the targets suddenly accelerated at amazing speed and vanished off the scope within seconds!

Nugent called over his senior controller, Harry Barnes, who in turn brought two more experienced radar men to watch. They had no solution for the remaining blips. At this busy airport there is also a second radar, in a separate building, which is a short-range system to guide planes in and out. Barnes called them on the intercom to ask if they were seeing anything peculiar. Controllers Howard Cocklin and Joe Zacko *were* . . . and it was exactly the same thing! Even more importantly, they got in touch with Andrews Air Force Base, who had also been monitoring unknown blips.

For three radar systems all to be recording this dramatic 'invasion' of the nation's capital was immediately significant. They knew a systems malfunction could not be to blame, but Barnes ordered his radar checked anyway. There were no faults. Meanwhile the targets had moved at speeds of up to 7000 mph, before stopping rapidly and then cruising about, behaviour patterns never witnessed before by any of the experts. What is more, they had intruded upon restricted air space – taking them right over the White House.

Various attempts were made by Barnes to get the Air Force to send interceptors after the objects. This should have required no justification. Yet he was at first informed there was 'not enough information', then that it was 'in hand', and finally that it was 'being taken care of', but nobody seemed to know who had the responsibility for the launch. Whilst the debate went on, at least two civilian aircraft flying in and out of Washington had been asked to keep their scanners peeled. Between 1 and 3 am there were two sightings of 'blue-white' lights whizzing past, or 'streaks of orange'. These sound like meteors that the alerted pilots misperceived in their anxiety. A ground observer at Andrews Air Force

Base also reported seeing a 'ball of orange fire' when he went to look for a blip that was on screen.

Finally, just before dawn, an interceptor *did* arrive from Delaware. It was too late. Nothing was visible.

Of course, there was no way to keep this out of the press. Blue Book faced blazing headlines and a real dilemma. Ruppelt flew to Washington, yet, inexplicably, go no co-operation. He was not even granted a staff car to interview the scattered witnesses. Use the bus, he was told! Then he was advised that he was spending too much time away from Wright Patterson (the UFO project home base) and if he did not get back he would be reported AWOL! Giving the perfunctory 'no comment' to the hungry press (which many doubtless saw as proof of a cover-up) he gave up in disgust.

Assuming that the Air Force are telling the truth about Ruppelt's role, it is very hard to imagine why he was not ordered to solve this case double quick. To be more or less shunted away from it hints at the possibility that it was considered too hot for Project Blue Book to handle. No doubt somebody at the Pentagon was trying to figure it out.

Then it happened all over again! At about 9.30 pm on the night of 26 July (one week later) more blips were recorded at Washington. The local press got wind of this immediately and a reporter rang Ruppelt within minutes of the start of the encounter, to ask what the Air Force was doing about this new invasion. However, Ruppelt, the head of the government's UFO team, had not even been told about it! Still smarting from his treatment the week before, he told the journalist (in understandable anger), 'I have no idea what the Air Force is doing; in all probability it is doing nothing.'

Whilst the press pondered this new 'cover-up', Ruppelt was fired into action. Regardless of hurt pride, this was his job. He phoned Major Dewey Fournet, an engineer consultant to Blue Book, because he lived in Washington DC. He told Fournet to get himself and anyone else he considered useful to the airport as fast as possible. Fournet, a radar specialist with the project called Holcombe, and Al Chop (the Air Force press officer) all arrived at the radar sets in time to see the unknowns and listen to ground-to-air communications as pilots were steered towards them.

Two Republic F—94 Thunderjet/Streak jets arrived at 11.25 pm (no delaying tactics this time!). As they did, the many reporters who had heard what was happening and had flocked to the tower were ordered out. The pretext (air force sources called it this themselves) was that communication techniques with an interceptor were confidential. As Ruppelt points out, this was nonsense, since anybody with a radio set could hear them when they liked! The truth was that most of the Blue Book personnel in that radar room believed this would be the night when indisputable proof of alien UFOs was finally achieved. This historic moment must be evaluated by the authorities first — before the press were told (*if* the press were told).

Over several hours there were visual sightings, many radar trackings, jets closing in on lights, only for this and the radar blip to vanish when the aircraft got near. Then, as the plane flew by, the blips would often come back again! The games went on until dawn, but without any final proof, just more unexplained events.

Even so, all those in the radar room were persuaded that the targets were 'very probably caused by solid metallic objects' and Fournet, in his report, pointed out that the screens also showed targets created by the weather. Since they were easily recognisable to the experienced operators, this was not the answer to the fleet of unknowns.

Despite this, at a press conference 48 hours after the UFOs had gone (for good), and even though it was admitted, 'we don't know the answer positively and there's no use pretending that we do', the Air Force verdict was given. The radar targets *were* caused by the weather — inversions or 'angels' (a form of mirage). The visual sightings were nothing but a few stars and meteors that everyone mistook in their excitement. Major General John Samford, director of Air Force Intelligence, called the conference (one of the biggest ever held since World War Two). The other main protagonists, Ruppelt, Fournet, Holcombe and Chop, were present but took a back seat. Most of the press, with some relief, accepted the solution. After all, they presumed, the US Air Force would surely not pretend there was nothing to worry about if the nation's capital really had been invaded by unknown phenomena.

In 1969, when the US government sponsored a scientific analysis of the UFO subject at the University of Colorado, radar expert Gordon Thayer concurred. His report does show that many of the visual sightings (especially those from the ground) probably were not UFOs. A great deal of suggestibility was around on these two nights. However, it leaves the radar returns at best only possibly explained. Remember that more than a dozen radar operators *saw* these targets. None supported the idea of mirages. The meteorological conditions were by no means perfect for such effects and have, of course, been duplicated many times since without the same results.

Dr James McDonald, an atmospheric physicist at Arizona University, was a specialist in such optics, and he looked at Thayer's data. His comment was that the conditions definitely could not have produced the effects seen.

It is also a little curious that the 1000-page final study report by Colorado University has only half a per cent devoted to this case, all of which is a fairly heavy account of radar optics. Yet, Dr Michael Wertheimer, a psychologist on the project, had gone to Washington DC on behalf of the group to investigate the encounters. He interviewed as many of the eye-witnesses as he could find. Dr David Saunders, another psychologist on the team, wrote his own 'alternative report' – published a few months before the government's official version. In this book *(UFOs? Yes!)* he *does* describe Wertheimer's work (missed out of the official project). He says of it, 'virtually every witness that Wertheimer talked with disagreed with Samford's temperature inversion explanation, observing that an experienced operator has no trouble identifying [one] . . . Wertheimer's own conclusion was that the sightings cannot be explained.'

Strange that a research project that cost the US tax-payer half a million dollars and was approved by the National Academy of Sciences as being objective should have mislaid this contradictory material and printed only the negative view.

It also certainly did not impress those within the Air Force who had been involved. General Samford may have had good reason to 'debunk' the story, but he was not present. Ruppelt had been (as an investigator). Fournet, Holcombe and Chop had all been witnesses. Within three years of the waving away of the Washington invasion, Ruppelt had left the Air Force to write a serious book admitting UFO reality and speculating that he was just a 'front man'. Fournet had quit to join a leading civilian UFO group, and Al Chop resigned his Air Force position to work as an adviser on a Hollywood documentary, released to big audiences in 1955. It told the full story about early UFO sightings.

Of course, this could all be coincidence; or it might mean that these people saw through the façade of official explanation and knew that something truly extraordinary *had* gone on.

It is strongly urged, however, that no indication of CIA interest or concern reach the press or public.

(CIA memo from acting Chief of Weapons and Equipment Division, 1 August 1952.)

The Air Force may have been satisfied that it had solved these incidents. More likely, it wished to create the illusion that it was satisfied. Clearly those most directly involved were not persuaded. Neither were the CIA.

The quote above, from a now-released (then top secret) memo, dates just two days *after* the Samford press conference. The Washington DC invasion had in fact provoked an intense desire for positive action in this major league intelligence service. So far as we know, although the CIA were in receipt of documents initiated by the Air Force intelligence units from 1947, August 1952 was the first time they made a real move into UFO investigation.

The plan that the public should be misled about CIA interest is also explicit in the statement – just one of several *direct* proofs that there has been a UFO conspiracy. The immediate consequence was the creation of a scientific panel to review the UFO data and decide what to do about it. Of most concern to the CIA was the genuine belief that an enemy could ride in amidst a wave of real or fabricated UFOs and perform a sneak attack during the confusion.

Ruppelt and Blue Book do not seem to have been aware of why the CIA were interested, and he was allowed to assume that the scientists would be taking their recommendations to the president if they voted in favour of the UFO. Blue Book had bets on the outcome and the odds did not favour anyone who rejected UFOs!

It is quite illuminating to read Ruppelt's 1956 account of the science panel meetings, when it was still top secret. When compared with the actual report (released in part through the Colorado University study in 1969 and in full under Freedom of Information later) it is plain to see that the head of the Air Force UFO team was himself duped.

In December 1952 the CIA were secretly trying to decide which security-cleared scientist should chair the panel and implement decisions already taken to defuse public interest (this was seen as the only way to stop that danger of sneak attack). In other words, whatever UFOs are, if nobody reports them they will not be a threat to us. One 'scientist' was proposed on a 3 December memo, 'because the latter is probably the most expert man in the country on magic and general chicanery'. These were evidently major job specifications for the UFO conspiracy.

By January 1953, when the panel convened, a renowned physicist had become its chief. He was Professor H.P. Robertson. Others were chosen as much for their CIA clearance as anything else. Those without such clearances but who were involved in Blue Book (e.g. Ruppelt and Dr J. Allen Hynek, the Air Force science consultant) got shut out of some sessions. There was Professor Sam Goudsmit (enemy weapons technology and intelligence), Professor Luis Alvarez (future Nobel Prize winner, who had worked with Robert Oppenheimer on the atom bomb), Dr Lloyd Berkner (a rear admiral as well as a physicist) and Professor Thornton Page (an astronomer and weapons expert).

It is hard to conceive of a more formidable panel. *All* were physical scientists. This shows better than anything how, despite public assertions to the contrary, in 1953 the US government believed UFOs to be very *real!*

6 AN AMERICAN CRAZINESS? – 1953

Some military officials are seriously considering the possibility of interplanetary ships.
  Air Intelligence Memo, 27 October 1952.)

Three thousand miles from Washington DC, about the time the CIA panel met, an RAF pilot and his science officer were on another secret mission.

The officer was Flight Lieutenant Cyril George Townsend-Withers (later to become a senior scientific officer, specialising in radar and working with the MoD at the rank of Wing Commander). It was a crisp, sunny winter's day in early 1953 and they were flying a new experimental Canberra aircraft, not yet into production.

The jet had been stripped of all removable parts to make it as light as possible. With this modification they were able to leave the RAF test base at Boscombe Down in Sussex and soar to 55,000 feet, then a record for the aircraft. At this lonely elevation they could be sure of no company and complete freedom from the problems of the atmosphere. This was necessary in order that they could test a new breed of radar being fitted to the plane.

Cruising over Salisbury Plain just after noon, Townsend-Withers picked up a strange blip on his screen. It showed an object travelling five miles behind them and maintaining station. His immediate reaction was to curse the return of the 'anomalous propagation' effects which they had gone to so much trouble to avoid. Having soon established it was no such thing, however, he became very aware that this was an image of something real – something actually flying right behind them.

The science officer went up to the turret to take a look at the sky behind the aircraft. Sure enough, glinting in the sun or pouring out a fantastic amount of its own light, he could make out a round shape trailing in their wake.

Townsend-Withers called his pilot on the microphone and told him that he could see an unknown. He suggested they try to fly faster and outpace it. They reached 225 knots but the thing would not be shaken off. So the pilot initiated a sweeping radius turn, which meant that they lost the target from the radar because it was rearward facing only; but it was not to be gone for very long.

As the Canberra came around from its turn the object swung back into view. It was dead ahead. Both men could now see it, as they raced through the sky.

For half a minute they were on a collision course with the unknown, swiftly trying to calculate what to do next. In those seconds they had a very clear view. They could see that the object was completely unlike anything which they had ever encountered before. It was round, like a thin disc, but with two small tailfins at the rear. It seemed to be metallic and enormous, and it was simply sitting there waiting for them to fly right into it.

During the decision about evasive tactics to get out of its way the UFO suddenly made this irrelevant. It flipped vertically into the air and climbed upwards at an astonishing rate. 'Fifty, sixty, seventy thousand feet – as quick as you could say it.' Leaving no vapour trail, wake or detectable sound, the thing vanished within just a couple of seconds way into the blue.

Of course, the two RAF men knew that they had encountered something utterly fantastic. In 1986 Townsend-Withers was still describing it as 'a reconnaissance device from somewhere else – that is all I could say about it.' No earth-bound aircraft looked like it, behaved like it or could reach such a height. They knew that some sort of official report was essential, but who would believe them? They had heard tell of 'flying saucers' – garbled stories carried by the media. The assumption was to treat these as an American craziness, something 'Yanks' were seeing but nobody else. Certainly not conservative, stiff-upper-lip British airmen.

However, when they did report, the reaction on the ground was surprising. Townsend-Withers says, 'once we satisfied them it was not a Russian plane they just weren't interested'. He *was* debriefed by the radar manufacturers, who were convinced their system was working perfectly. The radar return had definitely been of a real object. Boscombe Down also apparently channelled the report through to the Air Ministry (now the Ministry of Defence) and told the science officer in confidence, that they had a project evaluating UFO sightings from the point of view that they might be extra-terrestrial. This, of course, was not to be made public as it could be interpreted as governmental support for the idea.

Yet this project never contacted Townsend-Withers again. A classic daylight UFO sighting, with two experienced officers as witnesses, radar back-up and a near collision with a secret mission, was practically ignored. Townsend-Withers was almost as concerned by such a lack of action as he was by the UFO encounter itself. Surely somebody, somewhere, was taking note of such things?

Two RAF intelligence officers who were in the US on a classified mission brought six single-spaced typed pages of questions they and their friends wanted answered.

(Captain Ed Ruppelt, describing his time at Project Blue Book in 1953.)

The Townsend-Withers experience was *not* the first involving British witnesses, not even the first involving the RAF. However, none of the others (nor indeed the Salisbury Plain sighting itself) were known to the public. So the belief in UFOs as an 'American Craziness' had become quite dominant. There were those who regarded the whole UFO business as the product of the times – post-war nervousness. The fact that UFOs were being seen *globally* was known only to a few intelligence services at this time, and they appeared in no hurry to make that news public.

We will see some of this world-wide evidence later in the book, but we can understand why the events in Washington DC in July 1952 had major repercussions in Europe. A British MoD official was sent to America to discover what was happening (seemingly as a forerunner of the meeting Ruppelt describes above). This high-level visit was advised by Ralph Noyes (later under-secretary in charge of the department at the MoD which handles UFO reports). In 1952 Noyes was at the Air Ministry, on the staff of Air Chief Marshal Cochran, and sat in on cabinet level discussions about the Washington flap. He recalls Cochran grunting, 'I thought Vandenburg had put an end to this in '49' – a clear reference to the rejection of the Estimate of Situation stating that UFOs were alien, by the USAF Air Force Chief.

Noyes heard nothing more about what occurred following the intelligence missions to the USA, but a new spate of encounters quickly ensured that the British government could not brush the UFOs away, even if they had wanted to.

On 19, 20 and 21 September 1952, just eight weeks after the Washington invasion, a NATO exercise, 'Operation Mainbrace', was rudely interrupted by UFOs.

Mainbrace took place in the North Sea around Britain and lasted several days, using naval and air resources. Three major sightings are known to have taken place during its term. These must have had a big impact on all NATO allied attitudes to this 'craziness'.

First, on the 19th, an object appeared in mid-morning above Topcliffe Airfield, North Yorkshire. It was round and silvery. One witness said of it, 'it rotated around its vertical axis and sort of wobbled'. Many air crew on the ground (and some civilians) spotted the thing. A meteor jet was scrambled and the RAF pilot got close enough for the description just quoted. The UFO then turned west, then south-east (showing it was not windborne but in controlled flight) and flew off.

The next day a similar object appeared over a US carrier ship out with the fleet between England and Scandinavia. An American photographer was on board doing a story about the exercise. He took pictures of the sphere, which was ascertained *not* to be a balloon. These pictures have never been released.

Finally, the mini-wave ended on 21 September, when six RAF jets out above the North Sea saw a 'sphere' heading towards them, coming from the direction of the fleet. They tracked it, lost it, and found it had now appeared directly behind them! This was precisely the behaviour of the objects seen over Washington DC. One brave meteor pilot gave chase, but the UFO accelerated away and he was totally outrun.

This disturbing interest in NATO manoeuvres in the wake of what had happened over Washington must have increased tension. Ruppelt, referring to his intelligence visitors a few months later, said in his 1956 'memoirs', 'I was told by an RAF exchange intelligence officer in the Pentagon that [these reports] caused the RAF to officially recognise the UFO.'

All of which makes perfect sense of why Flight Lieutenant Townsend-Withers and his pilot were told that there was a British MoD investigation at the time he reported his encounter. Townsend-Withers adds that in the 1960s, when he was a senior MoD officer, he had several discussions about UFOs with relevant people in Whitehall. The project was even then supposed to be based at Farnborough, Hampshire, and staffed by RAF intelligence. It took UFOs very seriously, and probably still does.

There is only one problem with this parade of consistent stories. The British government publicly refute them. They claim that no such investigation was ever undertaken. Whenever UFO groups request information on cases they discover via the RAF witnesses (who like Townsend-Withers assume that after the expiry of the thirty-year rule for withholding secret data it is all right to talk) they get the same answer. No UFOs exist, no study occurred, and no files are kept for such alleged eventualities.

Nevertheless, as you will see later in this book, we again have a lie. This time it can be proven a lie by documents recently released.

Meanwhile, back in the USA the Robertson panel had concluded its five-day review of the non-existent problem, on behalf of the CIA. The scientists looked at some cases, especially photographic evidence from military witnesses, heard Ruppelt tell them about the disturbing non-random distribution of sightings over 'sensitive' areas, were given a detailed technical study by Major Dewey Fournet which (whilst he was 'biased' by having *seen* the Washington radar blips) argued that the flight characteristics of UFOs could not be matched with any earth technology, and heard Dr J. Allen Hynek tell them as science adviser to the project that there were unexplained cases and more funding was needed.

This was pretty hot stuff. Exactly as the Project Sign team in 1948 had concluded, the entire Blue Book staff had gone the same way in endorsing UFO reality. That obviously led to the termination of most of their project work during 1953 and 1954. Hynek alone remained, largely because as a civilian scientist he was less of a threat inside the project (where he was willing to keep quiet to retain access to the cases) than outside of it (where he might have significantly rocked the boat by alerting colleagues to the value of the evidence).

However, the CIA team were having none of this. Duplicating Vandenberg's response from a few years before, they went even further. UFOs, they said in their secret report (now released), should be stripped of 'the aura of mystery they have unfortunately acquired'. Means to do this were considered, ranging from twisting the truth to allow universal debunking and getting Walt Disney involved in the creation of cartoon films that made UFO sightings look silly. Monitors on UFO groups and investigators were also proposed, because these people were a threat to 'Operation Debunk'. They had 'potentially great influence on mass thinking', especially when 'widespread sightings should occur'.

If you think about these recommendations, which were carried out, they are rather sinister. Not only do they involve distorting the truth, hoodwinking the public and character assassination, but also concern surveillance on private citizens merely recording factual observations.

Of those who were members or attendees at the Robertson meetings, all the Blue Book personnel went on to become public advocates of the UFO mystery. Dr J. Allen Hynek, when eventually freed of his commitment to the Air Force, devoted his life to the scientific study of UFOs and became its greatest champion.

Concerning the five panel members who retained CIA ties, we know little. However, one of them at least changed his mind. In 1980 that man, Dr Thornton Page (now with NASA) said, 'The panel underestimated the long duration of public interest in UFOs . . . it also tended to ignore the five per cent or ten per cent of UFO reports that are highly reliable and have not as yet been explained.' In 1985, reviewing some of my comments on early UFO history (of which this part of the book forms an expanded version) he added, 'as one who was involved in much of it', that this was both 'accurate and revealing'.

On 8 December 1953, the CIA evaluated things one year after the study had made its proposals. It was pleased to note that sighting numbers had fallen dramatically, due it believed to the success of the implemented policies. However, there was 'still a role' for cases 'of possible scientific intelligence value'. It noted how such a course of action was a risky one, because serious UFO proponents were aware of the change in tactics and might point this out, fostering the image of a cover-up. The CIA conclude, 'The panel's recommendations might have been interpreted by a fanatical saucer "believer" as "debunking".'

I would be fascinated to know what anybody else might objectively describe them as!

7 THE ALIENS ARRIVE – 1954

Of course the flying saucers are real – and they are interplanetary.
(Air Chief Marshall Lord Dowding, head of the RAF during World War Two, August 1954.)

The year 1954 was to prove another crucial time in the UFO story. The UFOs ditched their seven-year love affair with the USA and moved to Europe. Italy, France and Britain became the scene for a dramatic new wave, centring on October, which was significant because it marked the commencement of an entirely new phase: a class of cases that we now call the 'Close Encounters of the Third Kind'. These involved sightings of the pilots flying the UFOs.

But first there was to be another very close aerial contact – involving a BOAC (now British Airways) transatlantic flight. The stratocruiser (Callsign 'Sierra Charlie') left New York at 9.03 pm (GMT) on 29 June 1954, bound for London. Captain James Howard was in command. Lee Boyd was first officer. Navigator was Captain H. McDonnell.

They were at 19,000 feet, airspeed 260 knots, on a fine clear evening. It was now after midnight into 30 June (GMT) but locally still light as they crossed Canada bound for Goose Bay, Labrador, where a brief refuelling stop was necessary.

Howard saw the object first 'moving off our port beam at a lower altitude at a distance of maybe five miles'. It was one large cigar shape and six smaller black ovals, milling round like baby animals being fed by their mother. As Howard watched, the retinue climbed up through thin cloud towards their aircraft, maintaining this pattern around the 'mother ship'.

One by one the crew were called to look. Captain McDonnell, being interviewed for the first time when tracked down by investigator Barry King in 1978, remembers how everyone tried to find an answer. 'Someone suggested flak, but that sounded a little ridiculous and was hastily dropped.'

Because of the position of the aircraft, its heading and the direction of the setting sun, they also knew it was not a reflection of themselves on cloud. The changing angle of the sun's rays (enhanced by the aircraft's eastward path) caused the object to *appear* to alter shape, although McDonnell does not believe this was a real effect.

After about fifteen minutes' observation, Captain Howard ordered Lee Boyd to call Goose Bay and tell them of their escort. The Canadians promised to send up an interceptor. Almost immediately this message was sent out the six mini UFOs 'entered' the big cigar (three from above and three from below) and the thing then 'shot away'.

The BOAC crew never saw 'Pinto One', the interceptor, but they understood that Goose Bay had the UFO on radar and were sending the jet towards it. The commercial aircraft landed at Labrador on time (1.51 am) and was met by Canadian and USAF officials, including intelligence officers. Howard and Boyd were hustled away and 'debriefed'. McDonnell says that flight logs were taken by USAF personnel, a definite breach of procedure. He was also questioned about the aircraft's speed and direction, but this was only short and his two colleagues were gone some time. Take-off was delayed because of this.

Arriving back in London later that day, Howard and Boyd were called to the Air Ministry. An official explanation was then offered to the press. What they and some of the passengers had seen was a phenomenon associated with a solar eclipse – one that had not yet begun when the sighting took place!

Some months later McDonnell met up with Howard in Pakistan. It was the first occasion schedules had thrown them together since the incident. McDonnell asked what had happened at the Air Ministry and was told, 'Sorry, I can't say. You know the score.'

In 1969 the University of Colorado looked at the case during its study programme. Gordon Thayer (the man who solved the Washington DC affair) suggested it had been a mirage. He admitted there were problems getting this explanation to work and ultimately concluded with one of the most bizarre statements in the whole report. Whilst not retracting his mirage proposal he added, 'This unusual sighting should therefore be assigned to the category of some almost certainly natural phenomenon, which is so rare that it apparently has never been reported before or since.'

Surely if anything qualifies for the term UFO (an unidentified flying object, remember), then this is it! Nevertheless the report concluded that there was no such thing.

As this case was echoing around the Air Ministry corridors, the October wave arrived. One of the first major cases involved Flight Lieutenant Jimmy Salandin, who took off in his meteor jet at 4.15 pm on 14 October 1954 from North Weald Airfield in Essex. Climbing over Southend at 16,000 feet, two circular objects shot past him at 'nine o'clock high'. 'One was silvery and the other gold', Salandin said. No sooner had he recovered from this than a third object began to head straight for him. It had 'a bun-shaped top, a flange like two saucers in the middle and a bun underneath. It was silvery in colour and could not have been far off because it overlapped my windscreen.'

The very near miss with such a big object really shook up Salandin. Experienced in the air as he was he had to 'fly around quietly for about ten minutes' to recover. He had been so scared that he utterly forgot to fire his gun-camera button. 'The thing was right in my sights,' he says ruefully. Imagine the sort of pictures these might have been.

Whilst Salandin was understandably more concerned about his safety than pretty pictures, others *have* taken film. No gun-camera films from RAF jets have ever been released (and only one from a USAF jet), but our old friend Ralph Noyes, when in charge of the MoD archives in 1969, says that they *were* there. The refusal to make them public can only make us contemplate what might be on them. If the films show nothing of any interest why withhold them?

The next two weeks saw hundreds of close encounters as good as this one from all over Northern Europe. Britain's first alien sighting came then.

On 21 October at 4.45 pm a shiny disc-shaped object approached the house of Mrs Jennie Roestenberg, a young mother. With her were both her children, who were terrified at the thing. It had a large transparent window in the front, and gazing down from this were two figures in turquoise blue 'ski-suits', covering them from head to toe. They had high foreheads, white faces, and gazed down with a look of concern that was not exactly friendly or unfriendly. They also had blond shoulder length hair.

The UFO had made a hissing sound, which upset the children more than anything. Wisps of vapour came from the rear, where a purplish light was also seen glowing as it left. The object had hovered very low over the farmhouse for about fifteen seconds, before it returned from the 45 degree tilt angle it had assumed (rather like a Harrier jet does now when hovering – but not in 1954, of course!). When the UFO began to spiral upwards Jennie and her children fled indoors and hid under a table.

This case was not publicised at the time, received little attention and yet is all that more impressive for that. I remember when I first saw the isolated house at Ranton, a village in Staffordshire, in 1975, and also heard Jennie relate the tale so convincingly that I considered the idea that we might not merely be dealing with strange flying objects but objects manned by something more than human.

The aliens' manner of looking at the Roestenbergs was the thing that stuck in her mind. When she described it I found myself thinking it was not unlike the way we might study a sick animal.

In 1967, Coral and Jim Lorenzon, American investigators who formed a civilian group fifteen years earlier (just about the oldest still in existence), published a review of such cases, called 'Flying Saucer Occupants'. They recorded 98 cases at that time. Only 11 had pre-dated 1954 and in the 1954 wave no fewer than 40 were logged. This shows the dramatic importance of this new type of encounter.

The aliens had arrived.

I still do not know why the high order of classification has been given and why the denial of the existence of these devices.

(Dr Robert Sarbacher, writing on 29 November 1983, about his involvement with the super-secret [MJ-12] UFO study project at the Pentagon in the early 1950s.)

In the USA the Robertson panel and CIA actions had forced Captain Ruppelt out of the Air Force. He could not put up with their policy to explain away the inexplicable. They could not accept his positive stance on UFOs. It did not tie up with the policy of debunking. 'Don't mention the unknowns', he was continually told.

However, whilst this policy had some limited temporary effect in America, the coincident move across the Atlantic by the UFOs themselves, and the new interest provoked by the occupant sightings, ensured that the mystery did not die. It is easy to imagine the UFOnauts having determined not to be debunked into oblivion *and* show they were visiting the planet, not one single country.

Project Blue Book did continue, under a new hard-line chief. It only made statements when absolutely forced to by press interest in sightings. Clever juggling tricks with the statistics made it appear that the number of unknowns had virtually disappeared. In fact this was simply because if *any* answer looked right (with or without any evidence to support it) then a new label 'Possible' was invented. At the end of the year, the truly solved cases were lumped together with the 'Possibles' and all were regarded as explained!

Another thing which aided Blue Book was the rise in what were called 'Contactees' between 1952 and 1955. Unlike the serious reports of UFO occupants, which matched all the characteristics of the real UFO mystery, these were isolated but highly influential stories of a wild and extreme nature, and utterly lacking in credibility.

Several people wrote books claiming that they had talked to aliens, ridden in their spaceships, and even visited planets that circle this star or another one. Prominent was George Adamski, a café owner on the slopes of Mount Palomar, where there is an observatory. By buying a toy telescope he was able to con a lot of people into believing that he was somehow an official astronomer. His several books, beginning with *Flying Saucers Have Landed* (1953), told of inter-galactic voyages and trees and rivers on Venus and the moon. In pre-spaceflight days nobody could disprove them. Now we can see how absurd they were. His dreadful photographs also convinced only those who wanted to be convinced.

It may seem rather quaint to think of these dotty stories a long time after they were written. However, in 1953 and 1954 they had a traumatic impact. Not only did they utterly destroy any hope of scientists taking the UFO subject seriously, but they began to turn many investigative journalists away, and doubtless made the average enquiring mind assume that *all* UFO tales were equally daft. They set the subject back twenty years at a time when the evidence was getting so good and governmental denials so unbelievable that (without the contactees) anything might have happened. They also made UFO researchers very wary of listening to anyone who claimed a sighting of occupants, thus preventing public spread of the fact that serious close encounters of the third kind *were* beginning.

There are those who see in this the hand of some devious intelligence agency. No released papers offer any real evidence for that, and it may have only needed one or two people 'set up' to claim such ridiculous things. Others would inevitably follow as all the cranks, money-makers and religious fanatics jumped onto the bandwagon. It is a fascinating idea to ponder, and a brilliantly successful plan if that is what it was.

One of the first British offerings was published after the October 1954 wave. Called *Flying Saucers From Mars*, it was a claim by one Cedric Allingham that he had met a Martian in Scotland the year before. The book had the usual madcap astronomical theories about 'Martian Canals' and some photographs that were even worse than Adamski's. It caused quite a stir at the time and did as much damage in Europe as Adamski's did in the USA. The only problem was that Cedric Allingham mysteriously vanished and, after a discreet inverval (during which the publishers claimed he was 'sick') his death was reported. This prevented any interviews.

In 1983 I was approached by Chris Allan, a remarkably thorough UFO investigator, who claimed to have tracked down some leads and uncovered the identity of the real author of this contactee book. There was no Cedric Allingham. In fact the book was hoaxed by a man who, three decades later, has become a famous TV personality. He was also well known in UFO circles for his frequent outspoken dismissals of the subject for the BBC. Once he replied to a letter of mine, saying categorically that 'UFOs are absolute rot!' He refused to discuss the matter any further.

I took some persuading that this man had hoaxed the contactee book and never admitted it. The joke seemed too good for it to have lasted thirty years. However, I soon realised that whenever this man wrote negative pieces about UFOs it was the Allingham case he used to boost his argument. He was just about the only writer on the subject mentioning it at all (everyone else who knows the field long ago relegated it to the rubbish bin). It did seem coincidental. Then, checking sources and contacts of the man and his publishers, I found that Chris Allan appeared to be correct. It was an open secret.

In the three years since then I have learned from many other sources (including close personal friends of 'Allingham') that Chris Allan was correct in his identification of the culprit. Indeed, I wrote to the author long before Allan decided to publish his results, advising him that he had been found out, and that whilst it was not my place to tell him what to do, and I had no intention of stealing the thunder of Chris Allan, he might consider coming clean on his own rather than be exposed by some Fleet Street newspaper. I received an angry letter back threatening me with legal action if I ever said a word. Frankly, after that, I wished Chris Allan all good fortune in bringing out the truth.

In 1986 I had the cause to speak to this man whilst working on a BBC radio series. He was very helpful, wanted to speak out against UFOs on my programme and had evidently forgotten all about my letter. During one of our conversations the Allingham book was raised by him; I was unable to take the repeated insults he was slinging out at Chris Allan and merely advised that we both knew he had been involved, but that was the end of the matter, I did not want to discuss the contactee subject on air. I was interested in UFOs. At this point the BBC personality backed out of the programme and instantly refused to speak to me further, perhaps an indication of having something to hide.

A few weeks later Chris Allan published his accusations, which *were* picked up by Fleet Street. These said that TV astronomer Patrick Moore had been the man behind *Flying Saucers From Mars*. Since I have not been sued, and nor has Chris Allan, and the allegations have (three months later) not been refuted, I leave you to draw your own conclusions about what this all means.

At the same time as the brief craze of the contactee was wiping out years of serious UFO study, deep below the surface it seems the Pentagon was stirring. The super secret UFO project (possibly MJ-12, the so-called scientist-intelligence unit) had noted the rise in alien sightings and doubtless knew which to take as genuine.

Indeed, over the years we have accumulated a number of rumours (some of which have been accompanied by signed statements and even legal affidavits) which tell not only of the supposed UFO recovery at Roswell but also dead alien bodies, retrieved then or later.

This is, of course, a highly controversial area. It is possible that this group of people are telling lies, or are even implanted like the contactees to downgrade the credibility of the UFO field. Nevertheless, they do form a body of testimony and are part of the UFO story which must be examined. One alleges that President Eisenhower first saw this absolute proof of the extra-terrestrial nature of UFOs on 20 February 1954 (ironically the same week as 'Allingham' claimed his contact!). Officially, the President had an emergency dental appointment that day and was missing for several hours (a most unusual event for a man who is always followed where he goes). The dentist's family seemed remarkably reluctant to confirm this story. And according to sources at Muroc Air Force base, Eisenhower went there and saw dead aliens! Comedian Jackie Gleason also later told his wife (and she said he was ashen-faced and seemed to be serious) that his friend Eisenhower had let him in on the truth, and shown him the proof of UFO reality.

Stories like these are all very well, but they are just stories. Far better is the written testimony of one of the scientists supposedly involved! Yet this man, Dr Robert Sarbacher, has admitted to Californian investigator William Steinman that he *did* know about the secret UFO project, and has since confirmed details to Jerome Clark – who as editor of *International UFO Reporter*, one of the most prestigious journals in the field, was formerly highly sceptical of all such claims. His view has altered dramatically.

Sarbacher's 'Who's Who' listing is large and impressive. He is termed an expert on 'instrumental physics and communications engineering' who worked with the Navy Department, researched guided missiles for the Pentagon and now ranks high at the Washington Institute of Technology. This man has so much to lose by making false statements it is hard to believe that he is not being honest. Yet what he says is incredible.

Supposedly, in the mid-1950s MJ-12 *was* in possession of real dead aliens! He was invited to participate in the top-level project to learn all about them. He says, 'John Van Neuman was definitely involved. Dr Vannevar Bush was definitely involved, and I think Dr Robert Oppenheimer also.' These are big names – exactly the sort you would expect to be chosen for such a monumental task.

Bush, in particular, has already been associated with the study by others. Dr Wilbert Smith, a prominent radio engineering scientist with the Canadian Department of Transport, had headed their 'Project Magnet' in the 1950s. This had examined UFO-related propulsion systems, and he claims that during his work he knew about MJ-12, saw part of a crashed UFO, and spoke to Dr Vannevar Bush (the project head).

These could all be fabrications, but it is hard to understand why famous scientists should make such claims unless there is substance in them, particularly as they do seem consistent with one another.

Notice also that whenever scientists are involved in official UFO projects they are rocket experts, engineers, propulsion researchers, nuclear physicists and so on. This seems to suggest that, regardless of the public pronouncements that the subject was the province of the psychologist or sociologist (i.e. misperceptions and hallucinations), several different official bodies had individually concluded quite the opposite.

Sarbacher further tells us that, during the Eisenhower administration, 'I had been invited to participate in several discussions associated with reported recoveries (of UFOs and entities)'; but he was unable to be active in this work. Nevertheless, he did receive official reports on his desk at the Pentagon. Of them he recalls that 'certain materials reported to have come from the flying saucer crashes were extremely light and very tough. I am sure our laboratories analyzed them very thoroughly.' This matches well the claims about the Roswell crash debris. Sarbacher, however, as the quote on page 49 explains, has no idea why this data remains classified.

What about the aliens themselves? Sarbacher says, 'instruments or people operating these machines were also of very light weight, sufficient to withstand the tremendous deceleration and acceleration associated with their machinery. I remember in talking with some of the people at the office that I got the impression these 'aliens' were constructed like certain insects we have observed on earth, wherein because of the low mass the inertial forces involved in operation of these instruments would be quite low.'

If this is true, the consequences are awesome; but only those who were there know for certain.

8 A WARNING FROM SPACE? – 1957

I, frankly, feel there is a great deal to this.
  (Senator Barry Goldwater, writing on UFOs to a constituent, 31 August 1957.)

Levelland in Texas, is a small town set in the far west of the state. Only 100 miles from Roswell, site of the alleged UFO crash ten years before, its flat near desert plains were again to become the focus for a major UFO event.

The town is a cotton-manufacturing centre and has but a few thousand inhabitants. On the mild night of 2/3 November 1957 a fair proportion of them came into direct confrontation with this mystery.

It began at 10.30 pm when thirty-year-old Korean war veteran (now a farm worker) Pedro Saucedo and his friend, Joe Salaz, were driving their truck on a road four miles west of the town. Suddenly, a flash of light rose up from a field beside them and resolved into an object heading right for the windscreen.

'When it got nearer,' Saucedo explained, 'the lights of my truck went out and the motor died. I jumped out and hit the deck as the thing passed directly over with a great sound and a rush of wind. It sounded like thunder and my truck rocked from the blast. I felt a lot of heat.'

The object was a yellowish torpedo-shape and had streaked away in the direction of Levelland. Determined to get away from there, once the engine and lights sprung back into action, Saucedo made tracks in the opposite direction, towards the small village of Whiteface. Here, at 10.50 pm, he placed a call to Levelland police. Officer A.J. Fowler took this and understandably mistook the semi-hysterical state of the witness as drunkenness. The report got filed in the usual repository for that sort of thing!

Fowler was soon to realise his error. The amazing occurrences of that night continued about one hour later, when he received a second call. Car driver Jim Wheeler had been on the same road as Saucedo's truck, but four miles *east* of Levelland. He had met up with a huge egg-shaped object that was sitting on the roadway! As he prepared to swerve out of the way, his engine and lights died. He was about to leap from the car and hightail out of the desolate spot when the 'egg' climbed vertically, blinked once and the terrified driver's engine and lights returned to life as if by magic.

Fowler had little time to act upon this new development. As midnight struck the third call came in. This time the witness was Jose Alvarez, who had been ten miles north of the town. He too had almost run into a glowing ball of fire perched on the road. His car and engine lights then failed. The UFO had risen and the car had regained its power. After initial scepticism the patrolman was very perturbed. All three witnesses had evidently experienced almost identical things.

Levelland police immediately contacted Sheriff Weir Clem, who, with his deputy, set off to try and round up the UFO! Meanwhile Fowler continued to receive call after call. Most of them were ordinary citizens reporting this 'ball of fire' that was floating around the town. There were now too many for there to be any prospect of some game or collusion.

At 12.15 am another car was stopped by the UFO. The driver, Frank Williams, was at Whitharral − north of Levelland and quite close to where Alvarez had undergone a similar experience. Williams saw the yellow ball, lost power and sat in his car watching it; but he also observed a new twist. The oval object pulsated, and as it did so his car headlamps went in and out as if synchronised. Then, with a thunderous roar, the UFO climbed into the air and his car returned to normal.

Now quite certain that something very weird was going on, Fowler telephoned Reese Air Force Base, about thirty miles away. They had no traffic in the area. By 12.30 am Fowler was telling local reporters, 'We are besieged. [The callers] are driving us crazy.'

Fifteen minutes later, as Sheriff Clem and his deputy toured around the outskirts of Levelland searching for the object, another call came in. This was from truck driver Ronald Martin, who was very close to the spot where Saucedo had his original encounter more than two hours before. He saw the same orange ball of light land on the road, and noted that it straddled the entire width. He also lost the electrical power to his vehicle. Then the light turned bluish/green (making it very similar to the 'green fireballs' which had plagued the area in the late 1940s and defied Project Twinkle's attempts to evaluate them). Eventually the object rose up, changed back to an orange colour and Martin was able to drive off.

The final incident in this incredible repeat performance came at 1.15 am, from a different road north of Levelland. Truck driver James Long went through a very typical experience. Clem and his deputy sped to the area and at about 1.30 am themselves saw an enormous egg. It was described by Clem as 'looking like a brilliant red sunset across the highway. It lit up the whole [road] in front of us for about two seconds.' In this case there was no interference with the car. A second patrol vehicle (with officers Lee Hargrove and Floyd Gavin) witnessed the whole thing from a position behind Clem on the road. Ahead of them was fire marshall Ray James. He saw the object as well and *did* experience effects on his car. However, this was only a partial impedence of both lights and engines, which quickly returned to normal.

After retirement in 1975, Sheriff Clem gave a more graphic account of what he saw. 'The object was shaped like a huge football and had bright white lights,' he told investigator Don Berliner. 'No living human could believe how fast it travelled. The thing was as bright as day. It lit up the whole area.'

Many cases, and seven of them involving engine and lights failure, all came within the space of three hours. The following morning an eighth example was called into the police headquarters by Newell Wright, a college student who only reported after insistence by his parents. He had been east of Levelland at 12.05 am, totally unaware of all the other events. Suddenly his ammeter jumped to 'discharge', then fell back to normal as his engine cut out. At this point he had seen nothing and assumed there was a major fault in his car. He got out and opened up the hood to check this out, but could find nothing amiss. Slamming the bonnet back down he chanced to spot for the first time a greenish oval on the road in front of him. Desperately he leapt back into the car and tried to reverse out, but it was useless. It was a couple of minutes before the UFO rose, swerved north (towards the place where ten minutes later Frank Williams had his encounter) and Wright was finally able to drive home.

Officer Fowler estimates he had at least two dozen calls that night from people seeing something. Sheriff Clem, interviewed by journalist David Wheeler in 1977, said that after the publicity over the next few days the number of witnesses rose to about a hundred. For so many to involve a dramatic loss of engine and lights as the UFO came close is significant. Close approaches had been reported in UFO cases on many occasions *without* the interference to a vehicle. Why, on this night, did proximity of the UFO result in such a serious consequence?

The behaviour and pattern of these events seems almost purposeful. It strongly implies an intelligent plan behind it. No known natural phenomenon occurs in such a repetitive manner or with such major effects. The whole affair cried out for detailed investigation and once more brought the UFO subject before the eyes of the world. However, ten years later when the University of Colorado got their half million dollar grant to study UFOs for the government, the Levelland sightings were not investigated. Instead a contactee who had communication with a universe populated by bears was studied!

The amazing night at Levelland could not be so easily avoided by Project Blue Book. Their official investigator arrived on 5 November but only interviewed two of the witnesses with stories of complete engine failure. Alvarez, Long, Martin, Wheeler and Williams were ignored. In a two-page report the conclusion was 'during the period 2 – 4 November 1957, the area of Levelland, Texas, was undergoing a rather heavy electrical storm . . . all witnesses experienced seeing the same 'streak' lightning . . . The storm stimulated the populace into a high level of excitement . . . and resulted in the inflation of the stories of some of the witnesses.'

In other words, there was a storm, they all saw lightning, got carried away and invented the rest. Quite how eight sets of witnesses managed independently to imagine exactly the same car-stopping scenario, or read precisely the same UFO shape into this lightning bolt, was conveniently never discussed. The job was done, because most people (outside of Levelland) trusted their government to be honest. If lightning was the answer, then so be it.

Unhappily, the government were *not* truthful in this case, as in many others. The Levelland affair must have been a big headache to them. It had to be killed off quickly. It was the sort of thing that was ripe for detailed scientific investigation, study of the vehicles and so forth. That would have been catastrophic for 'Operation Debunk'.

Shortly after the Blue Book had explained away the case, Donald Menzel, one of their chief allies as a UFO vigilante, took up the gauntlet. He was primarily interested in mirage effects, but that would not do here, of course. So instead he proposed that the form of lightning was not ordinary – it was 'ball lightning'. In 1957 that remained a controversial topic. Many atmospheric scientists still felt there was no such thing as floating globules of electricity created by storms. Now they are more open to the possibility, but still (thirty years on) would agree – almost to the last – that ball lightning is very rare, does not form repeatedly, is never as wide as a road, or stable for minutes on end, and has no effects on car engines and lights.

Now consider Sheriff Clem's personal account of the weather that night. 'There were a few, thin, wispy clouds in the sky, but not enough to obscure the moon.' What happened to the electrical storm? It lasted *two days* according to Blue Book, making it one of the wonders of the Texas weather phenomena in recent memory – *if* it had happened!

Atmospheric physicist, Dr James McDonald, from Arizona University, checked the local records for the night of 2/3 November 1957. Guess what he found. 'Completely antithetical (conditions) to conductive activity and lightning of any sort . . . there was not even any rain falling during this period, nor had more than a small amount fallen hours earlier that day.' In other words, there was definitely no storm!

Sheriff Clem recalls that the police consulted a local weather expert to look into Menzel's ball lightning theory. He had laughed at it. Journalist Wheeler also obtained full records for the weather at Lubbock that night (the nearest recording point), and provided facts to support both Clem's memory and Dr McDonald's claims. The clouds were thin, at 8000 feet, with a temperature of 50°F and a light wind of eight knots. There was absolutely no trace of the fabled electrical storm.

So how did Blue Book get away with their explanation? Well, notice how they speak of the period 2 – 4 November, when the sightings had ended only an hour into 3 November. Why bring up the 4th at all? On *that* day, twenty-four hours after the encounters, there *was* a storm. Whilst it was not centred on Levelland, and storms are by no means uncommon in Texas at that time of year, it produced a fair bit of rain and some lightning. It was utterly irrelevant to the UFO events; otherwise why were there no incidents at places elsewhere than Levelland, or during the storm period itself?

As Don Berliner says in his review of his interviews with witnesses, 'stripped of this make-believe storm, the Air Force explanation simply falls apart.' This has to make you wonder why it was considered necessary to come up with little short of a pack of lies to defuse interest in this significant case.

Ever since the Russians released 'Sputnik' there has been a great increase in the number of flying saucers and other UFOs reportedly seen by people all over the US.
(FBI status report, dated 12 November 1957.)

Journalist David Wheeler uncovered another fascinating fact about the Levelland cases. At 3 am that same morning, the White Sands Proving Grounds, a couple of hundred miles west of Levelland, produced another dramatic encounter. The public relations office released details (presumably without the blessing of Blue Book!). This explained how two military policemen on patrol had seen a ball of fire 'two hundred feet long and seventy-five feet wide'. It landed in the desert. Two more men were called out and they saw the hovering object blink on and off and depart at a 45° angle.

The landing site was beside some rather interesting disused bunkers. They were remnants of July 1945, when the very first atomic weapons explosion had taken place at this spot!

No wonder the FBI expressed deep concern at the return of the UFOs, which in truth had never been very far away. They had seen an even more astonishing 'coincidence', if you are brave enough to dismiss it as that. One month before, on 4 October 1957, Earth had entered the space age, when 'Sputnik 1' was launched by the Russians. This was no more than a metal football kicked into orbit. Rather more significant was 'Sputnik 2', which carried the first life form from our planet beyond the pull of gravity. That honour fell to the dog Laika, who never came home, of course. In the history of our world, when the book is finally written, Laika's adventure

58

will be remembered while the petty squabble of World War Two will be relegated to a footnote. It is certain that any alien visitors watching over us would know (perhaps better than we did in 1957) the major importance of that footstep into space.

Laika was launched on 3 November 1957, hours after the events at Levelland − which were reported before anyone there could possibly have known about the secret venture.

In the years since 1957 'vehicle interference' or 'car-stop' cases have become a new pattern. About 1,000 such events have been well documented. Yet in no instance, so far as we know, has the interference ever produced an accident. Were the effect to be the product of a natural phenomenon (like ball lightning) then there seems no reason why it should always strike at cars out on lonely roads, away from other traffic and in situations where the impedence will not bring danger to the occupants. Surely a car-stop would have happened whilst a vehicle was rushing down the M1 or the freeway at 100 mph, with disastrous consequences. The fact that it never has offers more inferential evidence that they are the result of a conscious plan, a demonstration by some intelligence that they can control our feeble technology, but have no wish to do so in a harmful manner.

In 1947, when the UFOs had first appeared, they flocked around the sites of our atomic weapons development. Now, *exactly* at the time when we make that historic step into the cosmos they return to this location and give a fantastic demonstration that our electrical equipment is easily disrupted. Of course, since then we have gone on to build bigger bombs and to carry them in rockets guided by electronic systems.

Could it be that we were given a timely warning − and ignored it?

9 ALIEN CONTACT − 1961

It had been a pleasant vacation over the border into Canada, a few days away from all the pressure of being a social worker. The journey back to Portsmouth, New Hampshire, was several hundred miles long and tiring, but Betty Hill and her husband Barney intended to do it in one go. The easiest way was to travel overnight. So on 19/20 September 1961 they set off back on their southbound journey and planned to reach the Atlantic coast before breakfast.

On US Route 3, at about 11 pm, they became aware of a 'bright star' in the south-west. There is much controversy about this light, which seems to have hovered for a long time. Later, sceptics identified it as the planet Jupiter, then brilliant in that part of the sky. I have to agree. Nevertheless, for many cases like the Hills', there very often is a natural trigger. This certainly cannot explain the whole encounter, and it does appear that some outside force can manipulate the mind of a witness to make them see a star or planet as a UFO and use it to 'hypnotise' them into the correct state of mind.

Barney, who was driving, had to stop several times for his excited wife to look through binoculars at this 'dazzling jewel' which dangled before them, enticing them to drive in its direction. The road twisted through uninhabited mountains making the 'star' seem to snake about. All the while the couple were becoming more and more lulled into a strange state of mind by this light. Barney had tried to dismiss it as 'just an airliner', but Betty was now adamant that it had a 'pancake shape'.

All of the events so far could be dismissed. An excited couple, tired by a long drive, on a lonely, monotonous road and misperceiving a planet. If that was all there was to this case − and if the same kind of prelude to a contact had not since been repeated dozens of times − this might be acceptable. However, south of Indian Head, about two or three hours from the end of their journey, things took a strange new turn. The 'light' swung in front of the car, hovered above the road and was seen through the binoculars to be a flattened disc with a line of windows along its edge. A red light appeared to either side of the 'pancake'.

Barney stopped the car and threw open the side door. Taking his wife's binoculars he went out into the road for a better look. As he did so the UFO moved to his left. It was completely silent and was coming close enough to be quite visible even without optical aid. There were about a dozen *figures* silhouetted against the windows, which seemed to be looking forward through the glass at the entranced car occupants!

There was now a flurry of activity, as the UFO tilted and began to descend. The two red lights moved outwards, appearing now as 'fins' protruding like stabilisers from the body of the 'pancake'. The figures also began to hurry about as if they were preparing for something. Betty was extremely concerned about Barney's state of health. He seemed transfixed by the object and was muttering to himself, 'I don't believe it. This is ridiculous.'

The object was now close enough for an excellent view of the entities inside. They wore dark one-piece suits and walked about very smoothly. By this time the UFO was so near that it filled the entire field of view in Barney's glasses (certainly, Jupiter could not have done that!). He dropped them round his shoulder and began to cry hysterically. The 'spell' appears to have broken at this point. Screaming, 'They're going to capture us!' he jumped back into the car, hit the accelerator and sped off down the road. Later he admitted that the gaze of one of the 'aliens' (whom he called 'the leader') seemed to be burrowing into him, and he felt 'like a bug caught in a net'.

As they shot off they must have driven underneath the object. Betty opened her window and looked back but could find no trace of it. Then, just a few yards on, the Hills both recall hearing a strange 'beeping' noise from behind. The car began to vibrate. The very next thing either could later remember was Betty saying, 'Now do you believe in flying saucers?' and her husband replying, 'No.' There were more 'beeps' and they recognised that they had travelled some way down the road and were nearer home than they realised they should be.

The Hills knew when they got back to Portsmouth that something bizarre had taken place. They remembered the sighting, and were confused about how they had suddenly arrived further along the road. In addition they were a couple of hours later than they had scheduled. Whilst this might have been accounted for in some rational way, they did both find it most odd. Especially in connection with everything else. Nevertheless, there was very little they could do about the matter, and they made every effort to forget the experience. However, the UFO itself was reported and investigated by Walter Webb, a local astronomer.

It proved far less easy to forget the events than the Hills had imagined. Betty had a series of recurrent nightmares, during which she saw alien faces with large cat-like eyes and images of being carried on board the object. These *seemed* to be dreams and she assumed that her subconscious mind was worrying around the blank period in memory trying to come up with an answer for what had happened. This stubbornly refused to return to her. Barney also could recall nothing of that time.

Betty saw her doctor about these things. He sent her to see a specialist, Dr Duncan Stephens, and Barney accompanied her, mostly to offer moral support. He was finding it hard to sleep, but had no nightmares. Stephens' one-year course of trying to remove the symptoms via standard medical procedures (e.g. drugs), failed. Eventually he recommended them to Dr Benjamin Simon, a prominent Boston psychiatrist, who was noted for his use of hypnosis to remove memory blocks caused by traumas. It cost the Hills a fair bit to make these frequent visits one hundred miles down the coast. This shows that, whatever else you may say about this story, the after-effects were clearly real enough to warrant very serious concern.

It was into 1964 before treatment finally relieved all of the pressure. Both Betty and Barney were repeatedly hypnotised and independently came up with remarkably similar stories. This concerned being taken on board in a sort of cataleptic state, both being subjected to medical examinations and having a sort of conversation (verbally or mentally was not clear) with these aliens, who showed a star-map to explain where they came from. Not that it meant anything to the Hills!

Transcripts of the sessions were later written up by New England journalist John Fuller as *The Interrupted Journey*. It proved one of the biggest sellers in UFO history and produced world headlines in the mid-1960s. Later a TV movie was based on the book, dramatising the encounter as *The UFO Incident*. Barney did not live to see that. He died from a stroke, whilst still young in 1969. Betty, however, continues in the role of a kind of UFO guru. She enjoys this and has reported seeing countless lights which others who have investigated are certain can be explained as aircraft. Nevertheless, few question the sincerity of the original story.

That it may very well have been catalysed by the observation of Jupiter hardly seems to be considered. This is either used by the sceptics to reject the whole tale or is itself utterly rejected by the UFO believers. In fact, I think it is probably crucial. It began a whole new trend in the UFO phenomenon: weird close encounters triggered by very mundane things. The question to be asked is whether *someone* was responsible for forcing the Hills to make that fateful error of perception.

It is thought that perhaps 100 sightings a year might be subjected to this close study, and that possibly an average of ten man days be required per sighting so studied. The information provided by such a programme might bring to light new facts of scientific value.

(Part of the conclusion of the O'Brien commission set up to review Project Blue Book procedures in March 1966.)

As the amazing Hill 'UFO abduction' was being pieced together, Project Blue Book was trying hard to get rid of its burden of responsibility. In the decade following the 1957 Levelland encounters ufology had gone through what Dr Jacques Vallée (a young researcher who wrote the first scientific book on the subject in 1965) termed its 'dark ages'.

There were still sightings, of course, but the Robertson Panel recommendations had ensured that they were recorded less often and promoted as little as possible. In the 1952 Washington DC flap as many as 1501 cases were logged by Blue Book. Of these one-fifth were unexplained. The year of the Levelland 'demonstration' saw the next American wave (1006 sightings), but, thanks to the plans of 'Operation Debunk', only 14 of these (less than 2 per cent!) are officially called 'unknowns'. None of the Levelland or the White Sands encounters are included in those!

The years 1958 to 1965 (inclusive) clocked up 4487 cases (an average of over 500 a year, still), but only 113 got through the Air Force demolition process. In addition, there had now been many years of UFO stories. The media had heard it all before and it was difficult to whip up enthusiasm for 'just another UFO', however unexplained! Our own race into space and towards the moon was now also attracting the sort of attention that UFOs once had.

However, the situation was monitored by the civilian groups that had risen in the 1950s to fight what they perceived as the 'Blue Book cover-up'. Most felt sure things would run full circle eventually. In 1966 there was indeed a new wave of American sightings. Between them, 1966 and 1967 logged 2049 cases of which Blue Book managed to get rid of all but 51. Indeed a joke began to do the rounds at this time saying that, 'Every month there are 100 UFO sightings, of which the US Air Force explain 101.' There was much truth in the humour.

Having been so ingenious with their destruction of the UFO mystery, Blue Book found no takers for the project. NASA were amongst those who refused to get involved in the public relations headache. However, the 1966 wave had provoked Congress interest. Gerald Ford (on his way to becoming President) was outspoken in demanding action. He wrote to the Armed Services Committee chairman, Mendel Rivers, on 28 March and said he was not satisfied with government actions on the UFO subject, because 'I think there may be substance in some of these reports and because I believe the American people are entitled to a more thorough explanation than has been given them by the Air Force to date.' He went on to request that the House of Representatives hold a UFO hearing, inviting testimony from all quarters. Ford concluded, 'I think we owe it to the people to establish the credibility regarding UFOs and to produce the greatest possible enlightenment on this subject.'

What a shame he forgot all these worlds when he later entered the White House.

There *was* a brief hearing, as Ford had suggested. This was held on 5 April 1966. More importantly, however, the US Air Force set up a committee of scientists to advise them on the best way out of their UFO responsibility. Dr Brian O'Brien, an optical expert, chaired the group. There were five other scientists involved – notably a then young, now very well-known, cosmologist, Dr Carl Sagan.

The O'Brien committee made specific proposals that the UFO problem be handed over to the domain of science. It added that 'contracts [should] be negotiated with a few selected universities to provide scientific teams to investigate promptly and in-depth certain selected sightings of UFOs.' The full reports on all this work should be 'printed in full and be available on request', and Project Blue Book data (then still secret, of course) 'should be given wide unsolicited circulation among prominent members of the Congress and other public persons as a further aid to public understanding.'

Now this was an eminently sensible plan, which doubtless incensed the agencies seeking to keep UFOs under their control. In any event it was only introduced in a very limited sense. No files were released. No documents were circulated. One university was given half a million dollars to conduct a year-long study into 'selected cases', and you have already seen some hints about the sort of cases selected for or by this University.

Dr Edward Condon, a high-security physicist who had been prominent in the Manhattan Project, was the 'coincidental' choice to head the team. He set about things with a mind so 'open' that within days he was publicly joking about UFOs and saying the project was a waste of time. There was virtual civil war in the ranks, leading to a rival report by team members ('UFOs? Yes!'). Despite the 1,000-page 1969 survey ('A Scientific Study of UFOs') finding one-third of its cases unexplained, it advised the US government to forget all about the subject.

10 THE END OF AN ERA – 1967

There is no sensible alternative to the utterly shocking hypothesis that UFOs are extraterrestrial probes . . .

(Dr James McDonald, atmospheric physicist, University of Arizona, 22 April 1967.)

On 3 December 1967 Nebraska patrolman Herbert Schirmer had a close encounter of the *fourth* kind. Such things did not exist prior to the Betty and Barney Hill story. Now we use this term for any case where the witness claims not just to have seen a UFO, or its occupants, but also to be taken on board: an abduction!

The Schirmer case was particularly important, not only because a policeman makes an unusually convincing witness, but also because it took place whilst the University of Colorado was mid-way into its funded UFO project. It was a natural for their investigation. Here was something far more interesting than a light in the sky. A credible witness claimed he had come face to face with aliens. It had to require the most rigorous investigation.

In fact the Condon report spends just two pages on this case, and it is not that easy finding it. The heading merely says 'Case 42 – North Central: Fall 1967'.

Schirmer was a well-respected police officer, serving Ashland and its cattle ranching plains. He had been a US Marine and subsequently became the youngest man to rise to head of the town's police department. This was after the sighting. So his judgement was evidently not questioned by his superiors. Indeed, his commanding officer at the time of the Colorado University enquiry told the scientists (as they publish in their report) that Schirmer was 'dependable and truthful' and that he was personally 'convinced [the officer's] report . . . was not the result of hallucination or dishonesty'.

The patrolman had been on duty since 5 pm and was nearing the end of his shift. He was cruising around deserted roads on the edge of town because some cattle had been bawling and acting up and he wanted to make sure they were not creating any more trouble. He looked at his watch at 2.30 am, as he approached an intersection. Then, ahead of him, he saw red lights which he assumed were hazard warnings on a truck that had possibly broken down. Going to investigate, he was astonished to find that his headlights illuminated an oval object that was definitely not a truck!

The UFO hovered a few feet over the road, and the red light came from a row of small windows. Craning his neck out of the patrol car Schirmer watched as it emitted a screeching sound and climbed upwards (swaying from side to side at first). When it had gone he probed around the area with his flashlight for a few moments but, finding nothing, drove straight back to the station. He arrived at 3 am and entered a note into the log book. 'Saw a flying saucer at junction of highways 6 and 63. Believe it or not!'

He was not that well upon return, but did not make a fuss and went home without doing more than file this note. He had discovered a puzzle about the time, being certain that from first seeing the UFO (at 2.30 am) to his arrival back in Ashland was a maximum of ten minutes. Yet when he reached the station it was 3 am. He could not account for the missing twenty minutes. This factor only emerged when, after Ashland police released the story, the Colorado University team came to see him. Schirmer had certainly not made a big thing out of it.

The scientists who came were sufficiently impressed to invite him to the project headquarters at Boulder, a beautiful mountain city. Here he was to be subjected to an enormous battery of psychological tests – including the Rorschach (ink-blot), word-association and various personality profiles. Dr Leo Sprinkle, a psychologist from the University of Wyoming, was also flown in by the Condon team to perform hypnosis, after these other experiments, in an attempt to unlock the memory of the missing time.

The hypnosis *did* produce a memory. Inexplicably, the Colorado University report does not discuss it or the results of the various psychological tests. It merely comments: 'new information was added to the trooper's account'! A summary of this new information is available thanks to the hypnotist, Dr Leo Sprinkle.

A force apparently emitted by the hovering UFO 'towed' Schirmer's car up a slight incline towards it, having cut out the engines and lights in the same manner as at Levelland. Two entities got out and one projected a green glow all over the car from a 'box' that it carried. In a sort of trance Schirmer found himself getting out of his vehicle.

One of the figures stood right next to the policeman. The description will sound somewhat familiar already. The face was ashen grey, with a high forehead, and cat-like eyes. No hair was visible on the face, but the body was covered in a tight-fitting one-piece suit that had a balaclava helmet on top. The mouth was only a slit and when the alien 'spoke' it used a deep tone, slow and ponderous, which seemed to come without being spoken, as if telepathically transmitted.

'Are you the watchman of this town?' the police officer was asked.

Schirmer replied that he was. He was then led up onto a catwalk that ringed the UFO and finally inside it. Here a circle of 'drums' spun around, giving off multiple colours. The entity explained that this was a power source which used 'reversible electrical-magnetism' (words that meant nothing to the witness).

Both abductor and abductee then 'floated' up a sort of gravity-free elevator shaft to another level where Schirmer was shown a 'vision' (possibly, although the concept would be unknown to Schirmer in 1967, a hologram). This 'vision' was like a projected image of a sun with six planets. The alien alleged that they had come from another galaxy and were watching earth closely. They had landed to obtain some electricity from a power cable. Before being taken back to his car Schirmer was told, 'Watchman — you, yourself, will see the universe as I have seen it.' It was added, however, that he would only remember viewing the UFO from the outside.

After this memory had been triggered by hypnosis, the policeman was sure it *had* happened. Sprinkle advised the Colorado study for their report, 'The trooper believed in the reality of the events he described.' It was not in his field to say whether they *could* have occurred. Nevertheless, the Wyoming doctor was so impressed by all this that he spent the next twenty years investigating similar cases and is now one of the world's leading experts on the close encounter of the fourth kind. In 1980 he summarised his view, 'In my opinion the present evidence for UFO phenomena indicates (tentatively) that the earth is the object of a survey by intelligent beings from some other civilisation.'

The Condon team seem to have been remarkably *un*impressed by all of this one-sided support for the witness. They even noted that Schirmer had voluntarily *asked* to take a lie-detector test and that this 'showed no indications that the UFO report was other than truthful'.

So, why was such a tiny amount of space devoted to this major case, when dozens of pages in the report are given over to complex mathematical calculations about radar and atmospheric optics? They allege that the site showed no trace of radiation and thus concluded that there was no proof that 'an unusual object had landed on or hovered over [there]'. A real cop-out, if you pardon the pun!

Although they have *never* published any material to support their conclusion, and all that is summarised in the report itself totally refutes it, the final Condon Project counts this case as explained, because there was 'no confidence that the trooper's reported UFO experience was physically real'.

The hypothesis that UFOs originate on other worlds, that they are flying craft from planets other than earth, merits the most serious examination.

(Dr Felix Zigel, trainer of cosmonauts on the USSR space programme, February 1968.)

Hypnosis remains a controversial field. Subjects under its influence *can* recall information consciously forgotten. That has been proven by its use to bring back details to victims of a crime who may, for instance, not be able to remember a car registration plate. However, it also stimulates the ability to fantasise or imagine. All those who work with hypnosis professionally recognise that most so-called memories are a mixture of partially real elements and some frills added by the mind itself.

Of course, this has been used by the debunkers to great effect. They claim that all the UFO memories of 'missing time' are not to be trusted. On the other hand, everyone who has spent any amount of effort studying these cases quickly rejects that view. There are too many threads of consistency between the stories. Whilst each has its individual facets, which may well be distortion added by the mind of the witness, they also appear to be giving us bits and pieces of a fundamental truth. Extracting from each case the relevant portions is like building one jigsaw puzzle when the bits are scattered in a dozen different boxes containing twelve separate pictures. You must look for the parts that seem to fit the picture you want and then fish out those pieces. By doing this with the UFO observers, a story is emerging with often disturbing elements.

The aliens are said to be similar in description (often smaller than humans in stature). They often perform medical examinations on board the craft. They also use telepathy to communicate and demonstrate a mind-control facility that is awesome. Different home planets, names, origins and motives are given, which may be fantasy features added by the witness, but a thread that weaves the tales together concerns the alien's plan to help mankind by planting information into their mind, for later release when the aliens are ready.

Psychologists who have studied witnesses disagree. Whilst Leo Sprinkle was persuaded that Schirmer believed his story, Dr Benjamin Simon accepted this for the Hills only up to a point. He said that they believed in the UFO, but that Betty's dreams were just that and Barney had come to share in them (without realising it). Of course, Simon had the disadvantage that his case was the first. He had no way of knowing that after 1964 dozens of other people around the world would have exactly the same kind of encounter, with time loss and subsequent 'missing memory'.

Dr Aphrodite Clamar, a New York psychiatrist who became innocently ensnared in the mystery when she worked with one witness, has since studied the phenomenon as an ongoing research project. Recently she showed some of the standard psychological tests conducted on the abduction witnesses. These examined all the personality factors of the individual and are what doctors use to decide the state of mental health of their patients. The doctors saw the results 'blind' and had no idea that the witnesses claimed to have been kidnapped by a UFO! They all found the UFO witnesses to be normal, sane individuals, although one or two of the doctors were horrified when they were told the full facts about the people they had judged!

Clamar's work shows that the now several hundred people known to have undergone a close encounter of the fourth kind are *not* an abnormal sample, and if anything are differentiated by a *higher* than usual intelligence. This immediately makes the idea of 'mass psychosis' very difficult to accept.

I have been present at about a dozen hypnosis sessions carried out by British psychiatrists, mostly based in the prestigious St John's Street practice in Manchester. When these doctors were first approached they had no idea that the patient they were to hypnotise to a given date had claimed to have seen a UFO and lost a period of time (ranging from fifteen minutes to two hours in the cases I have sampled). This was important so as to prevent any possible leading of the witness. Although several of the doctors used have now done work with more than one witness, and so know what to expect, they on the whole know nothing about all the other claims from hypnotised witnesses and have no set views about the UFO mystery.

These experiments, run between 1981 and 1986 by Manchester solicitor Harry Harris, have involved a wide spectrum of humanity – including housewives, businessmen, a former RAF pilot, children and a British policeman. All sessions have been videotaped, giving Harris a unique and staggering 'library' of film that depicts these ordinary people reliving extraordinary events. It is extremely easy to recognise the probable fantasy elements and those parts which form the 'identikit' UFO abduction.

Many of the elements in both the Schirmer and Hill stories are contained, for example the cat-like eyes, grey skin, balaclava helmets, medical examination, use of a green ray, telepathic contact, deep, ponderous voice etc. To hear one witness make a comment in a session recorded months before, followed by almost identical remarks from a witness at another session (even with another doctor), who does not know the other case exists, is to say the least a shattering experience.

It is hard to view the tapes and keep your 'feet on the ground'. Being at the sessions, even asking questions of the witnesses as I have, is even more disconcerting. More than once the doctor has had to end the session because the witness (who is constantly under measurement for heart-rate etc) is reacting to the remembered fear of the occasion in a way that could endanger their health. It is difficult to believe that a fantasy would do that.

The case involving the police officer particularly impressed me. It was the first we conducted, involving three sessions (with two psychiatrists) during 1981. As I was involved from very soon after the sighting took place on 28 November 1980, and have met the West Yorkshire patrolman many times since, I am as satisfied as I can be that it is genuine. If it is, the connections with the Schirmer case are so incredible that the only real explanation for them would appear to be a deliberate plan by somebody to demonstrate intelligent intervention.

The policeman, Alan Godfrey, was also nearing the end of his night shift at Todmorden, a Pennine hill town. He had also had problems with some cattle and had decided (like Schirmer) to go on the spur of the moment for a run around the outskirts to see if all was well. At just after 5 am he saw a number of lights on the road ahead which he took to be a bus. On coming closer it turned out to be a dome-shaped UFO with a circle of windows round the middle. This hovered just above the road. His patrol car headlights reflected back off its surface. Then the object was gone. Alan Godfrey poked around a few moments and returned to the police station, where he found that the timings did not match and fifteen minutes were unaccounted for.

Under hypnosis he also recalled being taken from his car (which had suffered power and lights failure) after being hit by a strange beam. On board he was contacted by entities with grey/white faces that spoke telepathically and performed a medical examination. Before sending him back they promised (as Schirmer was promised) to make further contact in the future.

Alan Godfrey says he did not know about the Schirmer case in 1980, and many of the facts of his story are verified by colleagues. Three police officers on an adjacent force also appear to have seen the UFO heading for his patrol car. Considering the amazing parallels between the two cases, the options for solution are very few. This does seem like a contrivance to demonstrate that an intelligence is at work!

Yet, despite this dramatic new turn of events, the Colorado University project advised the US government to abandon UFO interest (Condon even later suggested that writers of UFO books ought to be horse-whipped!). In 1969 – after 22 years – official UFO study ended and Project Blue Book was closed. At least, that is what the public were told.

At the same time interest was mounting elsewhere. Space scientist Dr Felix Zigel began educating the Soviet people to report UFOs 'for science'. In October 1967 the British Isles was hit by its biggest UFO wave to date. There were many impressive cases, although not alien contacts (cautious British researchers were a few years in deciding to look out for the 'missing time' reports). Even so they led to questions in the House of Commons.

Major Sir Patrick Wall, a Conservative MP with 'defence committee' status, posed many of them, as he still does. The Labour government's Defence Secretary, Merlyn Rees, was involved because many of the sightings in this wave were made by British police officers. The Ministry of Defence admitted that they held records on sightings reported to them by the police (and via air bases), but that these were routinely destroyed at five-year intervals! There was some concern at this and an end was put to the destruction. All files from 1962 were therefore intact and, so far as we know, remain in the MoD archives.

According to *Sunday Express* journalist Robert Chapman, whose book *Flying Saucers Over Britain?* about the 1967 wave was the first truly objective survey published in the UK, the Ministry recorded 362 sightings in Britain for the year. He was able to get a figure for those unexplained, and this turned out to be about 11 per cent − four or five times the number 'Operation Debunk' was providing in the USA. This was extremely in accord with the figure all serious UFO investigators would claim.

These British files are retained via Air Staff at Whitehall (an under-secretary and a junior ranking). They are evaluated by RAF intelligence staff, and Merlyn Rees did assure Parliament in his November 1967 commons reply, 'This is not just an air defence matter. We have access to scientists of high repute − they have been consulted on all these matters.' No scientist has *ever* come forward in Britain to say he is (or was) one of these MoD advisers. So they are presumably tied fairly closely to the 'Official Secrets Act' which dominates all MoD thinking.

Both the Townsend-Withers (1953) and BOAC stratocruiser (1954) case would allegedly have been shredded before 1960. Certainly the MoD have long maintained that no records exist on them, and many other prominent British cases. As for the 1962 files (which they do hold), none can be released until expiry in 1992 of the usual 'thirty-year rule' that protects such documents.

Of course, Townsend-Withers also told us that the real files were not (and probably still are not) in Whitehall, but at RAF intelligence units. The scientific advisers presumably also generate some paperwork somewhere. None of this has ever been released, or even been admitted to exist.

11 OFFICIAL UFOs - 1976

Reports of unidentified flying objects which could affect national security are made in accordance with JANAP 146 or Air Force Manual 55-11 and are not part of the Blue Book system . . . reports of UFOs which could affect national security should continue to be handled through the standard Air Force procedure designed for this purpose.

(Memo, dated 20 October 1969, signed by Brigadier General C.H. Bolender, USAF deputy director of development. This is what led to the closure of the Blue Book six weeks later, and in 1987 the US government still refer to that closure as marking the end of all USAF interest in UFOs. As the memo shows that is just another lie.)

On the night of 19 September 1976 reports were received from witnesses around Tehran, Iran. They said that a strange light was in the sky. It was approximately 12.30 am and the thing was likened to a helicopter hovering with a massive searchlight. The Iranian Air Force officer who took the calls suggested that it was probably just a star.

B.G. Yousefit was this man. After several more calls, all repeating the story, he began to doubt his ready-made solution and realised he could make a capital error if he did nothing. So he went to have a look. Indeed, there *was* a huge glowing light which was immensely bright. He could not identify it and contacted Shahrokhi Air Base to launch a Phantom jet.

The Phantom took off at 1.30 am and headed north on an intercept course. The object was an estimated seventy miles from the plane, but so bright that it was easily visible. On 1 October the *Iran Times* published an account, purporting to be the recorded communications between Lieutenant Jafari, the Phantom pilot, and ground control. This was very revealing.

Jafari was 23 years old and broke through the sound barrier in his pursuit. As he closed on the object it was 'half the size of the moon . . . radiating violet, orange and white light'. It seemed to see that he was coming and shot away as he approached! Jafari tried, but failed to catch it. So ground control suggested he abandon the chase and return home. Almost the second he agreed to do so he called out, 'Something is coming at me from behind. It is 15 miles away . . . now 10 miles away . . . now 5 miles . . . It is level now. I think it's going to crash into me. It has just passed by, missing me narrowly.'

The pilot was so shaken by this event that he asked to be guided back to Shahrokhi. He had apparently lost all instrumentation and communication for a while, regaining them only after he broke off the intercept.

Meanwhile, at 1.40 am, a second Phantom had been launched. At a range of 27 miles from the object its in-flight radar locked onto the UFO and recorded a closing speed of 150 mph (although the jet was going much faster than that, so the object must have been travelling away). However, moments after the lock-on was achieved the blip accelerated forward. The Phantom went into afterburner and reached its maximum speed. It was still unable to close on the rapidly accelerating object.

The pilot and radar operator aboard this second phantom were about to suffer one of the greatest shocks anyone in the air has lived through. Suddenly an object was *ejected* from the UFO and propelled straight at them! It was a ball of light, estimated 12 feet in diameter, and seemed too much like air-to-air missile for comfort. Following instructions drilled in during Air Force training the pilot immediately launched a retaliatory strike. For the first time, so far as we know, an AIM-9 Sidewinder infra-red homing missile was about to be fired at a UFO.

It never happened. At that precise moment, all power on the aircraft instrument panel was lost. Communications (internally and with ground control) vanished. In absolute panic the pilot made a 'negative G' dive and tried to evade the 'attacking missile'. It was no use − the ball of fire kept coming at them, changing course and closing within seconds to a four-mile range. Then, in a perfect manoeuvre, the thing cut *inside* the twisting jet and, making a 'U' turn, flew back into its parent craft.

Communications and power returned to the Phantom, but the pilot decided that one warning was enough. In no way was he about to fire a missile at something evidently way beyond his comprehension. Instead, he and his radar man stared in awe as a second projectile emerged from the UFO and travelled vertically down towards the ground. They expected to see an impact explosion. Instead, the projectile landed and began to ooze light over a vast area. Meanwhile, the original UFO had accelerated to 'several times the speed of sound' and vanished within seconds.

The pilot took his Phantom down from 25,000 feet to 15,000 feet, all the time watching the glowing light on the ground to mark its position. Eventually the light extinguished, plunging the desolate terrain below into darkness. There was no point in remaining, but such had been the brilliance of the UFO and ground light that the pilot suffered considerable impairment of his night vision. It lasted long enough for him to have to circle Shahrokhi base several times until his eyes adapted. When the jet passed through 150 degrees magnetic on these circuits it lost all communications. A civilian plane in the Tehran area at this time also reported an exactly similar problem.

At dawn the pilot and radar man from the second Phantom were flown into the landing area by helicopter and pinpointed the spot where the projectile came down. It was a dried-up lake bed. Nothing was found there, but a 'beeping' noise was picked up on the radio. Landing near the point of strongest contact with this sound, they found an isolated farmhouse. The occupants claimed that on the night before they had heard a big noise (possibly the Phantom jet) and seen a brilliant light.

Six days after these events an official Iranian statement tried to squash the press stories. It said, 'Pilots made no attempt to open fire, and at no time did the aircraft's electronic gear fail to function.' It agreed the UFO *was* seen, that the Phantoms *did* chase it and 'no apparent explanation (exists) for what the pilots did see'. The rest was 'exaggerated'.

However, here lies the rub. For the account I have just given does not come from the Iranian press. Instead it is summarised from an American Secretary of Defence dossier on the case! This was released in August 1977 under the new Freedom of Information regulations (possibly because the Iranian jet chase was already public knowledge, UFO investigators having picked up the press stories).

The Defence Intelligence Agency had evaluated the incident and termed its value 'High (unique, timely, and of major significance)', adding that the 'credibility of many of the witnesses was high (an Air Force General, qualified air crew, and experienced tower operators)'. Considering the content of the accounts, it pointed out, this was 'a classic which meets all the criteria necessary for a valid study of the UFO phenomenon'.

This was pretty sensational stuff – and all coming *seven years* after the US government had officially lost any interest in UFOs. Not only had it *retained* interest, but it was evaluating cases at the highest level. The file has a circulation list which reads like a who's who address book of the US administration!

DCD [Domestic Collection Division] has been receiving UFO-related material from many of our science and technology sources who are presently conducting related research. These scientists include some who have been associated with the agency for years and whose credentials remove them from the 'nut' variety. The attached material came to my attention through these sources and it appears to have some legitimate foreign intelligence or community interest potential.

(A CIA memo released under Freedom of Information. It dates from 14 July 1976, proving once again that highly classified and unreleased UFO research continued years after the US government claimed to have given it up. If it applied in 1976 it probably still applies. Needless to say, despite requests, the 'attached material', whatever *that* was, remains classified.)

Memos such as this from the CIA prove beyond doubt that the closure of Project Blue Book in 1969 was nothing but a sham. Yet it is still referred to in all official releases on the UFO subject as grounds for why no action is taken on major sightings. Bolender's October 1969 memo demonstrates how Blue Book never handled the 'security' cases anyhow, and that some other (unknown) agency (MJ-12?) continues to do so. The CIA documents prove that science and technology staff (many, note, not one or two!) are conducting 'related research'.

In a nutshell, these pieces of paper sum up this book. For the US government to claim that UFO research does not go on in secret and is not considered of both scientific value and a possible security risk is to call their own secret records a lie. Since these records only match what common sense tells us *ought* to be going on, anything other than an open admission of the truth *would* be a Cosmic Watergate. It would also be an insult to your intelligence.

Another CIA memo (26 April 1976) proposes how they have 'officers and personnel within the agency who are monitoring the UFO phenomenon' and that the CIA should 'keep in touch with, and in fact develop, reporting channels in this area to keep the agency/community informed of any new developments'. What does this mean? It certainly seems to be suggesting that surveillance of civilian UFO groups is maintained, even that CIA agents set up their own groups, or infiltrate others, unless, of course, there are non-civilian 'reporting channels' to keep in touch with. If so, perhaps the CIA had better tell the Pentagon, because they claim not to know of any!

Either way this memo implies a major infringement of civil rights. We are either being lied to on a colossal scale, or spied upon!

Freedom of Information is a new concept in US law, and its use to release once-secret UFO files only began in 1977. Thousands of papers have come from the Air Force, FBI, CIA, defence agencies and others. Many more are denied under clauses in the act which allow material to be withheld if it might infringe national security to release it. Even more sensitive documents have probably never been submitted for possible release under the act.

If we can see what we can see from the files that we have, then imagine what lies in the ones that we do not!

If all this is true for the USA, then surely something similar applies in other major countries. The trouble is that Britain (with the Official Secrets Act) has the mirror opposite of Freedom of Information. The conspiracy is so much easier to maintain, thanks to that.

The object was described as being metallic in appearance and triangular in shape, approximately three metres across the base and two metres high. It illuminated the entire forest with a white light . . . As the patrolmen approached the object, it manoeuvred through the trees and disappeared. At this time the animals on a nearby farm went into a frenzy . . . The next day, three depressions . . . were found where the object had been sighted on the ground. The following night (29 Dec 1980) the area was checked for radiation. Beta/gamma readings of 0.1 milliroentgens were recorded with peak readings in the three depressions . . .'

(Part of a report submitted to the British MoD for its UFO records on 13 January 1981. Author was Lt. Col. Charles Halt, deputy commander of the NATO base at Bentwaters, Suffolk. It was endorsed by the UK commander, Squadron Leader Donald Moreland. The MoD contend that they took no action.)

On 27 December 1980, at about 3am, two US Air Force security policemen were patrolling the East Gate area of RAF Woodbridge in Suffolk. Woodbridge and its adjacent parent base, Bentwaters, form part of the NATO defence territory in Great Britain, owned by the MoD but staffed by the US Air Force. It flies Fairchild A—10 Thunderbolt tankbuster jets, large rescue helicopters and Hercules transporter planes. The two bases straddle Rendlesham Forest, a large Forestry Commission pinewood about eight miles east of Ipswich.

The patrol was a routine one, although it was Christmas period and things were quiet. The 'B' road through the woods, linking the small East Anglian villages, carried only a few voyagers returning home from Boxing Night celebrations.

The two servicemen spotted something odd in the trees outside the base. Thoughts of possible sabotage, or an air crash, raced through their minds and they radioed through to security control. This quickly established that the bright light was not an aircraft (none were flying). However, the control tower *did* have a radar target, and more intriguingly RAF Watton (a radar defence unit about forty miles north, near Norwich) had picked up an unknown object tracking across the coast and moving south towards them. They had followed standard procedures, reported to the MoD, and Bentwaters had already been alerted.

There was apparently much confusion at the base. Woodbridge was the lesser of the two units, although Bentwaters itself (where the officers live) is situated no more than a couple of miles north through the trees. The hour of night and Christmas spirit had all combined to make vigilance possibly a little down on par. Nevertheless something had to be done. The acting night commander ordered three security patrolmen out to investigate. They took a jeep part of the way, but could not get very far as the track petered out just beyond the gate. They had to continue into the forest on foot. The only light they could see ahead was the beacon of Orford Ness lighthouse, five miles distant on the coast. It blinked on and off, as it constantly did, but once outside the gate the proximity of the trees swallowed this up and they could see nothing but blackness.

One of the three men was Sergeant 'Steve Roberts'. This pseudonym protects his identity (as he requested), although I know his real name. The other two men (true names) were Sergeant Adrian Bustinza and then Airman First Class (now Sergeant) John Burroughs. They had no idea what they were out to investigate, but all had at least some familiarity with these woods at night. Roberts had been on base for several years.

Cutting along a path that slices through the dense tree growth they went about a half a mile from the gate towards a clearing (or field) where the lights in the sky had seemed to descend. Here they viewed an object, about the size of a mini car, which was conical or triangular (Roberts' sketch is akin to this but more like the traditional UFO disc). It was metallic, definitely a machine and poured light out across the forest. A pulsing red light was on top and a bank of blue lights (or windows) ringed the middle. It hovered just above the ground, floating on a patch of yellowish mist that might have obscured legs. Roberts says he did see these in a tripod formation.

The three men closed in, completely bemused by what they were seeing; but the object began to recede. The airmen gave chase and at one point a single patrolman (we believe John Burroughs) actually made an attempt to climb onto the thing or at least touch it and confirm that it was solid. He was in a deep state of shock, and like Barney Hill had been, practically hypnotised by its presence. He had to be dragged from the forest.

Meanwhile local farm animals were going crazy as the light oozed down from the thing and it climbed skywards. Unbeknown to the men some of these animals (a group of cattle) had fled into the back lane beyond the field. Here a late-night taxi happened to be travelling. It hit some, but was going slowly enough not to kill any. The farmer found his herd later and with another landowner got them to safety. He also assumed they had been frightened by air traffic down from the base (he saw nothing but the bright light). After causing a fuss and at first being told 'we know nothing', he threatened to take the matter further and this farmer (whose name was Higgins) got paid compensation. Nobody knew why he almost immediately left the area and went to farm hundreds of miles away. He was traced there by investigators in 1984, and confirmed some of these details, but would not state how much compensation he got for this apparently minor incident. His sole quote was, 'Whatever it were − it weren't enough!'

The story so far reads like a much-expanded version of the first half of the partially-quoted MoD memo at this chapter head. However, that memo was not released until June 1983, and then only thanks to pressure in the USA under their Freedom of Information Act. It should be remembered that, whilst the three patrolmen were indeed Americans, *all* these events took place on British soil, just outside a NATO base owned by the MoD and supervised by a 'landlord' British base commander who endorsed the memo. That memo went to the MoD for their action, but it is hard to believe that (seventeen days *after* the incident) it represents the first documentation about the affair. According to the MoD, not only is that true, but it also represents the *only* documentation on the affair!

Leaving aside whether you believe the British government stance that they literally ignored such a claimed intrusion (which *might* have been Russian paratroopers, a spy plane, anti-nuclear weapons activists or Arab terrorists to name but four non-UFO possibilities) we also have the very clear fact that this memo was *denied* by our MoD for two and a half years. During that period at least two people (local housewife and UFO researcher, Brenda Butler, and myself) made requests for information about the events. A telephone conversation with the UFO archives at the MoD in 1981 was even tape-recorded. Brenda Butler first wrote in February 1981 (less than two months after the events) at the suggestion of Squadron Leader Moreland, whom she and a colleague (Dot Street) *met* on base. He had assumed at this meeting that they were from the MoD, come to talk with him about the case! So he certainly did not deny it.

Every single one of these communications with our Ministry by British citizens produced a total denial of any knowledge about the incident, even though (once the memo was released to *Americans* in *America*) the MoD did accept that they had received it from the base in January 1981 and it was on their records. This was the first real *proof* of a UFO cover-up in Britain. Had that memo never been released in the USA I would now be telling you a story about the case which had no official documents to support it. Like all the others you would have to make your mind up based on the credibility of me (as a writer) and the witnesses I cite.

Ask yourself *why* the MoD tried to obscure these events from its own people.

The story as I have told it comes from the security man Roberts (who gave his account in confidence to Brenda Butler and Dot Street in January 1981, days after the events), and a radar operator at RAF Watton who independently told me later in the same month. He knew more than just the radar aspect, because USAF intelligence men had come to inspect the radar tapes and informed Watton of the visual encounters. When Roberts told Butler and Street they did not know me and I did not know them. Only later, when we saw the remarkable coincidence of the separately 'leaked' stories, did we combine forces in a battle for the truth. That battle lasted years, cost us dearly and took us to the MoD and the Pentagon. It eventually led to our book *Sky Crash* and a front-page banner headline story in the *News of the World*. When we finally got into the public domain some sense of the events of that winter's night it caused a furore and led to questions in the House and numerous media stories all over the world.

Yet still the fight goes on. For the British government continue to insist that they did nothing about the reports. A statement which, frankly, every one of us must hope to be a lie. If it is true then it would have grave consequences for the security of this land. If they *did* do something, why (now it is out in the open) do they still refuse to talk?

Perhaps it is because of the story that lies *behind* the 'Halt memo', as the explosive document is often called. As you will notice already, the eye-witness accounts are substantially more graphic than the report itself; although these were given immediately after the incident. It is also hard to comprehend why the British and American officers should wait so long to send an account to the MoD. That would be inexcusable, if it were true. Regardless of repeated MoD assertions in public and in writing since the memo release of June 1983, the statement that the incident was considered to have 'no defence significance' (their words) is meaningless. To judge this they would have had to act swiftly and to investigate. Both would require other documentation that they deny exists. They cannot have it both ways.

All the work, done on this single case, by ourselves and by American researchers (especially Ray Boeche and Scott Colborne of MUFON), has produced many witnesses. There is clear evidence that quite a few were 'advised' not to talk and more than once we have been unable to get beyond simple admissions that the story is true. Sergeant John Burroughs (whom we have recorded on tape) falls into this category. Whether his promotion since the events accords with his caution is a matter of judgement. The third of the trio of airmen (Adrian Bustinza) is out of the Air Force. He gave one superb interview (on tape) to Boeche and Colborne. This matched very closely the then unpublished Steve Roberts story which we had. After the interview Bustinza clammed up, went ex-directory and may have been in receipt of 'advice'.

Senior officers such as Halt (later made base commander at Bentwaters), Squadron Leader Moreland, Wing Commander (now Brigadier General) Gordon Williams, and the Base Commander in the wake of the events (Colonel Sam Morgan) have *all* endorsed the story. In Britain (before the publicity, it should be stressed) we found a number of civilian eye-witnesses to the UFO, including a man on the coast (Gordon Levett) who saw it arrive. The volume of testimony outstrips almost any other UFO case (possibly bar the Roswell 'crash').

Piecing together this fragmentary testimony is a painstaking process, but a quite dramatic one, because it contends that something far more significant really took place, for which the memo is just a pale reflection.

This 'Mark two' story differs in no way from the one given days after the events by our primary sources at Bentwaters and Watton. Yet, if it is correct, it turns the Rendlesham Forest case into one of the most important that has occurred in the past forty years. For it says the UFO landed, aliens were seen and made contact with the senior officers!

Roberts and Bustinza both told how the UFO was present for a sufficiently long period to enable senior officers to come into the forest. Jeeps and portable lights were ferried in, but these suffered electrical disturbance. The entities were small with large eyes and wearing one-piece suits (all the usual features). They were suspended in shafts of light underneath the object and, whilst no contact was verbally heard, several of those present independently assert that Gordon Williams seemed to have a personal close encounter of some description. Williams, whilst accepting the UFO story to be correct, has only said about this latter, 'If it were true I would write a best-seller.' If he were allowed to, of course!

There is also ample evidence that film was taken of the object and subsequent damage and flown to Germany, for USAF analysis. Two British civilian policemen are also supposed to have been present, having responded to a call made after the initial light sighting. Between 1981 and October 1983 (when the story first went public) Suffolk police consistently denied this claim. *After* the press stories they changed their minds and (whilst refusing to release log books to prove this or show them to any journalist) asserted that a call had been received on 26 December (the previous night) and that when officers went there all that was visible was the Orford Ness lighthouse. Subsequently shown ground traces they identified these as created by animals.

Whether or not it is significant must be left for you to judge, but, immediately prior to this sudden decision to comment, a BBC journalist and UFO debunker had gone on air to 'solve' the case as an initial sighting of a meteor (for which he had to allege that the date was the 26th of December and not the 27th, since only then did any possibly visible meteor whiz by), a later gross misperception by half the air base of the familiar lighthouse and subsequent false connection of rabbit holes at the site. All these features, very conveniently, turned up in the Suffolk police statement, although it should be stressed that not a single witness has ever given 26 December as the date. Several insist it could not have been that night as it would have meant their duty beginning on Christmas Day, which it had not. The civilians recalled that it was early into the

27 December because of the Boxing Night parties they had attended.

This says nothing about the gross improbability of misperceiving a lighthouse as a flying, metallic craft (an idea all the witnesses have laughed at hysterically) or how the rabbits which allegedly made the holes succeeded in being radioactive and leaping thirty feet in the air and crashing through the pine tree canopy (since that is where the most serious damage, first isolated by a trained Forestry Commission worker, turned out to be).

The debunkers really have excelled themselves this time. Nevertheless, as the story was promoted by the BBC, the *Times*, the *Telegraph* and the *Observer* (all the highbrow sources that reach places of influence) it has effectively wrecked any chance of those in positions of power doing anything about this crime against the rights of British citizens. This was the most audacious conspiracy ever perpetrated on you. It is time that you knew about it.

Do you recall the considerable fuss generated in May 1986 when very weak fallout from the Chernobyl nuclear reactor wafted across Britain? In December 1980 a much more serious nuclear hazard was inside our shores. You were not told then. You are still being lied to now.

Whatever did or did not happen in Rendlesham Forest that December night, it simply must have been the subject of an intense investigation. To believe anything else flies in the face of everything that the Thatcher and Reagan administrations have stood for. If these investigations found nothing of significance, then given the extreme media publicity for this case (unprecedented for any UFO story in the UK) it would surely have been simple to prove this without compromising national security or implying deep interest in UFOs. Everyone (be they sceptic, fanatic or UFO debunker) would have expected a proper evaluation of these extraordinary claims from 'numerous individuals' (to quote a later part of the Halt memo) all at a major NATO air base.

Instead we have had constant denials, sheepish admissions, failures to answer any direct questions, and at no time a statement that says the explanation by the media (i.e. meteor, lighthouse and rabbits) *is* correct. Such actions coupled with the totally unbelievable claim that no documents exist on the affair can only make one suspect that in this case the MoD are *afraid* to tell the truth.

The only information we have on the alleged 'UFO sighting' at Rendlesham Forest in December 1980 is the report by Colonel Charles Halt of the United States Air Force.

(A very specific reply from P.M. Hucker, at the MoD, to the investigation team on 21 August 1985.)

I can assure you that there is not a grain of truth in the allegation that there has been a cover-up about (these) alleged UFO sightings.

(Then Minister of Defence, Michael Heseltine, writing to Labour MP Merlyn Rees in November 1983 after the media furore about the Rendlesham Forest stories.)

The Rendlesham Forest saga is far and away the most confusing and important I have ever been involved with. It literally changed my life and convinced me that to behave as the MoD have behaved there not only is a cover-up but a cover-up of what at least is suspected as some major truth. Studying all the facts and witness statements it is difficult not to believe that an 'alien' object was in that forest. Whether or not some form of contact occurred matters less. The facts we do know with reasonable certainty are awesome enough.

It was certainly *not* a misperception of a lighthouse. Imagine half the US Air Force at the base being put into a state of panic by something they see every night! Is it even faintly tenable? Particularly when the 'chief lunatic', Charles Halt, was subsequently promoted and made full commander (with MoD approval)! Had it been even suspected that he had led the base on such a foolish exercise he would (I hope!) have been quietly shipped off somewhere else less strategic. In fact he stayed at Bentwaters for four more years.

Whether the promotion of the absurd 'solution' to this case, initially by journalist Ian Ridpath, then the BBC and by all those big-league newspapers, is coincidental or part of a carefully engineered plot is another thing you must make up your own mind about. I can tell you that twice, since we first brought the story to four million readers of the *News of the World*, BBC film producers have approached us and requested to make documentaries about the matter. On both occasions, despite receiving our full support, the programme never went on the air. In the first instance (October 1983) the producer, Doug Salmon, told us all his efforts were 'blocked at the highest level in London'. On the second occasion a December 1984 transmission date was even agreed, and put in writing. The show was cancelled shortly before then. The reason? 'Not enough information'! Two ITV documentary series have also expressed initial interest and then withdrawn that interest without explanation. Another ITV documentary series has sat on reams of material we have provided for three years without doing anything but periodically call us to ask 'What's new?'

All this action has produced so little result, concerning a major event on British soil. In the USA *two* documentaries (including a four-part series) have been made. In Japan two ninety-minute drama documentaries have been shown. We know of other programmes on the story. Perhaps it is only British conservatism. Perhaps the ridiculous lighthouse explanation has scored the victory it may have been designed for, or perhaps something more is afoot. I do not know, but it only increases my belief that much of our understanding about the UFO subject turns on this case.

However, ask yourself one question that I have asked many times since January 1981. Why have we learned so *much* about what went on in that English pine wood?

A security sergeant *happens* to tell two UFO investigators about what he saw a few days before, despite (if it had occurred) it surely being subject to undoubted top security. He asks for anonymity, although those who matter must know who he is.

A radar operator approaches a well-known local writer in a pub. That man, Paul Begg, puts him on to me. Secret information about the tracking of a UFO and what occurred in Rendlesham Forest is released.

Then, in spring 1983, a Colonel from the base approaches an American science magazine *(OMNI)*. This man, Colonel (now General) Ted Conrad, gives them his version of the UFO story. Aside from the alien contact aspect it matches the others. Conrad has refused to talk to anybody since.

Two months later, in June 1983, Freedom of Information 'leaks' out the sensational 'Halt memo' at the MoD. It escalates the case to a new level of official confirmation.

Finally, in August 1984, *after* the case has become known around the world thanks to our publicity, Colonel Sam Morgan (base commander when the case was being investigated) releases to us (without restrictions) a tape, recorded 'live' in the woods by Colonel Halt, Lieutenant Bruce Englund and various members of the team from Bentwaters, out to record the damage. The tape (which we had known about before, and indeed one of our investigation team had *heard* in 1983 when called onto the base by the then base commander, but which has always been denied officially) is like a soundtrack from a science-fiction movie. It not only records photographs, samples and strange radiation effects from all the landing site damage, but it gives a 'blow by blow' account as *more* strange lights are seen during this investigation! These later sightings are described on the Halt memo. The existence of the 'live' tape record of them is not. However, the validity of the tape has been confirmed by all those involved (including Halt).

Why has there been this very bizarre leaking of secret data? Coupled with the 'debunking' story it is almost as if we are being *fed* sufficiently tantalising material to keep interest in the case alive, but not enough to prove its status absolutely. Why, for example, have the photographs or irradiated samples been withheld?

The possibility of an 'education programme' to end the cover-up gradually was first mooted to me by a source in the House of Lords, when I gave a talk to a gaggle of Lords, Barons and MPs in 1980, days before this case happened. I was told that the truth about the alien nature of UFOs was to be released slowly. The world must be prepared. Films such as Spielberg's *Close Encounters of the Third Kind* (and presumably his later one *E.T.*) had been financed by the right money being placed in the correct hands at the appropriate time. This made it seem quite innocent, but the idea was to foster an acceptance of friendly, cuddly aliens and pleasant

UFO connotations in society as a whole.

Frankly, this came up in a discussion when several prominent establishment figures were having a drink with me at the House of Commons bar, and I do not even recall who said it. I treated it as a joke at the time, but I have since discovered that the same 'myth' has entered the UFO community in the USA from similar leaked sources. I have to admit, it would explain the very puzzling behaviour of those involved with the Bentwaters incident. Security trained officers just do not act like that, unless they have a reason. Once might be a mistake. Twice would be a coincidence. For it to have occurred repeatedly during the investigation certainly implies something rather more than that.

If you compare this possible move towards enlightenment with the manner in which the UFOs themselves seem to have been trying to educate us, then it makes even more sense.

The UFO story *has* gone through clear phases of activity, as we have seen in the previous chapters.

1) From 1947 to 1952 we had the era of first arrival – where the presence of strange, distant objects in the sky was initially confirmed.

2) In 1952 came a public demonstration that the military forces of our world could not cope with these things. We were utterly inadequate against them.

3) By 1954 the alien origin of the UFOs was being implied by the first real sightings of pilots or occupants.

4) In 1957, the ten-year anniversary, our steps into space were marked by emphasis of the fallibility of our technological equipment and a focus on atomic weapons sites. This was possibly a failed attempt to give a public warning.

5) During the 1960s, the UFOs seem to have concentrated on a new approach – getting round the back door of the military cover-up by secretly abducting witnesses and planting information into their minds. This has sowed seeds that are blooming and popping all around the world, spreading a cloud of germinating ideas in a manner so clever that the planners of the conspiracy cannot obscure it.

6) Somewhere along this line, into the 1970s, may have come the recognition that the cover-up must be dissolved. The dramatic decrease in sightings that groups worldwide have noted since the 1978 release of Spielberg's first movie *may* be the UFOs marking time, and waiting for the final resolution.

In the Rendlesham Forest story we may have seen the beginning of the end – or, at least, perhaps, the end of the beginning.

Part Two:

THE
UFO
WORLDWIDE

INTRODUCTION

There is no measurable UFO evidence . . . How do you prove something that doesn't exist?

(26 November 1977: Dr David Williamson, special projects division of NASA, after President Carter had asked them to consider a new study of UFOs.

In introducing the UFO story I have tried to show the main phases and suggest that it might be a strategic plan of some sort. It was rather top-heavy with cases from the USA and which occurred in the first two decades. Part of the reason for this is that I did not wish to repeat myself by giving more 'classic' cases between 1967 and 1987, although they are certainly available. If a plan there is, it originally focused on the USA, probably because it was the major industrial nation in the wake of World War Two. The plan has largely been one of gradual emphasis of its main points by process of constant repetition.

It is now becoming very clear to researchers around the world that in the aftermath of the Spielberg movies (be they relevant or not) UFO sightings are fast disappearing. Some have gone so far as to suggest that the UFO craze is over and we are now simply historians. It is not quite as bad as that. A few cases continue to trickle through, but the effect is very real and too long-standing and widespread for us to ignore.

Prior to 1977 the British UFO Research Association (for which I am able to give precise figures) recorded about 300 sightings a year. 1977 was the last big wave year the world has seen (following 1947, 1957 and 1967, which increases speculation about what might occur in 1987!). Here are the total sightings recorded by BUFORA in the years since: 1978 (443), 1979 (277), 1980 (118), 1981 (69), 1982 (29), 1983 (35), 1984 (25), 1985 (20).

The plunge seems to have bottomed out, but is unmistakable. Undoubtedly it is partly due to increasing sophistication of both witnesses and investigators. People recognise things in the sky they once misidentified (e.g. orbiting satellites), but this should have been matched by strange 'stealth aircraft' and 'remotely piloted vehicles' used by security forces. Even taking all the obvious things into account (including an apathy factor – UFOs are no longer the novel topic of conversation they used to be), the trend seems to reflect a real change in the behaviour of the phenomenon, especially as it is worldwide in extent.

Sophistication of investigators has allowed them to recognise that not all UFO reports are even possible evidence for alien craft. Every genuine researcher agrees that he can explain nine out of ten reported sightings as misperceptions of one form or another. He agrees with all the official studies that what really counts are the other 10 per cent. However, amongst these there has been a dawning realisation that there are strange natural phenomena still to be explored. The term UAP (Unidentified Atmospheric Phenomena) is now used to distinguish such things, that are probably on the fringes of physics, optics or psychology.

The cases in the first part of this book may not all be alien UFOs. Some could have mundane solutions, others might be UAPs. I have referred to them not because they are necessarily the best, but because they were important signposts on the route taken by the UFO story. In the pages to come we shall see more of the truly perplexing evidence.

Even if only one out of every hundred UFO reports offers potential evidence for an alien visitation (and I doubt it is higher than that), this still means a colossal surveillance of this planet by an intelligence from an unknown source: tens of thousands of *real* close encounters, like the fictional one at Devil's Tower, Wyoming, in the Steven Spielberg movie.

Whilst the cases you have read so far forged the UFO conspiracy, the true strength of the evidence lies in less celebrated stories, the ones that do not create newspaper headlines but do create as many headaches. It also lies in the curious connections which tie cases together. A small footnote leaps out from a witness description, something of a trivial significance to his sighting, but it jogs a memory about a previous report; and, sure enough, when the data banks are triggered, there it is. The same feature or behaviour pattern or even UFO itself has turned up before in an obscure case on the other side of the world.

Then you *know* something real is involved. Hallucinations do not agree on the fine details.

For example, I have a copy of the 22-page case file of a 1949 USAF investigation. It is labelled 'Project Sign', although by then it was the debunking Project Grudge that was in charge. Obviously that news had not filtered through the air base responsible for this file. I obtained the case with help from a US Navy physicist, Dr Bruce Maccabee, for a reason that will become clear in a moment.

The records show how on 24 May 1949, at 5 pm local time, an object was seen (from a boat on Rogue River, Oregon, USA) by five witnesses. The account is headed 'Unconventional Aircraft', as in 1949 the term UFO had not yet been coined for our language by Blue Book co-ordinator Captain Edward Ruppelt (just another of his fine contributions to the field).

Briefly, the account tells of how these witnesses 'while fishing on the Rogue River, near Elephant Rock' had 'seen an object described as being round in shape, silver in colour, and about the size of a transport aircraft'. It came from the east, then turned south-west and left no exhaust trail.

The various witnesses each tell their story in a pretty similar way. The disc appeared flattened and had a 'rilled edge' with 'a stabiliser fin' and a surface that looked 'wrinkled and dirty'.

Air Force OSI (Office of Special Investigations) checked the background of the witnesses as if investigating criminals. The impression received from friends, neighbours, workmates etc was favourable. Weather details ruled out any windborne object (e.g. balloon). No test aircraft were in the area, according to enquiries at Washington, but there was no radar coverage of this remote spot, and since light planes could fly without a flight plan through the area, the totally unjustified 'guess' (to put it mildly) was made that the witnesses had seen a plane of some sort. In the final conclusion the file includes these words, 'No data was presented to indicate the object could not have been an aircraft.'

No data was presented to say it was. The witness descriptions (which included some made close up through binoculars in broad daylight) make plain that no aircraft could look like this. Even more important, one of the witnesses (the man who first reported it) worked in the supersonic test laboratories of a major aircraft manufacturers. If anybody knew what a plane should look like, then it ought to be him!

This merely shows how brazen was the dismissal of extremely well-documented sightings of highly credible witnesses; but that is not my point.

You may have noted that there are considerable similarities between the Rogue River account and that which Wing Commander Townsend-Withers related to me in 1985. The two sketches make the connection very obvious. The Townsend-Withers case is a new bonus, however. I had already retrieved the Rogue River file for very different reasons.

A car factory employee from Bedfordshire had approached me with his story of a sighting made whilst at the Ramridge School, Luton, at 1.20 pm on a day in May or June 1957. This man, Bill Dillon, showed remarkable determination to recall as much detail as he could, making life very easy for an investigator. He had heard about the Rogue River case (which had, so far as either of us can tell, only ever featured as a by-line in an ancient UFO book), but this was enough to tantalise him. It sounded like the same thing he had seen, whilst a boy. So he wanted me to get the file (if I could). Then he would describe mountains of detail before we saw the file so that, if they tallied, this would be excellent evidence of a real UFO.

Indeed they do tally – in a quite extraordinary manner. The number of small correspondences is such that there is virtually no doubt that the same very strange object was seen . . . in May 1949 in Oregon and May 1957 in Luton.

I will not publish much of these specific details here, because I hope someone at Ramridge School during that sighting (Bill says many other children saw the UFO) will read this and give us their own account and sketch. That would further establish this already impressive 'coincidence'.

Nor does the sequence end with these two (possibly three) sightings. I have found several other closely similar stories since. One is a claim of a 'captured' UFO on the ground at a Kansas Air Force Base! Another is a series of four UFO photographs taken by Grant and Dan Jaroslaw at Mount Clemens, Michigan, at 2.30 pm on 9 January 1967. Nine years after the photographs stumped analysts the Jaroslaw brothers wrote to Dr J. Allen Hynek and changed their story, claiming now that they had hoaxed the pictures. Of course, the Rogue River file was not made public until the time of this confession (via Freedom of Information). When the pictures were taken it was still classified. The photographs *do* seem to show a remarkable likeness to what is in the Rogue River file and what Bill Dillon claims he saw in Luton eight years later. So, do we have another coincidence?

So far as we know there is no secret aircraft that looks or behaves like the object witnessed in all these cases. Yet it seems to have been in Oregon in 1949, Wiltshire in 1953, Bedfordshire in 1957, possibly Michigan in 1967 and several other places in between. If this is a secret test plane it remains very puzzling why the project ran for so long, was never developed and remains classified. In view of the daylight locations the pilot was hardly going to much trouble to conceal its passage!

Cases such as this are by no means unique. In recent years there have been several sightings of what British witnesses call a 'manta-ray' or 'jellyfish' UFO. Their accounts are very similar, and describe a flattened object of distinctive shape that moves with a quiet humming noise and travels mostly at night.

At first glance these reports are just another set of baffling UFO cases. However, aviation sources advise that the Americans have designed a 'Stealth' aircraft called the Lockheed F—19. It has highly advanced technology (including anti-radar detection and computer-controlled skin camouflage). Whilst it remains an open secret and there are no photographs of it, sources tend to agree that it looks like a 'stingray' (as one aviation expert referred to it in *The Times*) and that it is very quiet and makes only a humming noise. Several are believed to have flown from bases in Britain during recent years.

Suddenly, we now see the possibility that Stealth may well be deliberately used in test flights over populated areas, safe in the knowledge that it will be reported as a UFO when seen. After all, who takes UFO reports that seriously? Here is yet another reason for the UFO conspiracy. It provides the perfect smokescreen for the testing of revolutionary aircraft designs. Make UFOs respectable and this no longer becomes a possibility. The only place you can now test these things is away from the European front-line.

There is very little doubt that our UFO archives contain reports of secret test flights. The F—19 may only be one of these. There are rumours of military airships of an advanced design, and RPVs (or remotely piloted vehicles) have come under the scrutiny of researchers from the Yorkshire UFO Society in recent months. They believe these sophisticated drones are used in all kinds of situations, in the sure knowledge that they will be misidentified as UFOs and be effectively hidden.

Any UFO sighting in the vicinity of an RAF or USAF air base, or other military research unit, must be considered with suspicion by the alert investigator, and it is surprising that more aviation commentators do not pay more attention to UFO sightings.

There are even claims that some of our advanced aircraft technology may come from studies of UFO reports. In other words the UFO-like nature of the secret devices might be partially due to our research being based upon sightings, propulsion systems or (just possibly) captured hardware from the objects themselves. It is difficult to know how much of this might be true, but there is certainly evidence in American government documents that there *has* been research by the security forces into the propulsion systems *implied* by UFO reports. Who knows what might have come from this?

If the sightings are *not* of a secret test plane, then the consequence is obvious. These must be genuine, constructed UFOs which can only have come from some (presumably) alien source. That is why NASA were quite wrong in stating that there is 'nc measurable UFO evidence'. That is why it would be folly to overlook the potential in the UFO. That is why we must now take a quick trot around the world and see that this thing (whatever it is) belongs not to one country but to the entire planet.

The UFO truly is a global mystery.

13   UNITED KINGDOM – 1948

There have been countless radar 'sightings', many of them recorded on film, as the displays were continuously photographed. It would appear that the military could confirm without doubt the irrefutable conclusion that UFOs exist.

(Letter dated 22 February 1978 from an anonymous RAF radar officer, still subject to the Official Secrets Act. He described a 1955 experience at a top secret radar establishment and related a nine-minute tracking of six UFOs traversing Britain at the then impossible height of 87,000 feet and at 2800 mph.)

In late May 1948 Sergeant T.G. Jones, a wireless operator with the RAF, was one of four officers and two crew aboard a York transport aircraft. This had left home base at Tangmere, Sussex, accompanied by a formation of six meteor jets. The time was 11.40 am and they were cruising at 10,000 feet above scattered cloud on a typical English summer's day. Below them lay the Oxford/Bicester area and they were bound for RAF Acklington in the north-east, where they had a scheduled firing practice into the North Sea.

Suddenly someone noticed a glinting object, high above them. Communicating on the intercom all six people in the York and the six meteor pilots quickly established visual contact. It looked at first like a small silvery ball. As they discussed it Jones, who had a pair of 'Barr and Stroud' 6 × 30 binoculars, was able to focus on the object and see that it was oval-shaped and an estimated 100 feet in diameter. There were also three 'bumps' or protrusions, in a triangular formation, inset into the underside. Ground control further advised that they had it on radar and nobody knew what it was. It was stationary and above 25,000 feet.

All the meteors had oxygen equipment (perhaps the Mantell crash a few months before had left its mark even on the RAF!). Amongst the pilots, three had flown in the Battle of Britain, one was a Squadron Leader and another a visiting US Major (now a General). He was called Robin Olds, and Jones recalls his name because he married a Hollywood film star, Ella Raines, who visited the base and caused a stir.

Two of the jets went up to get a closer look at the UFO. They came within a few thousand feet of it. According to Jones, who saw their sketches a few hours later, they drew a flat-bottomed disc with a small dome on top. But as they approached the UFO took off from a standing start and shot vertically upwards out of sight, exactly the same scenario we have heard many times, e.g. from Wing Commander Townsend-Withers.

Upon landing at Acklington all the witnesses were asked to write a separate report, away from their colleagues. This was when Jones learned of the meteor pilots' observations and also that ground radar had tracked the UFO departing at the incredible speed of 1500 mph. Once these reports were gathered in the men were all advised that this was a secret matter and should not be discussed outside.

Sergeant Jones left the Air Force and took a degree in nursing, where he was working when he first sent me a detailed account in 1982. 'From that day to this,' he told me, 'as far as I know this little incident has been kept suppressed. What did we see? Why was it so hush-hush?' Maintaining silence over so many years, especially in face of public apathy and MoD ridicule, must try the patience of even the most security-conscious person. More than once, ex-servicemen like Jones have come to me saying, 'I know I should not tell you this — but after thirty years surely it won't matter.'

I asked Ian Mrzyglod, a local investigator near where the witness now lives, to look into the case further. Jones was at first very helpful, giving more details and filling out forms. He even promised to make enquiries to see if he could find the other witnesses, or at least their names. That may have been his fateful mistake. In any case T.G. Jones disappeared, and we were unable to get any further contact with him, despite Ian Mrzyglod trying for a year.

Coincidence? A sign of guilt? Did he just move away? Perhaps. This sort of thing happens often when you probe cases of this type, however. It is easy to suspect that the warning of silence is reinforced once it is known that a witness has talked.

The MoD have nothing on the case. Despite there being a high-ranking American witness alleged, neither does the USAF archive of cases. Perhaps the Freedom of Information Act will reveal something, But, like so many other hidden cases of this type, I doubt it.

14 AUSTRALIA – 1957

The evidence presented by the reports held by [the Australian Air Force] tend to support the . . . conclusion . . . that certain strange aircraft have been observed to behave in a manner suggestive of extra-terrestrial origin.

(Part of a report in the Royal Australian Air Force files, released in 1982. It was written by Melbourne University scientist H. Turner in late 1954 and is entitled 'Report on "Flying Saucers" '.)

Maralinga in the Australian outback is a fearful place. During September and October 1957 three atomic weapons were detonated there by the British, following four others the year before. The effect on the landscape was terrible. Director of trials, C.A. Adams, was insistent that 'no injury or damage would occur to people or livestock' and that the radioactive clouds were being carefully monitored; but the local aborigines knew nothing about the dangers of fall-out and, whilst precautions may indeed have been taken, it has been alleged that they were allowed back too soon. Some may not even have left.

The RAF were there in abundance too, acting as observers. There was very tight security. You could not even take tourist photographs without permission, and the rules stated that, once he had got his equipment back out of confiscation by the ironically titled 'Peace Officer', a serviceman had then to put in writing where he intended to film and that he accepted 'the legal penalties involved in unauthorised photographs'. He also had to ensure that his film was 'submitted for processing through the authorised channels'.

These intense restrictions do not seem to have got through to whoever controls the UFOs. They showed utter disdain for them!

One man at the tests was Derek Murray, now a Home Officer photographer and a highly reliable witness. His first-hand account of what took place at Maralinga poses many deep questions about what little we seem able to do in the face of these amazing craft.

The trials were over and in late October (possibly very early November) the party was ready to return to England. So it was a fairly relaxed routine by this time, and at 4 pm Derek was playing cards with a group of at least a dozen men. One man came rushing in to say there was a UFO over the site. They laughed at him, but he remained sincere. So they went out to satisfy him that he was just mistaking something simple. What they saw was something far from that.

They remained speechless for several minutes, seeing right in front of them something they had all heard about, of course, but had assumed to be a fairytale. This was no fairytale! 'Mind you,' Murray joked, 'it was perched there like a king sitting on his high throne looking down on his subjects . . . it was a magnificent sight.'

The object had a flat base and a dome on top and was silvery-blue metal. Indeed it was so clear that they could see what appeared to be plates on the side. There were also several squarish windows or portholes across the middle, but the whole thing was tilted at a 45° angle, maintaining this impossible hovering posture (which we have seen in other cases if you recall). There was absolute silence.

Several other people came out during this time, including the duty air traffic controller. He looked at it and then dashed off, saying he was going to find out what this was and who had sent it. Apparently Alice Springs and Adelaide were the only two possibilities. Both were miles away and neither knew what it was.

After about fifteen minutes of observation, dusk now falling around the Nulaba Plains, the UFO shot upwards and away at a silent, fantastic speed. The RAF men were entranced, but had no idea what to do. It was so far beyond their comprehension that the thing had gone before the shock wore off.

Derek Murray appears to be the only one of these many witnesses who has talked of this encounter, showing how deeply engrained the security regulations must be. Murray could, of course, be telling lies, but there is absolutely no reason to suppose so. He says, 'I swear to you as a practising Christian this was no dream, no illusion, no fairy story — but a solid craft of metallic construction.'

If it was, then alien UFOs *do* exist. There is no other viable alternative.

Recently the Maralinga tests have become the centre of a controversy, with claims that the men were used as 'guinea pigs' to judge the effects of an explosion. The British government categorically reject this, but in 1985 the Australian Parliament began exploring the possibility of reparations from the mother country and an enquiry was launched.

Extensive records exist about the nuclear tests, but attempts to discover any information on the UFO encounter have failed. 1957 is five years before the earliest records the MoD retain. So that course is a dead end. Bill Chalker, who is an Australian co-ordinator of sightings, has had access to the RAAF files in Canberra. He could find nothing about this dramatic incident.

Somebody, somewhere, must hold information about it. I wonder what the Maralinga enquiry might make of the tale!

Derek Murray returned to England on 4 November 1957, the day after a UFO made a frighteningly similar 'inspection' of the very first nuclear detonation site in the USA (see page 58). When linked with the launch of Sputnik 2 on that same day, a rather interesting pattern emerges.

UFOs have appeared in very restricted areas since 1957, but for these objects almost simultaneously to mark our first step into space and also hover over both the first nuclear test site and the most recent one (on the other side of the earth) seems to suggest that an intelligence was at work. This is not the behaviour of hallucinations, illusions or natural phenomena.

Salem, Massachusetts, USA, July 1952 (see Chapter 5). During July 1952 there was the first significant wave of sightings. Everyone was looking for UFOs. This case of modern witchcraft at ancient Salem came from coast guards, but is believed to be explained as room lights reflecting off the glass through which the shot was taken.

Puerto Maldonado, Peru, July 1952 (see Chapter 5). Nevertheless, there *were* genuine UFO pictures taken. This photograph of a cigar-shaped UFO emitting a vapour trail comes from a farmer and is unexplained.

Bernina Mountains, Italy, July 1952 (see Chapter 5). The same month also brought the first photographs of a landed UFO and its pilots, according to contactee Giamiero Monguzzi. He stuck by his story, but many UFO experts contend that this is a table-top model. (Photo: G. Monguzzi.)

Mount Palomar, California, USA, December 1952 (see Chapter 6). When the CIA became involved in UFO study, orders to debunk UFOs took hold. They were aided by contactees such as cafe owner George Adamski, who claimed that he flew with Venusians and took many incredible photographs of their craft. Long after his death the controversy about these photographs still rages. Are they the best ever – or too good to be true? Perhaps the whole show was set up by the security agencies to discredit serious UFO work.(Photo: The Adamski Foundation.)

Rouen, France, March 1957 (see photograph later in this section). If UFOs are real, why is the same craft not photographed twice? Answer — it may well have been. The similarity between this picture and the ones taken at McMinnville, seven years before, and on the other side of the Atlantic, are obvious.

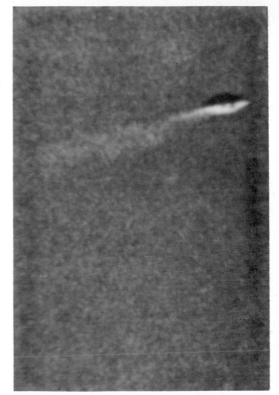

Namur, Belgium, June 1955 (see Chapter 6). The proof that UFOs were not an 'American craziness' came with first-rate sightings around the world, even in the wake of CIA-inspired debunkings. This is one of three excellent photographs by a postal worker showing a disc emitting a trail. The object flew *into* the trail by the final shot, proving its height.

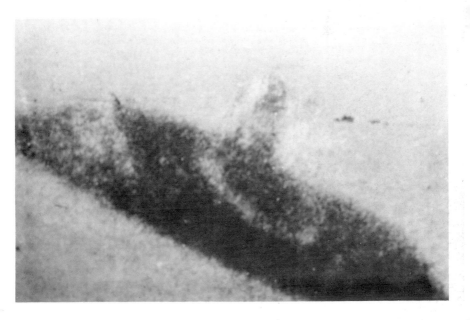

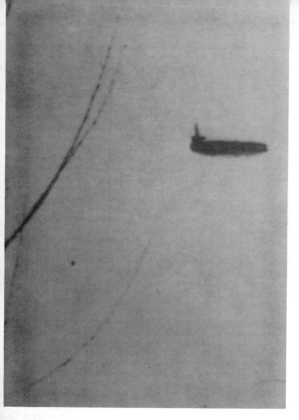

Mount Clemens, Michigan, USA, 9 January 1967 (see Introduction to Part Two). Two brothers took this daylight picture, one of several shewing the unusual object. Later they wrote to Dr J. Allen Hynek and claimed them to be fake. However, they are remarkably like a UFO seen in Oregon in 1949 and Luton, England, in 1957. The two brothers could not have known about either case.
(Photo: D. and G Jaraslow.)

Over Edwards Air Force Base, California (see Chapter 21). UFOs and aircraft have been featuring in many recent near-collisions. This picture, taken as a promotional shot for the B-57 bomber, may illustrate the attention being paid. Nobody saw the object at the time, but the UFO pacing the aircraft remains unexplained.

Near the moon's surface, July 1969 (see Chapter 22). Photographs by astronauts are very controversial and most are easily explained. This strange 'UFO picture', taken by Buzz Aldrin on the Apollo 11 mission when man first landed on another world, is perhaps evidence of alien interest in this historic event. NASA, however, say it is merely bright reflections off debris. (Photo: NASA.)

Kempsey, New South Wales, Australia (see Chapter 23). In July 1975 strange lights were seen around this Australian town. Glen Waters managed to photograph it. In another case the UFO was alleged to have smashed a local window, showing that physical effects *can* be produced. (Photo: G.Waters.)

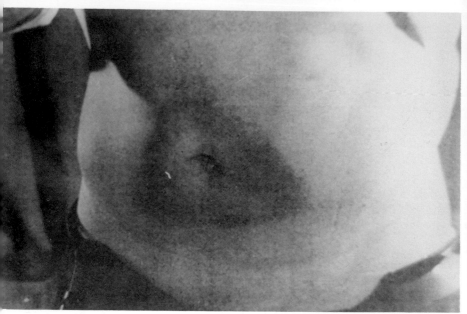

Southern France, November 1968 (see Chapter 24). UFOs sometimes emit radiation. In this classic case a beam of light from an object bathed the side of a house in which a famous biologist was standing, with his tiny son resting nearby in bed. Both developed weird red triangles on their abdomens, which recurred periodically at identical times — even when the two were miles apart and out of communication! (Photo: Aimé Michel.)

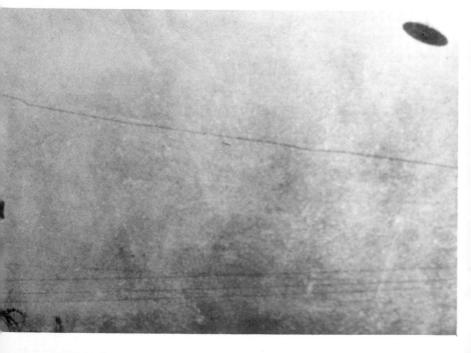

Trinidade Island, Brazilian South Atlantic, 16 January 1958 (see Chapter 26). A remote, uninhabited island. A ship with Brazilian navy personnel and scientists on board. A professional photographer and government investigation. All of this adds up to several photographs of an unexplained UFO.
(Photo: CUFOS.)

Falkville, Alabama, USA, 17 October 1973 (see Chapter 26). During a UFO wave, police chief Jeff Greenhaw (in his patrol car) chased this silver-suited figure. He lost it! Is this the only credible figure of an alien — or a cruel hoax played on the officer?
(Photo: Jeff Greenhaw.)

Left: McMinnville, Oregon, USA, 11 May 1950 (see Chapter 26). One of two photographs taken by farming couple Mr and Mrs Paul Trent. Considered one of the most impressive cases of all time, as it has passed scientific evaluation without explanation.
(Photo: P. Trent.)

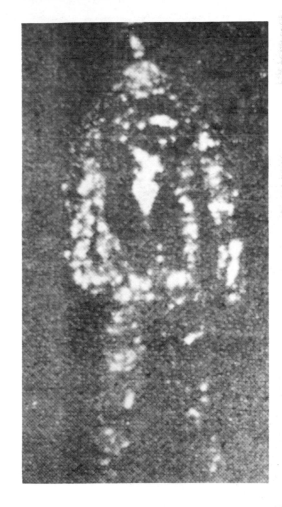

Gran Canaria, Canary Islands, Spain, 22 June 1976 (see Chapter 26). Many people (including Spanish naval personnel) saw this phenomenon. Photographs taken at Maspalomas were confiscated by the government, but one was later released with official files to an investigator. We do not know why.

Westbury, Wiltshire, England, August 1980 (see Chapter 27). Mysterious circles left in fields are *not* a new phenomenon. As the text explains, they have appeared in Australia for many years. The British rings began to be noticed in 1980. All are in cereal fields near Warminster — a once famous UFO hot-spot. Nobody has ever seen a UFO create the patterns, although the media speculate in this fashion each summer. Other ideas range from hoaxes to whirlwinds. Ian Mrzyglod and his group PROBE have investigated every angle and photographed the first circle within hours of it being discovered. (Photo: Ian Mrzyglod.)

Police in the province of Mendoza (Argentina) have stepped in to halt increasing concern about the presence of flying saucers . . . The authorities have issued a communiqué that the spreading of saucer rumours is an offence penalised by law. The penal code contemplates prison terms for people indulging in spreading unwarranted fear.
(*Buenos Aires Herald*, 7 September 1968.)

There have been many UFO encounters in South America and the press there thrive on them. Whilst some of the stories may be fabrications, borne from the paranoia the above article shows, hundreds of examples exist which bear a striking resemblance to those we know from elsewhere.

Of course, the language barrier is one difficulty. Most UFO research is done in the English-speaking lands (especially Australia, Britain and the USA). Not a great deal gets translated from the Spanish or Portuguese, and this untapped source would be unknown but for the efforts of the amazing multi-lingual former statesman, Gordon Creighton, who does this for the British journal, *Flying Saucer Review*.

I will summarise a typical case from the South American archives. It has a marvellous pedigree of investigation by Professor Hulvio Aleixo, a psychologist and UFO researcher who was actually called in to consult on the case within minutes of it being reported to Brazilian chief police commissioner, David Hazan.

The events took place at about 10.50 am on the morning of 14 September 1967, when sixteen-year-old Fabio Diniz was walking by the deserted grounds of an isolation unit at La Baleia hospital on the outskirts of the town of Belo Horizonte, an inland industrial centre. Whilst Fabio was still at school, he also sold Venetian blinds part-time, and this was his purpose in visiting the hospital.

He walked along an asphalt path lined by trees, adjacent to an empty football field. At this point he noticed an object *on* the field. It was shaped like a mushroom with a domed top and surrounded by a row of small 'portholes' and a thick central 'stalk'. This column was in contact with the soil.

The boy's immediate thought was that it might be a sort of fairground exhibition connected with a military recruitment drive then in progress, but as things became far stranger that idea was quickly rejected. A 'screen' that could be seen through (perhaps a 'force field' of some kind?) dropped like a canopy around the thing. Visible through this was a 'door' that had appeared out of nowhere and slid upwards on the column. From there two figures were emerging.

The entities were six feet tall, but looked human. However, they dressed in one-piece 'diving suits' of a greenish material, with the almost obligatory balaclava helmet hiding all of the face, except two very large eyes staring out. If you think this all sounds very familiar you are not wrong.

One of the aliens carried a bulky, tube-like implement in one hand. He went off in a circle around the base of the object. The other had a small 'probe' sticking up out of the top of his helmet and 'spoke' to the boy (although this may not have been verbally). The 'voice' spoke perfect Portuguese, and said, 'Don't run away! Come back!' Fabio admits that he was on the verge of escape and had turned to begin his run, but the creature then added, 'Appear here tomorrow. Otherwise we will take your family.' This threat, not surprisingly, terrified the youth.

After this sentence both of the strange figures got back into the base of the object and the door slid shut. The curtain also disappeared and the UFO commenced a slow vertical climb. Fabio took the chance and ran straight to the bus stop.

He was on his way home to tell his parents, when he realised that the shock could upset his mother (who was ill). So instead he went to the police station to report what had occurred. The scientist was therefore able to interview the witness less than two hours after the encounter, and stayed with him all day. When Fabio had recovered enough of his composure they returned to the landing site.

The doctor quickly saw that the boy was in shock. He was shaking, trembling and sometimes burst into tears. Aleixo's description of the witness at this first meeting includes, 'acute psychosomatic symptoms of fear and shock: his facial expression indicated anxiety and astonishment; pallid features, tremor of the hands, intense perspiration, pressure in the chest and rapid heart, verbal expression of fear, or insecurity in the presence of strangers . . . The correlation between the intensity of the emotional disturbance in him and . . . the incident remained constant over a period of several days (study) and was clearly perceptible in the tape recordings.'

The professor was certain that all these symptoms could not be faked.

At the landing site the police found some foul-smelling black material that crumbled easily. This was examined by Professor Roberto Murto, a geophysicist from the local university. It turned out to be made of iron, magnesium and silica with several trace elements (including quite rare ones such as phosphorus, titanium and zirconium). Murto did not know what it was or where it came from.

An impression which resembled a large footprint was also discovered in the dry earth. This corresponded in description and location to where Fabio had said the entities were, but it was just a print. As the police report said, 'the nature of this mark was not such as could either confirm or eliminate the possibility' that it was produced by the aliens.

The physical evidence being inconclusive, and no other witnesses ever being found, Professor Aleixo had to concentrate on the one he had. He next sought to discover if there were any pathological factors in Fabio's behaviour that might cause him to fantasise, hallucinate or simply lie. Truth drugs were given to him and the boy was (willingly) questioned using them, and in front of family, friends, neighbours and employers! He responded to the sort of imposition and trial that few adults would enjoy, with calm acceptance and insistence that he told the facts as they had happened.

No trace of any disorder was found. Nor did the use of various standard psychological tests discover any reason why the story should be discounted. Eventually, Aleixo was able to rule out all obvious causes, including 'organic poisoning, alcohol, psychedelic drugs, medicines or infection'.

Whilst the doctor admitted that hallucination can never totally be eliminated from consideration, 'the data gathered . . . indicate little room for such a possibility'. It certainly is difficult to imagine any UFO encounter which could be investigated more rapidly, thoroughly or objectively. That no conventional answer was uncovered, and that its details match quite closely with those reported by witnesses elsewhere in the world, can only help establish the significance of this baffling phenomenon.

Incidentally, Fabio *did* return next day as 'ordered'. Professor Aleixo went with him. The aliens failed to keep their rendezvous.

16 SOUTH AFRICA – 1972

Trace-landing reports number over 1300, and many researchers feel that an intensified study of such cases is the most direct approach to resolving the UFO enigma . . . UFOs are not available for study in the laboratory; physical traces are.

(Ted Phillips, researcher into UFO landing traces, commenting on cases such as the Rosmead, South Africa, landing.)

South Africa may not be popular with human rights activists, but it is not snubbed by the UFOs. It also has the distinction of generating one of the most ridiculous explanations the school of debunking has yet come up with. To explain a glowing UFO seen out in the bush by a farmer, we are told that the real answer was a sick elephant somewhat misperceived!

On 12 November 1972 another strange event took place at Rosmead, a small town about 12 miles from Middelburg in the East Cape Province. Philip J. Human, a local investigator, submitted the initial reports.

It began at 8 pm when three soldiers guarding a massive petrol dump at the town's army base saw something above the nearby tennis court, attached to Rosmead Primary School. They saw a red light 'similar to that on the rear of a motor car', that moved around in circles feet above the ground. Rifleman Petrus Nel and Fanie Rosseau were sure the light was *inside* the confines of the court. Their colleague, Gerrie Buitendag, could not be so certain.

As they were puzzling this out, Sergeant John Goosen and constable Koos Brazelle were at Middelburg police station looking out towards Rosmead through binoculars. They, too, could see a peculiar light above the town. Although they did not discover this until later, many of the local Afrikaans were witnessing the same thing, and fled in terror at the sight. One poor man was in such a hurry to escape the apparition that he ended up seeing stars of a different kind – running straight into a tree and knocking himself senseless for the duration of the encounter!

Half an hour after the light had been noticed, Harold Truter, school principal, arrived at his Rosmead home adjoining the tennis court. He was staggered by the sight that greeted him. The court was churned about, with huge chunks of surface tar dug up. A big light in the sky was moving vertically away, but he was more concerned by the catastrophe on the ground. He went straight indoors, called the Middelburg police and spoke to Goosen and Brazelle even as they were still watching the disappearing light. Needless to say, they wasted no time in getting over to Rosmead.

There were five main holes in the court, the largest about ten feet in diameter. Two 'spike' holes were also found. The entire scene of devastation had an oddly symmetrical look to it. Only the surface was disturbed. The layer of ash upon which the court was laid remained intact. None of the pieces of tar were overturned, and although some bits were deposited 200 feet from where they had been taken none were on the fence or gate. These only routes into the court were still locked without sign of tampering and there were no vehicle tracks outside. It certainly looked as if the only way the damage could have been done was by something coming from the air.

Detailed examination was carried out by the district police commandant, Colonel B.J. van Heerden, at first light. He discovered that a bluegum tree at the end of the court had suddenly begun to die and appeared scorched. None of the other nearby trees were affected.

Van Heerden made attempts to reproduce the damage by normal means (e.g. using spades and shovels). This proved impossible. The man who constructed the court was quizzed. Could a build-up of gas underneath have 'exploded' like a volcano? He pointed out that, had this happened, the ash beneath the tar would have been thrown into the air. Also the explosion would surely have been heard. Similarly nobody had reported a whirlwind, and for one to have deposited all the pieces the right way up seemed to be stretching coincidence a bit.

In the end the case went down unsolved – just one of those 1300 cases Ted Phillips spoke of in 1975 (that number has probably doubled since). Ground traces left by a UFO are not common (about one in 200 cases provide them), but over the years they certainly have compiled an impressive catalogue of evidence that the UFO – whatever it is – cannot be entirely an hallucination. Visions most definitely do not leave physical effects.

Radar tracked the objects over Lewiston, Montana, at a speed of seven knots. Two F—106 interceptors from the 24th NORAD region were scrambled at 02.54 EST, and became airborne at 02.57 EST. At the time of the initial voice report, personnel at Malmstrom Air Force Base and SAC sites K-1, K-3, L-3 and L-6 were reporting lights in the sky.

(Part of a Freedom of Information memo describing events on the night of 8 November 1975, when top security SAC [Strategic Air Command] atomic missile sites were penetrated by UFOs, seen visually and on radar.)

The depression left by the negative Colorado University report and the closure of Project Blue Book in late 1969 was very short-lived. In the autumn of 1973 the UFOs returned to America with a major wave that brought a flood of new books, civilian science groups, much public interest and the birth of the Spielberg idea to make the definitive UFO movie.

Most of the best cases came in mid-October, and undoubtedly one of the most important befell a helicopter crew at just after 11 pm on the night of 18 October. The matter was officially reported and can be found in a Freedom of Information document dated 23 November, signed by all four crew members and headed 'Near midair collision with UFO report'. However, even before the release of this file, the case was followed up. It was one of the first to receive weeks of research by the Center for UFO Studies (CUFOS) – a group launched that year by Dr J. Allen Hynek, the astronomer who for more than twenty years had been the silent UFO advocate as the official Air Force UFO consultant. Now he was determined to make up for lost time and speak out.

CUFOS included a number of scientists, such as Dr Jacques Vallée, whose books had been beacons in the decade before. There were also some renegades from the Colorado project, such as Dr David Saunders and Richard Sigismund – who had rebelled against the negative verdict. In charge of the helicopter case investigation (and author of the subsequent superb CUFOS case file) was Jennie Zeidman. She had been Hynek's secretary in Blue Book days and had been involved in other classified UFO work. She knew that the public official stance on UFOs was false.

Helicopter 68 -15444 was a Bell UH—IH Huey which was owned by the US Army Reserve. It had left Columbus, Ohio, for its home base of Cleveland, one hundred miles north. In command of the flight (sitting in the right front seat) was Captain (now Major) Lawrence Coyne, who had 19 years' flying experience and was very familiar with nocturnal missions. Beside him (front left seat), and actually flying the aircraft, was Lieutenant Arrigo Jezzi, an engineer.

The other two people aboard were Sergeant John Healey – a policeman and medical officer (sitting behind Jezzi) and Sergeant Robert Yanacsek, next to him. He was a computer expert. They were cruising at 2500 feet above the gently undulating terrain on a mild, clear night with many stars. Although there was no moon, they were easily able to see the ground below.

Healey spotted something first – a red light out to the west, slowly moving south. He did not think it important (just other air traffic of some sort) and mentioned it to nobody, but two minutes later (at 11.02 pm) Yanacsek also saw a red light through his window (to the south-east). After watching it for about a minute he decided it was probably a North American F—100 Super Sabre plane out of Mansfield, over which they were shortly due to pass. He told his commander. Coyne looked out, saw it, made a similar judgement and merely told the Sergeant to keep his eyes on it.

About thirty seconds later Yanacsek called out that the light had now altered course and seemed to be heading right at them. In the next few moments Coyne confirmed this, grabbed the controls from Jezzi and put the helicopter into an emergency evasion by pressing down on the stick and putting them into a controlled descent. Almost at the same time he called over the radio to Mansfield and was acknowledged. 'Do you have any high performance aircraft in this area at 2500 feet?' he demanded. There was no reply. After several subsequent attempts, and on other frequencies, it was realised that both UHF and VHF wavelengths were dead. The impedence was temporary (five minutes later they were working fine) but critical, given the situation they were in.

Mansfield later confirmed that they did not have any aircraft in the area. Nor, despite recording all ground-to-air communications, was there anything on tape from the UH—IH.

Meanwhile the red light was now much brighter and was still closing on the chopper. Coyne reacted swiftly again and increased the rate of dive, so that the machine was now descending at 2000 feet per minute. This was an action that would only have followed a perceived serious emergency. The altimeter showed 1700 feet at this point – so they were in definite proximity to the ground! Despite major 'G' forces Coyne was able to retain control of the aircraft at all times.

Suddenly the object had streaked in front of, and above, the helicopter. It stopped dead ahead for an estimated ten seconds and filled the entire windscreen during these horrific moments, as the Huey went almost straight down! Despite the stress all the crew men got a good look at it. They noted that it blocked out the stars behind and was like a grey cigar with a small dome on top. Yanacsek thinks he saw windows atop the dome. Nobody else did. The red light was on the front 'nose-cone' of the object, a white light lit the side and a green one poured from beneath. This began to swing around, as if it were a searchlight, and shone *into* the cabin bathing all four men in a greenish haze!

After this 'frozen tableau' of horror the cigar accelerated away rapidly to the west and soon appeared as just the white light. It then made an angled turn and moved off towards the north-west horizon. Healey was in the right position to be able to follow this for a couple of minutes before it was lost above Lake Erie. Jezzi and Coyne, up front, had far more important things on their mind. The helicopter was still in serious danger.

They had noticed, as soon as the UFO had streaked away, that the magnetic compass on the instrument panel was spinning at a rate of four revolutions a minute. Also, inexplicably, the altimeter now showed a height of 3500 feet and a *climbing* ascent at 1000 feet per minute. The stick was still pointing downwards and Coyne was reluctant to touch it. Moving it 'up' might produce fatal results. Of course, he had no choice and the aircraft was wrestled back to normality. They had got to 3800 feet before this was achieved. Next day the machine was thoroughly checked over. It was not at fault in any way.

Incredible as it may seem, the only reasonable conclusion is that the green ray from the UFO was acting like a 'tractor beam' that pulled the helicopter up through a couple of thousand feet. It is not difficult to imagine intelligent UFO occupants doing this to rescue the human crew from a potentially disastrous situation. Although Coyne had seen the altimeter at 1700 feet, because of ground elevation he realises they can only have been seconds from impact when the amazing rescue took place.

Detailed reconstruction of the event and analysis of the motion of the helicopter showed a one-minute duration of 'conflict' and a total of five minutes' encounter with the UFO. Investigation also turned up witnesses on the ground who saw the near collision *and* viewed the green beam. It had lit up the ground and the car where a woman and four children had been. The youngsters screamed at it and so they missed seeing how the helicopter avoided its near impact with the ground.

Jennie Zeidman points out, to anyone who might accuse these people of faking their story after the helicopter incident was publicised, that complex calculations based on their descriptions match perfectly with the helicopter crew accounts. It would be almost impossible for that to occur unless they had all seen a real event.

In 1974 the modern folk hero of the debunking school, aviation journalist

Philip Klass, produced a book entitled *UFOs Explained* – and solved the case. He is notorious for making sweeping assumptions, as he did in this instance, and I felt his wrath in November 1983 when I lectured (principally on the Rendlesham Forest Story) at a conference organised by the University of Nebraska. There were several eminent scientists on the bill, including Professor Hynek, and the incidental theme happened to be the cover-up of UFO evidence. Klass, unsuccessfully, tried to persuade the University hierarchy to cancel the three-day meeting because it lent sympathy to the Communists! The idea is so ridiculous it got the response it deserved – but it does show the lengths the debunkers will go to in order to prevent the truth emerging.

As for the Ohio helicopter case, Klass decided (without meeting the witnesses, seeing the helicopter or reconstructing the events – all of which CUFOS did) that they must have exaggerated a bright meteor. Apart from the fact that no meteor in the history of science has ever been visible for what is a theoretically impossible duration of five minutes, that meteors are incapable of creating physical effects, that they do not appear as domed cigars with red and green lights or that nobody else in the State of Ohio evidently witnessed this fantastic sight, it might be a reasonable suggestion! Of course, meteors do not perform levitation tricks, either.

It must be said that the 'green beam' has been reported by others (who I am quite sure usually do not know about similar cases) and that more than once this 'levitation' effect has accompanied it.

One case I recall in particular was investigated by the Yorkshire UFO Society and involved a British Rail worker walking along the tracks from Headingley, Leeds, to his home in the early evening of 12 February 1979. He observed a strange green light above him, but then had to move quickly onto an adjacent track as the Harrogate to Leeds train went by. Whether this was perceived as endangering the man is hard to know. He was quite safe. However, the green thing came low above him and seemed to suck him upwards into the air. It felt like a powerful magnet had pulled him about six feet skywards and moved him bodily along the track, depositing him unharmed further along. He stood petrified for a few moments, but then turned back and saw an oval with a misty vapour moving away. Needless to say he did not take this short cut home after that!

The connection between these two 'green beam' levitations has not, so far as I know, been pointed out before, but it certainly adds another little nugget of evidence to the growing persuasion that some UFOs must be intelligently controlled.

Something very superior to me influenced me with its power. It demonstrated to me that it was stronger than the whole army . . . I was totally powerless.
(Extract from the mysterious 'Talavera' witness interview, found discarded on a French train in 1981.)

Talavera La Real is a Spanish Air Force Base near the town of Badajoz on the Portuguese border. In the early hours of 12 November 1976 it staged either the most audacious hoax or one of the weirdest UFO tales ever.

Juan Benitez, a local UFO researcher whose work procuring official government documents we will examine later, heard of the case soon after it occurred but had to wait until early 1978 (after the principal witness had left the Air Force) before he could publish details.

Two witnesses were originally involved. They were José Trejo, a 20-year-old national service man, and Juan Carrizosa. They were in sentry boxes protecting a fuel dump inside the base at 1.45 am on a cool, dark night. Suddenly they heard a high-pitched whistle, like an electronic signal – which, according to Trejo, was 'so piercing it hurt our ears'.

It lasted only seconds, but after a pause began again. Trejo called Carrizosa over and they searched the area but found nothing. Five minutes later it happened a third time. 'We thought we would go mad,' Trejo said. 'It seemed our eardrums were going to be ruptured.'

Now some minutes after 2 am the silence descended once more, but with it came a new puzzle. A huge silent explosion of light appeared in the sky and lit up large areas for about twenty seconds.

A third patrolman, José Hidalgo, now arrived, along with a guard dog. He was making a routine tour of the perimeter sentry boxes and wanted to know if they had seen the big glow. He had done so, but had not heard the noise. After raising the alarm Trejo, Carrizosa and Hidalgo were all told to go out to the fuel dump and make sure that no saboteurs were breaking in.

Hugging the wall that rings the base, as it was pitch dark now, they were happy to note that the dog remained calm, suggesting all was well, but they loaded up their quick-fire rifles just in case!

Hearing noises in the bushes they let the dog loose. It ran in, but returned a few moments later, swaying as if stunned or drugged. It recovered and they sent it back a couple more times, with the same result. 'His ears seemed to be hurting. He was whimpering,' Trejo explained. Finally, the dog began to circle the group of men — a behaviour posture it is taught to adopt if it senses danger.

On the alert Trejo says he now 'felt' something, and turned to see 'a splendid light'. As he faced it full on he realised it was 'something absolutely extraordinary such as I have never seen before'. It was an enormous human figure about ten feet tall, glowing a phosphorescent green. This is rather reminiscent of a hologram, which glows by projected light. It definitely seems to have been insubstantial. Indeed, the legs were not visible and the body was made 'out of small points of light'.

Trejo was paralysed with fear and could not move his hands to fire. Then, 'I felt myself suddenly go weak . . . Before falling to the ground, I managed to shout to my comrades to get down.' On the ground, but conscious, he found his eyesight fading in and out. His chest was sore for at least twenty minutes.

These shouts brought Carrizosa and Hidalgo rushing forward. They had been some yards behind, looking in the opposite direction. Almost as one they fired about 50 rounds straight at the thing. Being about 60 feet from it, they are sure they must have had a direct hit. There was a 'photographer's flash' and then 'like the fading of the image on a television screen', the figure just vanished.

Such details match the impression that this was a projection of some sort, but where was the projector and who was the projectionist?

The two men helped the weakened Trejo to his feet. The entire base had been alerted by the gunfire and flared into life, but nobody found anything. At daybreak 50 men scoured the area. Not a single spent cartridge was found and, although the 'entity' was standing in front of the wall, this showed no trace of any marks. 'We simply cannot understand how it could be that not one of the shots hit that wall which was right there in front of us,' Carrizosa said later.

Over the next two weeks Trejo suffered bouts of blindness and temporary blackouts. He was treated in the Air Force sick bay, then transferred to a hospital in Badajoz for extensive tests. No physical cause was diagnosed. It was decided that the attacks were psychological and trauma-induced. Exactly the same situation has arisen in other cases (including an Essex teenager who had a frightening encounter in mid-Wales with subsequently induced spells of blindness, 'to stop himself seeing the thing again', according to his doctor).

After a month in the Air Force hospital in Madrid, where these effects gradually decreased, Trejo left the service and Benitez found him in good health at his interview a year after the events.

What happened to the dog is unrecorded.

Nearly four years after the first report, French UFO writer Geneviève Vanquelef told of the incredible sequel. If there is anything to the 'education programme' this may be yet another example of casually-leaked evidence.

On 18 November 1981, an employee cleaning a train bound for the Spanish border in France found a cassette tape discarded in an empty compartment. He took it home, found it contained a conversation in Spanish (which he did not understand) and ultimately gave it to a friend who chanced to be interested in UFOs. It had been recorded on the train (station names and other announcements were heard as background noise). The man who finally got the tape, Michel Rouanet, took it to a local UFO group (Orion) on 21 December 1981. Only then was it found that the tape contained an apparent interview between an unknown man and what purported to be José Trejo, the man involved in the Talavera case.

This has never been confirmed, as Trejo has gone out of contact. The voice is more sophisticated than that of the simple airman of 1977 when Benitez interviewed him. However, the conversation seems to suggest a reason for that – including Trejo saying, 'After this contact I felt an intense development of my brain. I experienced a sensation of superiority, of quickness of mind.' He also began to have psychic experiences, he claimed.

The tape begins and ends mid-stream and appeared to be one of several (so it looks as if it might have been left by accident). It is filled with 'vivid philosophical discussions', according to Vanquelef. Whilst many details match the original Trejo story, others do not. 'I saw a machine about 100 metres wide,' the witness now says. He adds that the entity got out and both he and the dog were hit by a 'discharge'. The dog 'leapt into the air and was burnt to death before it touched the ground'. Other details make plain that it is the same case, but he adds, 'I remained in a coma for three months. Everything I've said has been classified as a "military secret". One male nurse merely told me: if you were to hear all you've said you'd go crazy.'

Is this tape genuine? Was it set up and planted on that train to discredit the story? Or is it just a clever hoax? There are endless questions, and the peculiar similarity to the release of the Rendlesham Forest cassette tape has to be noted. Is this part of the education programme or part of the conspiracy? Who knows!

What we do know is that the whistling noise and projected image type of figure *has* been reported before. In particular an NCO in the British army wrote to me about his September 1968 experiences at the Dakelia barracks in Cyprus. He reported *before* the Trejo story came out – so there is no question of collusion. At 3 am one night his Turkish wolfhound fled under the bed whining. Then the NCO heard a dreadful high-pitched noise and opened the door to find a figure with no legs floating towards him. He slammed and bolted his door and sat on the bed with a loaded underwater speargun ready to fire! The noise disappeared, but the dog suffered permanent trauma. 'It was turned overnight into a devout coward,' the man told me!

These stories are so similar that it cannot be another coincidence.

19   NEW ZEALAND - 1978

Maybe, when [scientists] finally get around to studying all the information, interviewing all the witnesses and analysing all the movie footage, their findings might be worthy of consideration. Until then, I don't believe they have any right to expect their guesswork to be taken seriously.

(TV Reporter Quentin Fogarty, describing efforts to explain away the movie-filmed New Zealand encounters, *Flying Saucer Review*, 1980)

On New Year's Eve, 1978, a booster rocket from a Russian satellite, Cosmos 1068, re-entered the atmosphere over Britain. Thousands of people saw this spectacle. Fire brigades and police forces received calls about a 'crashing aircraft'. The slow-moving tube of lights was a much better show than the pathetic offering of Halley's Comet seven years later.

This major 'UFO' sighting, coming as it did just months after the release of Spielberg's movie, was prime fodder for misrepresentation. Yet most witnesses described it well, despite certainly never having seen anything like it before. There were not claims of landings, aliens, car-stops or ground traces associated with it. UFO investigators themselves isolated the cause of the sightings very quickly indeed.

Anyone who professes that the UFO is merely a product of human imagination, exaggerating strange but normal things in the sky, has to think very hard about the Cosmos 1068 story. It flatly refutes their arguments. It also has a bearing for what else occurred on that same night (31 December 1978) half-way round the world, for this was also well described, but *not* identified.

The booster rocket itself was very definitely nothing to do with *this* encounter, which became celebrated like no other – being the only UFO story to make the lead item on British TV news, for example.

The case actually began ten days earlier, on 21 December, when Captain John Randle, piloting a Safe-Air cargo freighter to Christchurch on New Zealand's South Island, spotted some lights over the coast off Kaikoura. It was 1.20 am and the radar at Wellington was tracking them too. Speeds of up to 120 mph were clocked.

For the next two hours it was like a rerun of the Washington DC episode. More radar targets, and more visual sightings occurred. Captain Vernon Powell and his first officer, Ian Pirie, were in a second Argosy cargo plane. Wellington radar informed them of several targets, principally one that was '10 o'clock to you, range 30 miles'. They had seen it first out at sea and it had 'tracked down to 60 miles (from Wellington) at 120 mph and has remained stationary for three-quarters of an hour and has now moved to about 20 miles to the west.' The Argosy crew followed these directions and saw a 'red glowing light out at our 10 o'clock position'.

This was just one of the occasions where radar-visual contact coincided.

The following week Australian TV reporter, Quentin Fogarty, chanced to be on holiday in New Zealand. The story of the aircraft sightings was floating about and there were witnesses alleged on the ground. Not to pass up the opportunity, his TV bosses asked Fogarty if he might get a local film crew and do a story for them. In fact he decided to go one better and persuaded Safe Air to let him fly in one of their Argosy planes on the duplicate run (it was a nightly route). With him went New Zealand husband-and-wife sound and camera team, David and Ngaire Crockett. Their trip (30—31 December) would be exactly the same as the one where the UFOs had appeared, thus adding atmosphere to the interviews which could be 'voiced over' the film.

At least that was the plan. The UFOs had other ideas!

Pilot that night was Captain Bill Startup and first officer Bob Guard. It was rather cramped aboard the plane and not at all easy for Davy Crockett to film with all the bumps and vibrations of a noisy aircraft that was not fitted with passenger seats owing to its exclusive use on the cargo run; but they flew to North Island without incident and got accustomed to the environment. After picking up a load of newspapers, past midnight and into the 31st, they set off south from Wellington for Christchurch, and the TV crew set up to get their film.

Around Kaikoura, as Fogarty was explaining that this was where the best UFO sightings had occurred, his 'live' recording was interrupted by Wellington radar confirming that they had more UFOs. Over the next half-hour or so, all five on board saw red and white lights pop up out of nowhere and disappear just as fast. The erratic and unexpected nature, plus the difficult conditions, made it hard for Crockett to get much on film, but Fogarty bravely battled on with his commentary, like a true newsman. He made this comment at one point, destined to become the title of his book about the affair, 'Let's hope they're friendly!'

Whilst Fogarty's account is fascinating in that he relates (very honestly) the aftermath of the story and how the TV company attempted to exploit the film that fate had given them, a clearer account of the sightings themselves (and the background of other events around Kaikoura) comes in

The Kaikoura UFOs, written by the air crew and radar operators.

Landing at Christchurch at about 1 am the plan was for Fogarty and the film crew to get off. Only Ngaire Crockett wanted to do that. Nothing would get her back into the air. Her husband and Fogarty were determined to go and see if the UFOs were still around and a local journalist, who had monitored the air-to-ground conversation, was very keen to take the sound girl's place.

They flew north again at 2.15 am and between here and passing Kaikoura the most spectacular sightings occurred. The now adept Davy Crockett got some good film, although the jarring of the aircraft and the constant refocusing does produce darting images that expand and contract in size, due not to the actual appearance and motion of the lights but to the camera. This has provided many false interpretations when people see the film and do not know the story behind it.

Within hours of landing Fogarty was on his way back to Australia with his priceless 23,000 frames of film close to his chest. He had no idea what would be on it, but there had been one domed UFO of classic flying-saucer shape that Crockett said he had captured.

The film was indeed sold around the world and shows many blinking lights, and other effects. It is slightly disappointing to the UFO expert, as all the shapes that seem to appear are evidently an effect of the camera and the awful conditions the photographer worked under. A few frames do show the 'domed UFO' Fogarty talked of, but there is debate as to whether that too is a focusing effect. The story was certainly hyped (probably overdone) and the fact that all the film really shows are a few coloured lights aided the cause of the debunkers. Certainly more poppycock has been written and spoken about this case than any other I know.

When TV news broadcasts (e.g. in Britain) began to show the film it was, of course, chopped about, edited out of sequence, and had no linking commentary. All the usual 'know it all' experts (not UFO investigators, but science reporters, astronomers, weathermen etc) were paraded in the next couple of days to tell the world what the film showed. Everyone had a different answer.

Of course, these people knew nothing about the film and less about UFOs. The answers they gave were often ridiculous. They ranged from the obviously absurd (Superman and Santa Claus going home!) to the seemingly clever. Even the head of Jodrell Bank got in on the act, and had an astronomical answer which could not have applied! We had boats, car headlamps, lighthouses, streetlamps, moonlight shining on cabbage patches and every visible planet in the solar system (although Venus and Jupiter were the favourites). The British Astronomer Royal disagreed and said the film likely showed 'meteorites'.

Naturally, all these answers could not be correct. Some were easily proven impossible. For instance, Venus was not even visible at the time! The UFO investigators remained aloof from all the fun and merely got on with the job of evaluating the case. By the time they had done so the media had long lost interest in this 'nine-day-wonder'. As far as the majority of the world's population knew, the film had been explained away (as any one of a hundred things, according to which TV station they had seen or newspaper they had read). When the full analysis was conducted only a few thousand UFO investigators remembered the case or heard the results.

Dr Bruce Maccabee, US Navy physicist, is a specialist in photographic cases. He obtained the film days later for investigation. Once satisfied that it was no hoax, he flew to both Australia and New Zealand and spent weeks on site interviewing witnesses. I met him several months later, when he presented his results and showed the full film a number of times. I must admit that I had been previously sceptical, viewing only the TV version of the five-minute film. Now I was more intrigued.

In 1985 I also established contact with John Cordy, who very kindly wrote to me out of a desire to get the story straight. He was senior air traffic controller on duty during the events of 21 December, and said of the many press accounts, 'some make me wonder if in fact I was there, or if it happened to someone else, so at variance with the facts are they'.

I am very grateful for his detailed notes and sketches, helping me to understand what is a very complex series of many events (which I barely skim over in this chapter). He has based them on the recordings of the communications that night which are, of course, far better than third-hand musings by a collection of 'experts'. Cordy does *not* support the spaceships idea, I should hasten to add. He merely contends that 'so far I have not heard a reasonable explanation for what we saw on radar and the aeroplane crew saw from the cockpit', but 'there are unexplained things in our atmosphere that science hasn't caught up with yet'.

When the BBC made a programme in their *Horizon* series in 1982 they used the Kaikoura case as an example and explained the radar trackings (unsatisfactorily I thought) as the old favourite – weather-induced temperature inversions. I asked John Cordy to comment on this. He said, 'there were not, on either night, a great number of short-duration radar echoes or "Angels" – the significant targets were of quite long duration. Most press reports seem to greatly inflate the number of targets and some make it sound as though the screen had measles!' He adds that he is positive that the few good echoes that correspond with visual sightings were solid objects. 'The target that moved out from Wellington to the south-east and then "hovered" – or remained stationary for almost an hour and then moved to follow the Argosy [i.e. the red light described before] was a good solid target all the time.'

Whether these were UFOs or, more likely in this case UAPs, something strange *was* seen. John Cordy has more than persuaded me that the air traffic controllers knew what they were doing. Surely the air crew knew what they were *not* seeing. This is typical of how the armchair experts can wreck a good UFO case, if you listen to them.

20 USSR – 1985

The sighting by the Tallinn crew has been investigated . . . The case is genuinely interesting, although we know of others like it . . . The only conclusion that can be drawn is that the Tallinn crew encountered what we call a UFO.

(Dr Nikolai Zheltukhin, USSR Academy of Sciences, vice-chairman of the 'Commission on Anomalous Phenomena', discussing the Aeroflot UFO encounter.)

Getting information out of the Soviet Union has never been easy. Getting UFO information from them has been next to impossible, but they do have sightings. One of the most dramatic occurred at an unknown date (possibly early 1985) and was first reported by the Soviet authorities on 30 January that year. It has some comparisons with the Ohio helicopter incident of 1973 and the Tehran jet chase of 1976. It is all the more fascinating, though, because the ordinary citizen of Russia has almost no access to such UFO reports. That sort of thing is strictly controlled.

The event concerned Aeroflot flight 8352 from Tbilisi to Tallinn. This was a Tupolev T-134 jet piloted by Tallinn-based crew. Captain was Igor Cherkashin (who had 7,000 hours in the air to his credit). His co-pilot was Gennadiy Lazurin, Navigator Egor Ognev and mechanic Mikhail Kozlov.

Things began to happen at around 4.10 am when the plane was about 80 miles from Minsk, travelling at 30,000 feet. According to V. Vostrukhin, who gave a poetic description of the official reports, the aircraft was 'all alone in the emptiness of space, in a block of glass with the stars as holes'. In other words, it was a clear night!

Lazurin first noticed something unusual. It was a 'large star', yellow in colour; but he knew that it was not really a star, especially when a 'blob' shot out from it and headed for the ground below (remember the Iran jet chase?). Lazurin quickly pointed this out to Kozlov, who suggested to his captain that they file a report. The blob had elongated into a beam of light and was now projecting a cone of brilliance towards the ground. All the crew could see it by this point.

As they watched, two less vivid (slightly wider) beams came from the object. A cautious Captain Cherkashin said, 'Let's wait. What do we report? We don't know what it is!' As he was musing over this, Lazurin

115

began to draw a sketch of what they were seeing, and the others were estimating its height, which given the absence of surrounding landmarks was very difficult but was 'guessed' at 100,000 feet! Yet, if so, this would be incredible, because the beams emerging from it were lighting up the ground miles below them, casting a greenish tint over trees, roads etc. It was as if some huge searchlight was playing on them. Then the big beam swung around and projected straight into the cabin, exactly as the Ohio helicopter crew had witnessed. The star was now visible as a huge light surrounded by concentric rings of different colours, an effect which may have been optically induced by its brilliance.

As the light 'flared up'. Lazurin yelled, 'It's switched on engines and is racing towards us.' Captain Cherkashin knew that he no longer had any choice. He told Ognev to call Minsk ground control, but as soon as he began to do so the light stopped its movement towards them.

The air traffic controller at Minsk was polite but sceptical. 'I don't have anything on my radar screen and I don't see this big light,' he told the airliner. Nevertheless they could see it! Now describing it as a 'green cloud' it had swung from side to side and dropped down to their level; indeed it had taken up station right beside them. As it cruised along, Cherkashin tried to crack a joke, 'They are giving us a ceremonial escort!'

Being much nearer the green cloud it now filled a considerable expanse of sky (several moon diameters) and they were observing a weird 'electrical' effect inside. There were multiple lights of different colours and fiery zig-zags that criss-crossed the 'vapour'. It lit up like a Christmas tree, Ognev told Minsk over the radio.

Suddenly the man on the ground cut into these descriptions: 'I can see flashes on the horizon.' The aircraft was now flying into visual sighting range of the ground controller and it soon became evident to him that he *was* seeing the spectacular light-show of the mysterious green cloud.

Meanwhile the phenomenon was behaving in an odd way. It was changing shape as if to mimic the plane! It developed an appendage and then 'became' a 'wingless cloud-aircraft with a pointed tail'. The yellow and green glow, like phosphorescence, was eerily intertwined.

About this time a stewardess came into the cabin saying that the passengers were getting a little concerned about the funny thing flying beside them. 'Tell them it's a cloud reflecting the lights of cities below,' Cherkashin suggested rather weakly. When the inadequacy of this idea was pointed out, he shrugged and said, 'Well − tell them it's the Aurora Borealis!', even though he knew it was in quite the wrong part of the sky and the answer was no match for what they were seeing.

A second Tupolev, flying in the opposite direction from Leningrad to Tbilisi, now entered the Minsk control zone. It was 60 miles from the scene of the encounter and radioed through that it could not see anything. The

Minsk director gave precise directions to this Captain and, when the second T-134 came within just ten miles of Cherkashin's aircraft, it saw the UFO. For a short while, as it flew by, the second aircrew were able to give a confirmatory account of the weird green cloud.

Down on the ground the control staff at Minsk were able to watch the green mass float over. Controllers at Riga and Vilnius on the aircraft's northern flight also saw this bizarre combination of aerial travellers. This lasted for more than an hour in total and the Tupolev only lost its 'escort' when making its descent for a landing at Tallinn.

When they were on the ground the crew discovered that the Tallinn approach radar had picked up two 'blips' on their screens trailing behind the aircraft. Even more strangely, whilst these targets remained solid the aircraft reflection kept fading in and out. The radar controller is quoted as saying, 'I would have understood it all had you been 'blinking' on the landing radar — but on the 'long range' scanner, that never happens. It simply *cannot* happen!' However it did.

When later questioned by the Soviet team of scientists that studies UFOs officially, the crew guessed the object to be 25 miles long! This is vastly in excess of what it must have been, as the experience of the second Tupolev shows. If it had been so large, they would have seen it from much further than they did. The scientists proposed that the error was understandable. Cherkashin's crew knew nothing about UFOs (certainly not of their supposed origin as alien machines). They had assumed that what they were seeing was some natural wonder, e.g. a radioactive cloud from a volcano. In this case the 'cloud' would be a long way off and enormous. If, on the other hand, it was far closer, then it would be considerably smaller.

The radar returns seem to confirm that it was small and close. Whilst we might try to find a rational solution to this perplexing encounter and dismiss the connections with other UFO cases, the truth is that we do not have a good answer. Like so many others, it is a real mystery.

Part Three:

THE

UFO

PROOF

INTRODUCTION

I once went on a routine visit to the Pentagon, in my capacity as scientific adviser to Project Blue Book, and I asked a leading official there why they failed to take UFO reports seriously. I was led aside and told, 'Allen – do you really think we would ignore something like this?'

(Dr J. Allen Hynek, astronomer and USAF consultant on UFOs, talking to me in August 1983.)

It is time to draw some strands together. You have read many stories, each of which could be supported by dozens of others just like them. You may be as sceptical as you like, but most of these cases are *not* inventions. They happened – often to very well qualified people. Many have been investigated by scientists and official departments. For some we actually have released documents proving their veracity. Countless numbers involve both visual and radar observation.

If anyone tells you that such a thing never happens – well, as you can see, it does!

Between all these wild tales there is an overwhelming fact: something is going on for which we do not have a simple answer. If you have come even this far in pursuing my arguments then I cannot ask for more; but for those who are still interested let us now explore a little more about just what the UFO does, and try to recognise why one of two positions simply must apply.

Either the authorities of all the major powers on earth speak the truth when they tell you that there just is no evidence that behind the UFO stories lurks something of concern to them. In that case it is hard to interpret such an attitude as anything other than crazy. When set against the mountains of evidence, the very least we might expect from intelligent people is an open mind and a desire to dig deeper.

Alternatively, if you find this hard to swallow, then these authorities *are* disturbed, and must be taking action. In that case there *is* a cover-up. You *are* being lied to. All of this mammoth conspiracy is maintained at great cost and great difficulty. No reason is obvious, but reason there must be. We can only hope it is an honest one.

One of these attitudes must apply. Neither, in my view, is comforting or acceptable.

21 AIR ENCOUNTERS

Pilots represent a very stable personality type with a high degree of training, motivation and selection. When they say they have seen something, you know they have seen something.
(Dr Richard Haines, NASA life scientist and specialist in UFO-aircraft encounters. Interview in *MUFON Journal*, October 1985.)

You must have noticed that there are many mid-air encounters described throughout this book. I lay stress on these for a number of reasons. I believe they have been under-emphasised before. Pilots *know* what various things in the sky should look like. It is part of their training. Someone on the ground may or may not be well-versed in the interpretation of the latest military jets or weather balloons, but when you are up there, miles above the earth, your very life might depend upon an ability to make a correct identification and react swiftly. If anything 'pressures' you into becoming a good UFO witness that must be it.

Secondly, if UFOs do exist and are flying about our atmosphere they must be more readily visible if you are already there. Down on the ground they might be a long way from you, or masked by clouds. Aerial encounters can be very close indeed, in fact so close that there are not insubstantial dangers of mid-air collision with a UFO.

As I was writing this part of the book, a Mexican airliner tragically collided with a light plane in clear, daylight conditions above Los Angeles. If this is possible with two quite identifiable craft, imagine the consequences when one of the conflicting travellers has filed no flight plan and comes from goodness knows where. It is certainly a sobering thought to contemplate the number of unexplained air disasters as well as the constantly increasing numbers of planes that cross the sky. The potential hazard of the UFO may not be one the frequent air traveller has given much thought to, but perhaps that is something we should now do.

Whatever UFOs are, they appear in the sky, and anything passing through that environment could collide with an aircraft carrying very vulnerable passengers. Whether UFOs are misperceptions of assorted things, new natural phenomena or alien spaceships, it might be very dangerous not to take their certain existence into serious account.

My fears have been intensified because, in this time of relatively few UFO sightings, the rate of UFO-aircraft encounters has risen dramatically in recent years. Perhaps the fact that we *seem* not to have had any catastrophes is one more part of the education programme, but if there is to be a new wave of sightings we cannot afford to dismiss the dangers. So I offer no excuses for offering a flood of brief synopses of a number of such cases. They by no means exhaust the possible total I could have chosen to tell you about.

I trust that you will be as disturbed by these facts as I am.

24 February 1979, north-west England, 2 am

A family in a village amongst the Lancashire Pennines first saw a brightly-lit UFO apparently descend into a quarry at Bacup. The husband, Mike Sacks, had my phone number via Jodrell Bank Radio Telescope (whom I assist in the investigation of UFO stories). He called me immediately, at 2.05 am, and said he was off to get his brother-in-law (a photographer) in the hope of capturing the object on film. As it turned out they did not find the UFO, but they did meet two police officers up in the quarry. It was now 2.35 am, and these 'bobbies' had spotted an orange ball of fire streak over the hills heading west. They had gone up to the quarry for a better look.

This orange ball was seen by at least a dozen people on its forty-mile trek to the coast. At Wigan a taxi driver followed it. A policeman gave chase in his patrol car near St Helens. A courting couple at Ormskirk jumped from their car when it began to glow orange – although *not* with flames of passion as they might have assumed! A plane coming into Liverpool Airport saw it. There were also several reports of radio sets being scrambled by terrific bursts of static as the thing flew over.

Very soon after this (at about 2.50 am) a caravan park at Scarisbrick, near Southport, was rudely awoken by a thundering sound that shook doors and windows. An orange light was racing out to sea. At 3.15 am, coming back in from the Irish Sea, the roaring orange light shook the pier at Blackpool, where security guards came rushing out wondering what on earth was happening.

Labour MP Robert Kilroy-Silk asked questions on behalf of the Scarisbrick residents. He (I think correctly) concluded that they had been disturbed by a low-flying jet aircraft travelling dangerously low. He was fobbed off with the story that an exercise involving American F-111 planes had been on and one of them must have strayed into this 'no-go' area. Low flying is certainly prohibited in such built-up areas at night, not least because there are three major civilian airports all within this zone (at Blackpool, Liverpool and Manchester).

Unhappily, Kilroy-Silk did not know about all the other encounters that night. He was after quick answers. UFO researchers took months gathering together the data and plotting the witnesses onto a map. Many remained unpublished; for example, the Blackpool pier guards wrote direct to me and knew nothing about the other cases. There is little doubt that they all form a pattern.

I pressed the MoD hard about this case, but it took me years. At first they had merely referred to a 'special exercise' involving USAF F-111 jets that was on at the time. They did *not* say the UFO had been an F-111, just left you to draw that inference. The USAF categorically denied it. According to Colonel Schrihoffer at USAF Upper Heyford, in charge of the planes, the west-coast sightings were 'definitely not F-111s — and that's official!' Eventually, after several tries, I got the MoD to back down at this, saying that 'clearly we were wrong', but that they had never proposed the F-111 as a solution anyway! In other words, it was still a UFO, and *that's* official! (I doubt, however, that this information was conveyed to Mr Kilroy-Silk.)

My best guess would be that a jet of some sort *was* seen over Scarisbrick and Blackpool, streaking out to sea and returning to base. It may have been RAF (possibly from Warton near Preston). These two locations are the latest in time and the only ones to feature the loud roaring noise. A jet (probably using after-burner to create the orange glow) would certainly produce one, so we are left with no answer for the earlier sightings (from the 2 am quarry landing through to the 2.35/2.40 am departure of the orange ball tracking fast to the west). That would appear to have been a genuine UFO. The Sacks family had an excellent close-up view and what they saw was certainly no aircraft!

It does rather appear that this UFO was detected and a jet aircraft scrambled to chase it. Being in a hurry, the pilot circumvented normal low-flying rules and sped off out to sea in pursuit of the unknown (which we must assume it never caught). The MoD hoped that the excuse of a USAF exercise and straying F-111 would get them off the hook and mask all these sightings. It worked, at least so far as the general public were concerned.

Now you can see the case as it really is, I think you will agree that my scenario makes far better sense.

11 November 1979, Balearic Islands, Spain, 11 pm

A TAE Super-Caravelle airliner with 119 people on board was on a holiday charter from Salzburg, Austria, bound for the southern sunshine of Tenerife. It had made a stop on the island of Majorca and was now between Ibiza and the Spanish mainland on its final leg, when near disaster struck.

At the controls was 34-year-old Francisco de Tejada and his co-pilot Sr

Suazo. They were climbing through 24,000 feet when a call came from Barcelona air control to advise Tejada to switch to an emergency frequency. He thought a plane may have got into trouble. In fact ground radar had picked up an unknown near the Caravelle. However, all Tejada got on the airwaves was a mass of static, and events rapidly took over before he could try again.

To quote the pilot, 'Two very powerful red lights . . . were heading towards us at the 9 o'clock position . . . I think there was just one thing. The two lights seemed to be set at the two extremities . . . The speed at which they came at us was staggering.'

The lights 'played' with the TAE jet, 'performing movements that it would be quite impossible for any conventional machine to execute'. Tejada responded with a cool instinct and banked the aircraft away from the oncoming lights. He immediately put them into a descent to 10,000 feet. Calling through to the passengers, he advised them to put their seat belts on but decided not to inform them that a UFO was making 'buzzing passes' at them. Instead they were distracted by being served with dinner!

At this point, with the lights still sweeping past him on frequent 'runs', he made the decision to divert to the nearest airport, which was Valencia, on the mainland. After confirming this decision (the radio now functioned) the lights moved back a bit but continued to follow them towards the coast. The Caravelle landed just before midnight and ground crew at the airport saw a red light over the end of the runway as they did! The poor holiday-makers were given no real explanation, just bundled off to a hotel for an overnight stay. Meanwhile the aircraft was checked and found to be undamaged.

Within 48 hours of these events Spanish UFO researcher Juan Benitez had spoken to Alfredo Espantaleon, TAE's deputy director. He had confirmed that 'the plane was forced to land at Valencia and we know that the UFOs were also seen by eye-witnesses on the ground, as well as by the pilots of several military aircraft.'

Apart from also speaking to Tejada and Suazo the UFO investigator was now on the track of these military witnesses. It transpired that both Barcelona and Valencia civil radar had recorded the object, as indeed had the Air Defence Command radar. This had shown the UFO making a 12,000-foot plunge in just 30 seconds, a frightening descent rate.

At midnight, when the civilian aircraft was out of danger, two Mirage fighters were scrambled by Los Llanos Air Base near Albacete. Their mission was to intercept the object. One Mirage pilot had a similar 'buzzing passes' encounter with the UFO. There were rumours that the other one got film of the event. If so, as it almost goes without saying, that film has never been released. The Spanish government Transport

Minister, Salvador Teran, flew to Valencia to supervise an enquiry, and a few days later said, quite assuredly, 'It is clear that UFOs exist.'

11 November 1980, north-east Spain, 6.40 pm

One year to the day after the TAE near-collision (by accident or design) it all happened again, only this time seven airliners saw the UFO!

They were flying into or around the Barcelona Air Traffic zone and three were in the vicinity of Maella, 100 miles inland. It would take too long to recount all the details, but the closest encounter seems to have befallen an Iberia Boeing 727, piloted by Captain Ramos. This was flying south-east to Barcelona at 31,000 feet. The sky was darkening but not fully dark. Suddenly a green light appeared almost dead ahead of them. 'It was like a sphere,' Ramos said. 'Or, rather, like an enormous soap bubble.' He made a reflex dive through several hundred feet and in under a minute the object was gone.

Ramos contacted Barcelona to demand to know what traffic might have nearly hit his 727. The reply was that the only aircraft nearby was a Monarch Airlines package tour bound from England for Alicante. Their crew had also reported the green light streaking across their path.

Moments later a Trans-Europa flight from Majorca to southern France, then over the Mediterranean, called to say it had also seen the object. As this plane was a hundred miles from the other two, sceptics have pointed out that if the same thing was seen then it must have been very high in the atmosphere to be visible over such a vast area. In that case it was very probably a meteor or some space junk from a rocket or satellite burning up. No such thing has ever been proven, as it is usually simple to do. People on the ground can normally see it as well. It is also worth noting that this is very like the 'green fireballs' from thirty years before, which meteor expert Dr Lincoln La Paz was certain were not natural. They could not have been bits of re-entering rocket (as there were none up there to re-enter!)

More importantly, ground observers at Barcelona airport *saw* the 'green soap bubble' come in at a steep angle, buzz the runway and then shoot almost vertically skywards. An Iberia crew on the ground, getting ready for take-off, saw the thing and blinked their lights at it! The UFO appeared to respond by going out!

One witness at the airport said, 'A machine that comes along in a horizontal flight, then changes course when one aircraft takes an evasive dive, then comes down and "buzzes" the runway and then turns off its lights when another plane flashes light signals at it – it is totally impossible for a machine that does all these things to be anything else but controlled by some type of intelligence.'

12 July 1981, Irish Sea, 2.30 am

A Dan-Air Cargo plane from Belfast to Liverpool was just crossing the Dee Estuary on its final approach when the crew observed a ball of yellowish/white light that pulsed in the sky below them. They called Liverpool Air Traffic Control, who confirmed a radar contact. When they landed they also logged a report with ground staff, but it was decided not to take the matter further and the crew were advised not to speak about it, because it was 'not policy' to do so.

Unbeknown to the Dan-Air crew (and vice versa, as the aircraft sighting had no publicity) two men were camping on Thursaston Common, a piece of high ground to the south-west of the Wirral Peninsula. This overlooks the Dee Estuary. The two men were watching a yellow light above a factory in Flint. After some minutes they realised that it was not on an aircraft, nor was it a hazard light on the chimney. Before they could work out what it was the light began to climb and then accelerated at rapid speed to vanish towards the Welsh mountains.

Although they did not remember seeing an aircraft pass over, these are quite common and the locations and timings are so exact that it appears the same events were witnessed. The MoD have no record of the affair.

21 June 1982, Brindisi, Italy, 11.15 am

Another Dan-Air jet, this time a passenger Boeing 737, had a UFO encounter when on a charter route from London Gatwick to the Greek island of Corfu. It was a bright sunny day and the aircraft was beginning its descent, passing through 23,000 feet just south of Brindisi. When first seen, the UFO was considered to be a tyre falling from an aircraft above them. Then they realised it was stationary and they were flying *past* it.

Both the Captain and first officer saw it, as did two passengers who were on a visit to the flight deck at the time. It was black and shiny, not unlike a doughnut, and they came within two miles of it, as it seemed just to hang there. They considered filing a report, but they were out of radar coverage (this is a notorious radar black spot) and they had been informed that no other traffic was nearer than 30 miles. So they waited until arriving back at Gatwick later that day.

Extensive investigation by Philip Taylor from the Royal Greenwich Observatory and astronomer Peter Warrington (commenced within hours of the sighting) failed to discover a conventional solution, e.g. a balloon.

19 April 1984, eastern England, 4 pm

Unfortunately, all I can say about this location is that it was a civil airport with full facilities somewhere in eastern England. Three air traffic controllers were witness to the events and broke civil aviation rules by not reporting the UFO. I must respect their confidence.

The reason for this breach of rules was that one of the controllers became very upset following the incident and requested that they study the 'book'. This stated that UFOs reported *to* them should be passed along. They chose to interpret that liberally as not applying to UFOs reported *by* them!

It was a bright, sunny day immediately prior to the Easter weekend. As only one plane was being talked down the radar was switched off. Whilst two of the controllers were concentrating on this the senior operator had come in to watch over them. He was idly glancing out through the windows of the tower when he saw what he took to be their aircraft landing on the wrong runway. By the time a brief exchange had ensued and the light plane coming in had confirmed it *was* making an approach to the correct runway, the thing was now very close. It was reflecting a great deal of sunlight off its surface.

The UFO made a steep approach and touched down briefly on the cross runway (intersecting the one that the aircraft was about to land on!). It then climbed almost vertically at an accelerating rate.

By this time all three controllers were watching the 'ball of light' and the senior controller was viewing it through binoculars. It appeared like 'masses of crinkled paper all reflecting light'. Within seconds it had gone from view, having streaked up at a speed well in excess of that which any conventional aircraft could achieve. The size was estimated as similar to that of a small car, such as a 'Mini'.

A call was put through to a nearby air base to see if any military traffic might have strayed off course. The military field had shut down for the holidays and its radar had just been switched off. So the controllers decided only to contact UFO investigator Peter Johnson and tell him the story that same day.

You may note the similarity with the touch-down and take-off of the 'soap bubble' at Barcelona Airport.

5 July 1984, USSR, 2 pm

This is a case that would doubtless have got away, but for the fact that the Aeroflot Tupolev flying at 35,000 feet from Leningrad to London was carrying many British passengers. The chief reporter was a retired experimental nuclear physicist who spotted what looked like a thick black pole protruding at an angle from a lump of fluffy cloud. It paced the aircraft for about three minutes before being obscured by cloud. During this time he pointed it out to several adjacent travellers, including a retired aircraft inspector, who was thoroughly puzzled. A woman sitting behind him remarked, 'That's a mighty long telegraph pole!' Sadly, no photographs were taken (although being a holiday flight many had cameras). Aeroflot do not allow them in the cabin!

11 June 1985, Inner Mongolia, China, late evening

Captain Wang Shu-Ting, pilot of a Chinese Airways Boeing 747 'Jumbo', was flying from Peking to Paris when another member of his crew alerted him to a yellow walnut-sized light that hung in the sky ahead of them. It glowed very brightly. At the time they were above 32,000 feet and Wang radioed to ground control that he was not about to take any chances. He asked for clearance to set down at the nearest possible airport. As if in response, the centre of the light vanished, leaving just a blue ring. Seconds later it disappeared. The incident would probably have remained hidden (like so many other pilot encounters do, supposedly because it might undermine confidence in the airline), but a few days later one of the crew (on another aircraft over the north-western Xin Jiang province) saw a very similar object. Wang decided that he had better speak out about the matter for the sake of other air crew.

19 May 1986, São Paulo, Brazil, late evening

Ozires Silva, president of the state-run oil company, was landing his private jet at an Air Force base near São Paulo late this evening, when he saw a series of multi-coloured lights blocking his path. Switching on his airborne radar he picked up several anomalous targets and decided that he had better abort the landing.

Silva radioed to the Air Space Defence Centre that he was going to chase the lights and find out what they were. Meanwhile, the sophisticated radar at the Defence Centre had already picked them up. They were moving at speeds between 160 and 990 mph and altogether about a dozen of them were detected over the next half-hour. Deciding they could not leave it up to a civilian pilot they scrambled six Brazilian Air Force Northrop F-5E jet fighters.

Brigadier General Octabio Lima, Air Force Minister, explained that, 'Since they had saturated our radar system in São Paulo and were interfering with air traffic, we decided that we must send up planes to pursue them.' All the fighter pilots saw the dazzling lights. One described them as looking rather like ping-pong balls, but they were all unable to catch them. At one point an unfortunate F-5E pilot was encircled by the lights. Seven came to one side and six to the other. He was utterly helpless, but they flew away again.

Eventually the fighters ran out of fuel and had to return to base, but the Defence Centre launched three Mirage III supersonic interceptors that had been armed with AIM-9 Sidewinder air-to-air missiles. They were determined to be prepared this time. As soon as the Mirages became airborne the UFOs shot away at terrific speed.

'It is not a question of believing or not . . . we have neither replies nor technical explanations for what happened,' the Minister later told disgruntled pressmen.

The next report announced that the Brazilian Air Force Ministry had 'summoned pilots of the interceptor jets to report on their sightings'. After that – not a word. On past performance we are unlikely to hear much more about yet another serious mid-air encounter, happening only a few weeks before the deadline for completion of this book.

Some of these cases might have answers in the long run, but the pattern displayed by these and many more cases (in several other countries during the past two or three years alone) seems clear. I hope you will pause and consider the possible implications.

If you are due to board an aircraft in the not too distant future, then I trust you will be able to do so without feeling a twinge of concern. Who knows what might be up there waiting for you?

22 SPACE ENCOUNTERS

They are there without a doubt, but what they are is anybody's guess.
  (Brigadier General James McDivitt, US astronaut, speaking about UFOs on 5 October
  1965.)

Whilst aerial encounters certainly give strong evidence that something
unknown is up there in the atmosphere, they do not prove an extra-
terrestrial origin. It should be realised that UFO researchers (myself
included) are stating beyond question that *unexplainable* phenomena exist;
the theory that they are vehicles manned by an intelligence beyond earth is
merely a proposition. You might think (with good cause) that there is a
great deal of inferential evidence that some UFOs (certainly not all of them)
appear to have an intelligent design and seem way beyond our capabilities.
However, other ideas about what they are and where they come from
cannot be ruled out.

Just one possibility (given all too little consideration in my view) is the
suggestion that UFOs might be 'timeships', not 'spaceships'. They *are*
flown by intelligent beings far past our level of technological development
and they *are* extremely interested in us at this critical time in the planet's
history. However, they are human. Humans from our far future. Aside
from the fact that this would actually make more sense of what we see,
including the human appearance of the entities and their long-standing
observation of us, it does have another advantage. For UFOs *not* to be
'timeships' we will virtually have to rule out any prospect of time travel
ever becoming possible. For if it does – even thousands of years from now
– surely the era when we entered space and built our first weapons capable
of destroying the planet would have sufficient interest to attract visitors. If
we do not see them, they do not exist. If time travel is ever possible, it
seems by logical application of the circumstances almost certain that the
UFOs *must* be them.

Of course, the visitors themselves might wish to create the false
impression that they were from space. That could explain why they play
games and act out roles based on our current science-fiction concepts. In

this way the truth is not perceived by us, but if that truth is suspected by the authorities, then it offers an even bigger incentive to cover-up. These 'aliens' would know all about the future, our future, because to them it is the distant past. Imagine the power *that* would put into somebody's hands!

Leaving this question aside, *if* UFOs are some form of alien travel vehicle then we might expect sightings during our own brief trips into space. Have astronauts seen UFOs?

The answer is yes and no. There are stories, explanations and rumours. The rumours contend that the real space encounters (e.g. sightings of UFOs *on* the moon) have been covered up. This may well be a case of taking the conspiracy theory to its extreme, and whilst we can never disprove it I have to say that there is *no* reasonable evidence for such a claim. There have been alleged photographs showing these 'UFOs' that have somehow escaped the cover-up. They have found their way into some of the less reputable tabloids and hysterical UFO books. Without exception, in my opinion, these have satisfactorily been shown up as hoaxes. It is remarkably easy to doctor one of the thousands of NASA photographs so that quite explicable lens flares, reflections and floating bits of debris beside the space capsule look like a UFO.

Indeed, many of the claimed UFO sightings during actual missions have a similar solution. Almost without exception the astronauts knew at the time (and sometimes cracked UFO jokes that were later taken seriously!) or very soon identified the probable truth about the light or blob seen outside their window.

The *only* case that has stood the test of time involves the Gemini 4 mission which ferried two men into orbit. On 4 June 1965 only James McDivitt was awake as they floated above Hawaii. He then saw an object 'like a beer can with an arm sticking out'. The astronaut took two photographs using two different cameras through the tiny window, battling with the rolling motion of the capsule that quickly took them into the glare of the sun. He certainly could not explain the object he saw and, even eight years later on a TV chat show, was still discussing it in UFO terms, 'we were never able to identify what it could have been'.

The Colorado University investigation failed to explain this case and called it 'a challenge to the analyst'. The McDivitt photographs were not released, but NASA did hastily issue two which both they and McDivitt apparently knew were *not* the ones of the UFO! Allegedly they did this to assure journalists there was no cover-up, but the strange action hardly does that. Both McDivitt and his then employees are positive that the photographs show sunlight reflecting off a window bolt, and only two blobs are visible – nothing like the 'beer can' object the astronaut verbally described.

As to where the genuine pictures went, McDivitt says he searched all the mission film and was unable to trace them. That said, there were dozens of spoiled pictures where the sunlight glare had flared them out. It was more than possible, he guessed, that this was the reason for the failure to find the ones he sought. Whilst this could, of course, represent a conspiracy, I do not see anything in the facts to give cause to doubt McDivitt's version of events. This leaves us yet to explain what it was that he saw.

James Oberg is one of the least nasty of the UFO debunkers — as close to a compliment as most of them deserve, I am afraid! It would be very unfair of me not to commend him on the excellent work he has done demolishing most of the legendary astronaut sightings. Most serious UFO researchers, certainly outside the USA, have never made a big deal out of these stories, but he persuaded the BBC *Horizon* series, when they made what remains the only important TV documentary on UFOs in the past decade (the supposedly objective 'Case of the UFOs', transmitted in 1982), to waste a lot of time on these astronaut cases. This had to be at the expense of the sort of real UFO evidence you have met in this book, which was hardly given a glance by the BBC.

The sceptics still concentrate on isolated cases they believe they can explain, and, like a sleight-of-hand conjuror, try to divert attention from the hundreds of others which are not so easy to wave away.

Oberg was a USAF officer in 1976 when he first resolved (to his satisfaction, if not McDivitt's) the Gemini 4 encounter. He is now a NASA flight controller and space journalist (according to a 1980 personal profile on him). He specialises in the cases he is best suited to judge, and recently has been claiming that virtually all Soviet UFO cases (e.g. the Aeroflot encounter over Minsk) are misperceptions of secret Russian space launches. Of the McDivitt case, he says that the astronaut mistook his own booster rocket, drifting in a nearby orbit. His evidence seems persuasive. The window was dirty, the space voyager's eyes had been sore, and his colleague on board had failed to recognise the booster once before.

McDivitt's reply to these arguments is that he had been tracking the booster for an experiment and so was quite familiar with it. He makes no claim that what he saw was a spaceship, only that it is unexplained. Nevertheless, another UFO debunker, aviation journalist Philip Klass, sent McDivitt a still taken from movie-film of the Gemini booster asking if this was 'his UFO'. Without hesitation, the astronaut replied, 'I very quickly identified the object in the photograph as the second stage of the Titan rocket which launched us. I am sure that this is not a photograph of the object which I have described many times and which many people refer to as the Gemini 4 UFO.'

So, the lack of all but this possible space UFO may support the time travel rather than extra-terrestrial version of UFO origin; but another interesting clue has arrived very recently, through the Freedom of

Information Act lawsuits of 1985. Ray Boeche obtained a wad of documents through the Defence Intelligence Agency. Most are the usual sort of material these actions have brought many times. Two refer to a previously unheard-of 'Project Moon Dust', which appears to be space-related.

The first, from the US Defence attaché in Rabat, Morocco, is dated 18 January 1967. Forwarding press cuttings, it says, 'the page one coverage afforded this sighting demonstrates a high level interest in the subject of UFOs and presages further reporting which could be valuable in pursuit of Project Moon Dust.'

In forty years of UFO study and eight years of Freedom of Information Act requests, no trace of this UFO project had ever emerged. Had the attaché merely got the name for the USAF project (Blue Book) incorrect? This was still operative in 1967. The answer is no, because the second (more detailed) documents come ten years *after* all official interest in UFOs supposedly ended; but Moon Dust is still active!

The 21 August 1979 memo comes from La Paz, Bolivia, and amongst other interesting circulation points went to the Foreign Technology Division of Wright-Patterson Air Force Base, former home of Project Blue Book! As such it seems to be an example of one of those cases which 'could affect national security' that 'are not part of the Blue Book system', if you recall the memo that led to the project's closure.

The seven-page file headed 'An info report, not finally evaluated intelligence', 'Title: Moon Dust', relates details of an object that *fell* from space near Santa Cruz. In other words, Project Moon Dust (as the title rather suggests) is concerned with recovered objects from space!

Allegedly, a 'whistling sound' followed by a 'fire ball' had resulted in an explosion near Buen Retiro. The next day 'a small aircraft that had three lights' was seen over the explosion area. This was searched in daylight by local residents who found 'a sphere . . . not heavy' which was picked up and taken away. A precisely similar sphere had fallen a few days earlier near Cotoca, the report claims.

It continues, 'these spheres were real balls of fire when they entered the atmosphere because of the friction and after a high speed fall hit the ground. However, in the area where they had been found, there was no sign of the impact, as though the spheres had landed smoothly.'

They are described as light and fragile but undamaged, except for an explosion that has destroyed the interior, and one hole in the outer skin. The metal is 'similar to copper, kind of dark with light spots. [It] has apparently been exposed to very high temperatures.' Each sphere was three feet in diameter, weighing about twelve pounds.

According to Colonel Ariel Coca, director of the Bolivian Air Force Academy, 'the sphere is made of special light alloy but very resistant', suggesting space travel *was* a design feature. 'A study' was proposed 'to determine its origin . . . in case it contains radioactive substance'. US Defence attaché, Colonel Hamilton, says it is perfectly round in configuration and reaches up to a man's knees when stood on the ground. The hole is nine inches in diameter. Movie film was to be forwarded to the Defence Intelligence Agency for Moon Dust evaluation.

Naturally this is all we know about this intriguing story.

23 WHEN THE FORCE IS WITH YOU – UFO EFFECTS

There is certainly a need for much better data collection in electromagnetic (EM) cases, and a greater effort to duplicate these effects in the laboratory under controlled conditions.
(Stanton Friedman, nuclear physicist, now a full-time 'space science UFO investigator'.)

Those who say that the UFO story is simply a collection of anecdotes (be they from housewives, airline pilots or astronauts) are mistaken. The phenomenon can create *real* effects that are very consistent and demonstrate that a physical force (not a hallucination) is present. It is puzzling why most scientists continue to ignore this important truth.

We saw how the Levelland, Texas, events in November 1957 produced a new type of case – the 'car stop'. This has now accumulated to such an extent that two detailed catalogues are available, recording hundreds of examples. There are many clues within these dossiers which the scientist could get his teeth into. We do not know what is causing these electrical systems to be scrambled, but something most certainly is.

A good early example of the 'car stop' defied even Blue Book's 'Operation Debunk' policy and became one of only ten unknowns for the year. It is a nice simple illustration of what the UFO can do to a witness who gets close enough when circumstances (whatever they are) chance to be right.

On 26 October 1958, Alvin Cohen and Phil Small were driving their car quite slowly on a twisting road near Loch Raven dam, north of Baltimore in Maryland. The road is so bad, with a cliff to one side and river on the other, that speeds of 30 mph are fast on it. After rounding a corner and first seeing the object, they crawled forward at about 12 mph, as this was the safest speed at which to keep on course and watch the UFO.

It was 10.30 pm and the object had appeared over a metal girder rail bridge that crosses the road and river ahead of them. It was 'a large, flat sort of egg-shaped object' (Cohen) and 'glowing with an iridescent glow . . . it occupied approximately one-third of the bridge at the height it was at (estimated 150 feet maximum)' (Small).

They inched closer, puzzled and confused by the huge thing. As they got to about 75 feet from it both engine and lights failed. Small, who was driving, says in the Blue Book report, '[it was] as if you had your points go up, or somebody took the battery out of the car . . . I tried to put the ignition system on but there was no whirring or anything'. He braked the car to a halt a few feet further along.

There was nowhere to run on this barren road, although they both felt like hiding from the looming intruder. Cohen said, 'So we got out of the car and put it between the object and ourselves. We watched it from that position for approximately thirty to forty seconds.' There was then a flare of light. Small says, 'This light seemingly was blinding and approximately at the same time we felt a wave of heat. It didn't seem like the heat of a burning object but something like an ultraviolet light or some kind of radiation.'

Coincident with the explosion of light came a 'thunder clap' of noise, 'something approaching a plane breaking the sound barrier' (Small). Within ten seconds it had risen vertically and vanished. The speed of climb and brilliance of the glow made the egg shape vanish inside a powerful light that blotted out all other features.

Immediately they found that the ignition worked again, and turned around and drove to a phone they had passed. A patrol vehicle came out to them within minutes. After taking statements the men felt their faces were burning, although there were no visible signs. However, as a precaution (because they feared the burns might be caused by radiation) the two men drove themselves to St Joseph's Hospital in Baltimore, where they were examined. The doctor noticed their faces were a little flushed but after a very superficial examination (heart rate, pulse etc) sent them away. Within a couple of days the effect faded.

Police did discover that some people at a restaurant a mile north of the bridge had heard the explosion (and what was presumably its echo from the canyon cliffs). As there was no storm around it was noticeable to them as most unusual.

This was one of the cases that first impressed scientist Dr Jacques Vallée enough to study UFOs in a serious manner. Owing to his credentials and being a student of Professor Hynek, doing a PhD in America, he was allowed access to the Air Force files on this case when it remained secret and had got no publicity. There was no conceivable motive for this case being hoaxed.

The first similar event I became involved with has many correspondences and also remains deeply impressive in my mind. It occurred on a night of incredible UFO activity in the Pennine hills of Lancashire and Yorkshire at the start of the major spring wave that dominated Britain that year.

Jeff Farmer and Brian Grimshaw worked on a night shift at a textile mill in Nelson, a small town near Burnley. It sits at the foot of Pendle Hill, a brooding place with folklore and witchcraft legends dating back centuries. The two men did not know that as from late on the previous evening (8 March 1977) many people had seen a weird light in the sky, including a coachload of people who had been frightened by it. They also did not know (indeed nobody in the UFO field did, until David Clark and Granville Oldroyd secured access to old police records during a 1985 investigation) that an almost identical case (without car stop elements) had occurred in the area in 1915!

At 3.10 am on 9 March, Farmer and Grimshaw had dropped off a canteen worker and were on their way back to the nightshift. The Nelson town centre, with terraced houses, was deserted, but they saw a light coming down out of clouds that swirled around Pendle Hill, and became puzzled enough to slow down and watch. It resolved into a sausage-shaped object (although their sketches show it far more like the Loch Raven egg than this might imply). It radiated an orange glow from its edges and multiple lights from a brilliant emission in the body itself.

As the object approached, heading south-east, it was seen to be at about two or three times rooftop height. When very close by, the car lost power. Lights and engine faded out. In the silence they could hear the object emitting a low humming noise as it hovered above them.

The men had got out of the car *before* the engine stopped, and although the lights faded to a dim glow they did not go out totally. Grimshaw, who was driving, said, 'It did not shudder, as when petrol runs out, but stopped instantly as if someone had pulled out the wiring.'

Out in the open the object drifted above them 'the size of a double decker bus' and the lights 'just seemed to be moving . . . They were all different. It looked as if you were looking at the exhaust of a car when it is red hot . . . The red and the orange stood out a lot [but there were] pink, green, blue and black . . . they were criss-crossing, going straight . . . it's hard to explain.'

These simple Lancashire men, very unsophisticated and having no way with words, easily conveyed the absolute confusion and terror of a UFO close encounter, in some respects far better than had they been able to wax eloquently about it. There was a mist around the object, held like a cloud to the surface. This is fascinating, because the presence of an electrostatic field is definitely suggested by what the men say they felt whilst stood in the open right beneath the object. This was a pressure on their heads and shoulders, creating a 'tingling' ('like you get when you rub your hand against nylon'). This field could have attracted particles of dust or vapour to it, thus creating the cloud.

Jeff Farmer panicked at the situation. Grimshaw says, 'his legs were shaking. He said to me, "Let's get away now!", and I said, "What can we do?" Then I got in the car and tried to start it. Even the ignition light wouldn't come on . . . I put the key in and nothing happened. It didn't turn over. It was dead.'

After what appears to have been about five minutes (quite possibly less) the object moved off towards Manchester. Then, as Grimshaw says, 'The first thing I noticed were the lights . . . They came back on again properly. Then the engine just started up.'

They drove back the few hundred yards to the menswear factory, arriving at 3.20 am. Both now had pounding headaches. A few hours later Grimshaw's eyes began to water. This effect persisted several days – long enough to be seen by our investigation team when we arrived. They also felt unwell enough not to be able to eat for a couple of days. These effects were put down to the stress of the situation by the witnesses. Jeff Farmer was so disturbed by the affair that he refused for a long time to talk to others about it.

Brian Grimshaw struck me as one of the least likely people I have ever met to have invented his story. He knew nothing about UFOs, save what he remembered from sensational press stories. Coming from that part of Lancashire myself I was able to translate his heavily accented language and understand perfectly what the electrostatic field had done to him, when he said, 'I were all of a tingle. It pushed down on mi head and mi hair all stood up. I'm buggered if I know what it were.'

Manchester Airport had nothing in the area at the time. The weather was in no way conducive to ball lightning or any other such fanciful idea. The car (a 1968 Vauxhall) was examined by us. New points and plugs had been fitted five weeks before the event and the car had been thoroughly serviced. This was because Grimshaw had already made tentative plans to sell it to a dealer in part-exchange for another one. After the encounter the only lasting effect was that the radio set did not work. New fuses failed to resolve this problem.

In my view the validity of this case is further stressed by the simple fact that if you have just arranged to sell your car the last thing you are then going to do is make up a story that it has just stopped for no reason!

There was a second car stop during the British wave. During a downpour on 5 June 1977, a car and motorcycle were both partially impeded by a glowing pinkish egg shape at Barnard's Castle, Durham. In this fascinating case sufficient heat (described as radiative as at Loch Raven) was generated by the encounter during the observation to enable the motorcyclist's wet leather gear to evaporate dry and become permanently wrinkled. There were sunburn, sickness and headache effects in this case too.

Half-way round the world on 2 July 1977, Keith Basterfield records that some occupants in a car also saw a reddish glow pace their car and cause it to lose power for 20 seconds. It had to be clutch-started. Whether there were any after-effects on the human witnesses is sadly not known.

The argument that these egg-shaped UFOs are natural phenomena (UAPs perhaps) takes a knock when you realise that identical effects are reported in cases where entities are seen.

On 12 August 1975 USAF Sergeant Charles Moody had finished his shift at Hamilton Air Force Base, Texas, and went for a late night drive to cool off. Sitting on his car bonnet admiring the fine night, he saw a bright disc of light descend to the ground about 100 feet away. He felt a tingling sensation over his body as he leapt into the car and tried to drive off. The engine would not fire. When the UFO departed and he did go home he discovered that an hour of time had vanished.

Being in a sensitive position he reported the affair and was studied by doctors at the local army hospital. By now he had developed a red blotchy rash over parts of his body and the suggestion of mild radiation sickness was mooted. Drugs were administered but he was able to carry on working. However, gradually, bits of memory came back to him. He got as far as recalling small beings with large eyes and one-piece suits inviting him on board. Then, as news leaked out to a UFO investigator, who interviewed him, Moody was suddenly posted abroad. The Army hospital, whilst recalling the case and the treatment, claimed all the medical records had mysteriously 'disappeared'.

Despite the unsatisfactory nature of this case, the red rash after a close encounter is very common, too common to be unconnected. Whilst researching a radio programme on UFOs in 1986 I found a woman, by pure chance, who in 1947 had been travelling across desert into Tibet with her husband and a Gurkha guard. They all saw a floating object that attracted a swirling cloud to it (the electrostatic field again?). Afterwards all witnesses independently reported a red, itchy rash that covered only the parts of their bodies exposed to the air.

Another case I have studied in detail concerns a young receptionist (now herself a medical representative) who had an encounter with a domed object near her Bolton home on 23 January 1976. She described (I am sure without the slightest connection with the Nelson case, which had not yet happened, do not forget!) a force that 'pressed down on me from above. It almost pushed me into the ground. It made me tingle or vibrate, almost like an electric shock.' Her teeth chattered and subsequently fillings crumbled to powder (requiring emergency dental treatment). Next day she was sick and began to develop a red rash over her arms and neck.

This woman, Shelley, is one of the most convincing witnesses I have met. Yet her encounter also contained a time lapse (which under hypnosis has revealed an apparent on-board contact with aliens performing a medical examination). She was also visited by two strange men after the experience who seemed to be from the military or government and to know exactly what physical symptoms she had.

There is no doubt in my mind that a real force is involved in these cases.

24 WITNESSES WHO GLOW IN THE DARK – UFO RADIATION

In such cases, however, if radioactive material actually were present, the possibility that it was placed there by humans cannot be ignored.
(Professor Roy Craig, physical chemist, dismissing all anecdotal evidence for UFOs that emit radiation, in half a page of the Colorado University UFO project, 1969.)

The UFO has an interest in atomic installations. That much we have seen. Perhaps this is because the UAPs, as natural phenomena, are dangerous by-products of our nuclear exploration (all the more dangerous because science laughs them off as 'silly UFOs'). Alternatively, perhaps, some intelligence (alien or even our own future descendants) are issuing warnings about the abuse of such power. Either way it is something to concern us, especially when coupled with the cases in the last chapter that show evidence of some energy source associated with UFOs.

Beware – the worst is yet to come!

In Britain, controversy surrounds the proposal to build a pressure-cooled water reactor system at the Sizewell power station in Suffolk. This has been the subject of a mammoth public enquiry, and although the local people will continue to show hostility (especially in the wake of the Chernobyl disaster in the USSR) most suspect that the advance of nuclear power will never be halted.

The tiny village of Leiston is the nearest main habitation to the coastal plant. Aside from being in the shadow of the reactor, it also sits at the northern end of Rendlesham Forest, home of the dramatic events of 27 December 1980. In that case radiation traces were left in the pine trees, if you recall.

That is by no means the only time strange things have gone on in the immediate vicinity. Woodbridge and the surrounding woodland has generated many UFO sightings, sitting in the BUFORA files when I skimmed through them. Like the thousands of other cases investigated and then put onto computer they remain a body of significant testimony which I doubt very much the Sizewell enquiry (although it heard just about everything else!) was not made aware of. It is tempting to consider that someone, somewhere, has been making their views felt in the way *they* know best!

On 24 February 1975 a postal worker walking his dog on the beach a mile from the reactor saw a rotating greenish cloud that changed shape and came in from the sea. It resolved into a pear shape. Doubtless you will have noticed the points of similarity with the Aeroflot 'cloud aircraft' case ten years later.

The UFO on Sizewell beach was investigated by Peter Johnson, a long-time local sleuth. He found that the witness had recorded a sharp, tangy odour coming from it (which appears to have been ozone gas that must have resulted from ionisation of the atmosphere in the vicinity of the encounter). The dog became terrified and fled, by some irony to the sanctuary of the reactor's perimeter fence! The startled human simply watched it float away. Brenda Butler, an investigator and co-author on the 'Sky Crash' story in Rendlesham Forest, tells me that this man was unwell after the experience and lost his job because of it. What happened to the dog I do not know. Perhaps his good sense in getting out of there saved him drastic after-effects.

Drastic after-effects are a fair way of describing what happened to Gordon Levett's dog. He was an eye-witness to the Rendlesham Forest events of late December 1980, when he spotted a fluorescent green object come in from the direction of the Sizewell reactor, drift over his house at Sudbourne and vanish into the forest. His dog, who was being put into a shed for the night, became ill soon after the close encounter. It died. The vet diagnosed some form of poisoning, but did not know about the UFO. Gordon Levett did not know about the 1975 Sizewell beach encounter. Nor, of course, did the Aeroflot crew know about either case. Clearly these events prove that some *real* radiating energy is involved. This is no hallucination. As witness José Trejo said after the Talavera Air Force Base case, 'Hallucinations don't kill dogs.'

Local fishermen around Sizewell also know about 'green fireballs' that pop out of the sea. By coincidence (or was it?) around October 1983, when we first brought the Rendlesham Forest 'Sky-Crash' to the world through the *News of the World* newspaper, a wave of green fireball sightings occurred, almost as if to mark the occasion! For example, at 4.50 am on 15 November 1983 those on board the fishing boat *Alison Teresa* out of Harwich saw a green ball of fire move slowly across the sky. There were some suggestions of a meteor, which *might* apply in isolated cases, but not when the green fireball mystery is so repetitive.

You have already heard me mention the exact same phenomenon in and around the American missile and atomic development sites in the first few years of the UFO story, and how meteor expert Dr Lincoln La Paz rejected this theory. I have talked to former RAF pilot, Gerry Mitchell, who saw three green fireballs over the massive Shell Oil Refinery at Carrington near Manchester. This place has also generated several other classic encounters. Another oil refinery at Pitsea in Essex has also produced a green fireball story. There are almost certainly many others lurking in the records. It seems to me unlikely these are more coincidences.

But for a friendly contact at RAF Farnborough (whom I will not put into difficulties by naming) the fact that a more disturbing case took place over Rendlesham Forest might not have come to my notice. It happened on 24 August 1984 and my friend sent a copy (handwritten) of the accident report memo that gave a first description of the events.

At 12.55 am that night, a Britten-Norman Trislander cargo plane from Stansted in Essex was heading for Amsterdam over the forest. It was at 5000 feet. The pilot felt a 'bump' in the controls, and then later noted that the right engine had seized. Fortunately, a Trislander has *three* engines so it was possible to continue and make a somewhat scary but otherwise uneventful landing in Holland. Inspection there showed substantial damage to the left propeller, control runs, cables and right engine. From holes in the fuselage it was obvious that a metal object had struck the aircraft, because pieces of metal debris were still embedded!

The report called these 'metallic objects, foreign to the aircraft'. It added that the meteorological office had failed to identify the debris as being anything to do with a radio-sonde or weather balloon. The memo even said, most intriguingly, 'Examination of a radar recording indicates no other aircraft or "identifiable objects" in this area at the time.' Of course, that means there *were* other targets on the radar, as is always the case, and that one of these 'unidentified objects' may have been of considerable interest.

I tracked the aircraft down at Stansted and contacted the freight company who owned the Trislander with the appropriate registration mark. The chief officer of the company, Kondair, replied on 19 December. Mr D.A. Hughes said, 'The flight to which you refer did depart Stansted at 00.38 hours (GMT) on 24 August 1984.' He added, however, that it would be up to the pilot concerned whether he personally responded any further to my enquiries.

Meanwhile, in January 1985, the local East Anglian press mentioned the story (tucked away as a bit of information within its 'Air Scene' column on page 21). A cartoon depicted an angel sweeping nuts and bolts off a cloud and hitting the unfortunate aircraft! A few new details were added. The Civil Aviation Authority (CAA) had now specified that the object the plane had struck was not 'a UK weather balloon', leaving the door ajar for it to be one from somewhere else. One of the holes was described as 'four inches by one-half inch' and the 'three items' recovered were said to be 'one resembling a tyre valve, and two short cylindrical sections (one of which was magnetic)'.

This hardly seems very alien, and I suggest that the CAA ought to have been able to resolve this very quickly. I have monitored the situation since but, more than two years later, the cause of the incident seems not to have been found. The very fact that the accident chanced to occur where it did makes it of UFO potential, and I cannot say this thought was squelched when the CAA decided to make it clear (although I had gone out of my way to offer no hint of a suspected connection) that the Trislander was 'not in collision with a UFO'. (In any case, since a UFO is an unidentified flying object, that is precisely what the Trislander *was* in collision with!)

On 5 February 1985, I confess to my surprise, the pilot did write to me. His very helpful letter explained that after six months nobody knew what had occurred. 'Unfortunately, we do not have any idea as to the cause of the event and can only surmise it was a weather balloon possibly many hundreds of miles from its place of launch.' Indeed, this may be the answer, although I would not have imagined it to have been that difficult to back-track wind directions to check the relatively small number of launch sites it could have come from; and presumably the rest of the balloon fell to earth in August 1984 over Suffolk. Yet nobody appears to have reported it. It must have been fairly substantial to survive such a long journey and cause such damage on impact.

That the CAA were less impressed by the idea comes from a second memo (this time copied direct to me). It contains a photograph of the debris, which looks remarkably fresh and free from marks. They appear utterly terrestrial. Unless some aliens, familiar with our jargon (in which extra-terrestrial spaceships are often called 'the nuts and bolts theory') are having a good laugh by offering us real nuts and bolts! At the end of the memo the Aviation authority ask, 'Has anyone any ideas?'

In October 1985 the *Observer* newspaper carried a report by David Keys entitled 'Nuts and bolts from the blue'. This is a short article about the rising number of incidents involving bits falling off aircraft; i.e. doors, parts of a wing etc. It is not very encouraging if you chance to live near a busy airport, as sooner or later one of these bits is going to do serious damage. The Kondair story, although rather out of place, forms a postscript, basically saying, 'The Islander [sic] affair is perhaps the most bizarre of all the incidents so far, but it shares at least one common characteristic with most of the others − the identity of the "guilty" aircraft almost always remains unknown.'

Of course, if we are to believe the initial CAA memo about the radar track then there was no guilty aircraft in the Rendlesham Forest accident. At least, no aircraft in the sense that Keys and the *Observer* obviously implied. Keys further says that the CAA, having got nowhere in their investigation, had even approached the MoD. I hope they got further than we did over the December 1980 Rendlesham Forest events! Allegedly the

MoD could not help (surprise, surprise) and it was now being speculated that 'space junk or military objects may have been responsible'.

I make no claims about this case, which may eventually have a rational solution, but it seems to me well worth noting that the (so far as we know) only alleged UFO crash, and the sole collision between an aircraft and a 'UFO' over Britain, have both taken place over the same area – the area which has been plagued by green fireballs in the past. The area where radar was developed during World War Two, where there is strong evidence to suggest that British nuclear weapons were partly developed and where now the first potentially catastrophic civilian nuclear power station may be built.

There are more definite UFO connections with some destructive cases. For example, the events of 8 February 1981 must be considered of some significance. On that date a Frenchman named Collini was working in his garden at Trans-en-Provence at approximately 5 pm. He heard a low whistle or humming noise and glanced up to see a strange glowing mass descending towards a terrace at the foot of his land. Before he could respond it climbed skywards again, still whistling.

Rushing to the scene he discovered that the thing had evidently touched the ground, because there was a circular imprint and some indentations. A rather upset M. Collini called the local police right away. The Gendarmerie (as you will see in Chapter 29) has a unique role in France. The government fund a UFO research programme on a permanent basis and the scientists in charge use the police task force as preliminary field investigators. The Gendarmes are trained in how to do a UFO study and determine quickly if the case is important enough to warrant flying in the scientists.

The Gendarmerie took samples of vegetation and soil before the day was out. Then, after interviewing M. Collini, they decided to call in the scientists. The witness was studied by a psychological laboratory who found that there was no reason why he should not be telling the truth. According to Jean Velasco, engineer in charge of the team, 'There was great internal and external consistency between the various versions of the witness's report and the minimum element of subjectivity.'

Physics and chemistry units also analysed the samples and a bio-chemical research laboratory examined the vegetation. This gave three independent checks on the physical evidence. Some of the results proved startling.

The soil had been compacted and heated to between 300 and 600° C. Minerals such as zinc and phosphate were left behind *only* in the affected area. The wild vegetation here was carefully studied by the National Institute of Agricultural Research, under Professor Bounias. Between 30 and 50 per cent reduction in the chlorophyll content of leaves in the immediate vicinity was noted. The younger the shoots the worse the effects, and detailed mapping showed that there was a direct relationship between the amount of effect and distance from the centre of the landing site. Velasco said, in 1985, 'the correlation phenomena—distance appears beyond dispute'.

What caused these significant changes in the local conditions? Had the witness spread chemicals over the ground and made up his story? Indeed not. Velasco says, 'The effects on plants in the area can be compared with that produced on the leaves of other plant species after exposing the seeds to gamma radiation . . . a considerable amount must be applied to produce a disturbance equal to that observed at the site.'

We are in fact talking about 10 rads: not enough to create serious life-threatening circumstances to a human, but more than was left in the wake of the Chernobyl accident during May 1986. The results led the French scientists to conclude that a trauma induced by an intense electromagnetic field (presumably associated with the UFO) had been responsible. It is rather interesting to compare this case with the landing in Rendlesham Forest, England, just six weeks earlier. If a thorough scientific evaluation of the soil and tree damage had been carried out then, would it have provided similar evidence? Indeed, as samples *were* taken (the tape-recording clearly relates this as it happened!) perhaps such a study *was* done and is being kept secret.

There does seem to be a rather strange double standard here. There was quite a government outcry against the Soviet Union for hiding from the world the radiation hazard after the Chernobyl explosion, but at least the Russians did talk after a few days. You have *never* been officially informed about what went on in Suffolk and Trans-en-Provence, both decidedly closer to most of western Europe than Chernobyl. Yet the French police were on the scene the same day and the British police now admit they were too (and the MoD have long admitted that they had a report on the radiation traces some days later).

It should not be up to me, through a UFO book, writing to a few thousand people. This is something that is dishonest for any government to obscure. Are you satisfied that (whatever UFOs may or may not be) those in authority hid these facts from you?

Ironically (or was it?) just as the Colonels, Majors and other officers on Bentwaters base were out in Rendlesham Forest recording their testament to a conspiracy, collecting evidence of the radiation effects, far across the Atlantic an even more serious radiation spillage was taking place!

The case has been thoroughly examined by Houston space-shuttle engineer John Shuessler and NASA scientist Dr Alan Holt, via their part-time capacity as UFO researchers. They have become so disturbed by the so-called Cash/Landrum affair that they have devoted years of their lives to a quest for truth. Being similarly ensnared by the 'Sky Crash' in

Rendlesham Forest I know how they feel.

Restaurant owner Betty Cash, her employee Vickie Landrum and Vickie's young grandson, Colby, were driving back from a trip to check out a rival establishment. It was a mild winter's night, just after 9 pm on 29 December 1980 (which, taking time zones into account, is *exactly* coincident with the last part of the tape then being made in Suffolk!).

The three people were driving on a road through a pine forest (one of dozens of little 'coincidences' that link these cases). They were near Huffman, Texas, just outside the space city of Houston, where NASA headquarters are. (Believe it or not, RAF Woodbridge also has ties with NASA, via the 'Aerospace Rescue and Recovery Squadron' lodged there to recover astronauts.)

Betty Cash and the Landrums saw a diamond-shaped object appear on the road ahead pouring out flame and light. Vickie told her grandson that it was the end of the world and Jesus was coming. Instead the UFO just hovered there. They felt waves of heat and had to get out of the car to escape the oppressive atmosphere. Betty stood at the front of the vehicle feeling her wedding ring burn into her finger. Colby became so hysterical that his grandmother had to take him back inside. This decision might have been one of the most innocent yet important of Colby's life!

Suddenly a large retinue of helicopters came thundering over, heading for the stranded UFO. They seemed to shepherd this away. Colby was petrified by the roar of the large twin-rotor Chinooks, as it formed such a contrast with the silent UFO.

Schuessler, Holt and colleagues at the UFO group MUFON made a search for other witnesses and found some, especially who had seen or heard the helicopters, which is rather odd because no agency admits liability for the Chinooks! For such a large flotilla of noisy helicopters to fly within ten miles of Houston without being detected is practically impossible, and there are very few sources that could fly so many of these aircraft. Their denial is even more astonishing than the denial of the UFO.

Following this terrible night all three witnesses became ill. Colby vomited over the bed. Each suffered headaches, diarrhoea, 'cooked skin' burn effects – symptoms that again point towards radiation sickness. Even more significantly, they each lost clumps of hair over the following weeks.

Vickie and Colby (partially protected by the car body for much of the encounter) recovered substantially after only a few days. Betty Cash was so ill that she had to spend weeks in hospital (including a long spell in intensive care). She lost half her hair growth. Many physical problems not directly produced by the encounter were provoked by the trauma and she has rarely been out of hospital for more than a few weeks in the years following the incident.

Having seen the photographs that the MUFON team took at various stages during the investigation, the rapid decline in Betty's health and the less serious (but no less worrying) effects on Vickie and Colby Landrum are all too plain. For anyone to suggest that they did this to themselves is absurd. Yet the only other solution is that the object was a UFO.

The US government, of course, deny all knowledge of this event. For them to say that neither the object nor the helicopters are known about is either an outrageous lie on their part, or they are calling the witnesses liars. No other option really fits. I cannot see any prospect of a nation as security-conscious as the United States allowing a radioactive unknown object and a dozen noisy helicopters to parade above a road just a few miles from NASA without them knowing full well what was going on.

Of course, the Americans did not attempt an intercept. Why was this? Were they holding back deliberately? Did they understand what was happening? I have heard it suggested that the radioactive UFO *was* American, a nuclear reactor that was leaking, for example. If it is true that they would fly such a thing over populated terrain at such a time of day then it would present almost as big a scandal as a UFO conspiracy.

Either way there are many answers owing, but we are getting no answers at all.

The ridiculous way in which we are expected to believe such audacious statements has driven these three witnesses to *sue* the US government. Betty Cash is demanding both compensation and recompense for her extensive medical fees (which in a country without a national health service can be catastrophic). This promises one of the most fantastic legal battles in history — provided UFO investigators can find the money to help these three tragic victims of circumstance get the one thing they deserve: justice.

UFOs, whatever they may be, are usually quite harmless. They are also, fairly often, explicable. However, they can at times be very dangerous. If the government of your country refuse to issue a health warning then I must do so. I do not wish to exaggerate the risks, nor to create the impression of dastardly aliens shooting humans with their radioactive ray-guns. It is not like that at all.

UFOs can seriously damage your health.

25 SUPERNATURAL CAUSES – UFO FATALITIES

Location of the occurrence: Not Known
Time: Not Known
Degree of injury: Presumed Fatal
Opinion as to cause: The reason for the disappearance of the aircraft has not been
determined
(Part of the conclusions to an Australian Department of Aviation accident investigation
report, May 1982, concerning the loss of Cessna 182 VH-DSJ.)

In March 1978 I did not have any idea where Risley, Cheshire, was. It is
mere chance that I now live half a mile from the spot where late on the 17th
of that month a Warrington service engineer, Ken Edwards, had a fatal
encounter with a UFO.

Ken was returning from a union meeting in south Manchester and had
turned off the M62 onto a slip road that now feeds the Birchwood village
development. In 1978 Birchwood was not yet built and the road was known
only to those locals who took it for a short cut. It eventually branches into
an older road that passes a sloping embankment on one side and a high-
security fence on the other. The fence demarks the boundary of the UK
Atomic Energy Commission administrative centre, where there are also
experimental and research facilities. That a UFO encounter should take
place here is, I suppose, just another coincidence (I hope that you are
getting pretty sick of that word by now!).

A glowing white mass appeared to Ken's right, on the embankment, and
drifted down into the centre of the road as he slowed the van to a halt. For
a few moments there was a staring match between the engineer and the
'thing', before two beams of light emerged from round eyes and struck the
witness where he was holding the steering wheel. The mass then moved
onward and passed straight *through* the security fence into the Atomic
Energy complex, vanishing over the top of the embankment at the far side
of the wire.

Ken Edwards and his wife were plagued by all manner of reporters and
religious societies after the police gave their story to the *Warrington*

Guardian. From here it found its way to Fleet Street. So bad was this that they were driven out of their home for a few days, just to escape the pressure. They did not want all this attention. I was very impressed with their matter-of-fact approach and disdain for all the silliness that went on about them. By misfortune the movie *Close Encounters of the Third Kind* was soon due for release and the Sunday tabloids had marvellous fun with such inane titles for their stories as 'Ken and a flasher from outer space'!

Because of this it was a couple of weeks before the dust had settled enough for me to intrude on the family. However, colleague Peter Hough had seen them both for a brief time only three or four days after the sighting. So it was possible to compare notes. The witness had sketched a humanoid figure with arms protruding from its chest but no other features save the eyes and white glow. He has always alluded to the thing as a 'figure' — and, of course, it could just as easily have been a ghost as in this case there is absolutely no justification for the media's UFO label. I was never as certain myself. I had the impression that the 'thing' had been more a blob of energy which Ken might have interpreted as a figure.

After the object (whatever it was) had vanished through the fence Ken was left in a profound state of shock, but he drove the mile or so home and was treated by his concerned wife (chiefly it would seem with liberal supplies of medicinal whisky). 'He was white, shaking and petrified,' she told me. She drove him to the police station at Padgate, who returned with the gradually recovering man to the research centre and searched the area for several hours with UK Atomic Energy security guards. One thing was clear. The fence was undamaged. It was just not possible for anyone to have gone through it as Ken had claimed to see.

A number of things followed. Ken Edwards was unwell, but it was never possible to be sure this was not a result of the trauma. When we timed the journey and his arrival home was compared it soon became apparent that about 45 minutes were not accounted for. We could correlate this because, as both Peter and I saw, his watch had stopped at the time he alleged that the encounter had happened and was still not working when I met him. Even so, Ken himself did not regard this as significant. He believed that he had sat in the van for all the missing time frozen to his seat. However, as the vehicle was in the middle of a fairly narrow road this seems unlikely, but not impossible, of course.

Furthermore the insides of the fingers of one hand (the one that had been exposed to the beams of light from the thing) were coated by a faint sunburn — needless to say not real sunburn in England during March.

It was quite amusing for me to see these marks on Ken Edwards. For one of the key scenes in Spielberg's movie is when character Roy Nearey is stopped in his van by a UFO and struck by lightbeams. The part of his face exposed to the beams is 'cooked' by the ray and the part in shadow is not.

Nearey's wife in the plot says she will tell everyone he fell asleep under a sunlamp! Ken Edwards had not seen the still unreleased film. Since I was helping Columbia with promotion I was able to see the irony. As millions thrilled to the fictional exploits the UFO enigma had given a real demonstration of this exact effect!

Another point which the hasty wave of ludicrous press attention had missed was that the radio transceiver in Ken's van had been demolished. The engineers at work who tried to fix it reported that a tremendous power surge had swept through and literally exploded it beyond repair. Since it had worked on the day of the sighting and did not work the next time he came to use it (less than three days later) it seems reasonable to connect the two incidents.

This case was one of the earliest close encounters either Peter Hough or I investigated. In retrospect a great deal we should have done was never possible. Our excuse was that both of us had full-time jobs, and of course in 1978 the scientists of Britain laughed at UFOs and we did not have the money to pay for costly laboratory tests on the watch or the radio set. Peter does note that when he visited the site a couple of days after the encounter he found a dead rabbit on the embankment close to where the thing had first appeared. It showed no marks to indicate it had been run over, or indeed how it had died. It may be irrelevant, but we have wondered many times what might have been learned had we been able to have that rabbit studied.

I moved to Warrington about two years after the experience and had kept a semi-frequent contact with Ken and his wife for a number of reasons. I felt that serious UFO investigators owed a debt in view of the abuse handed out by less ethical colleagues. In addition there was a chance that some memories might return if indeed there was more to the missing time than we currently knew. However, all that Ken ever did recall were vivid dream images reliving the experience over and over. Although he did have several phone calls from people requesting to carry out hypnosis (one man saying he was associated with NASA!) none gave names and none ever called back when Ken said he was unsure about the idea.

There was good reason why Ken Edwards had put the case to the back of his mind. In the year following his experience, whilst only in his mid-thirties, he began to feel progressively tired and unwell. Treatment failed and cancer of the kidneys was diagnosed. He had surgery at the beginning of 1980. However, he did not fully recover and cancer of the throat was then discovered. Just four years after the UFO encounter he lost his fight for life. To the end Ken never associated the illness with the UFO, and his doctors almost certainly did not know about it (Ken did not tell them). It is impossible to say that the two things are related, but in view of the known effects in this case and the clear evidence of radiation in other UFO sightings I do not think we can rule it out. I am sure Ken would have wanted me to warn of the potential danger, so that anyone else in the same situation can have regular medical check-ups immediately after being struck by beams from a UFO. It always pays to be cautious.

This is not the only possible UFO-related death that I have sadly been involved with. The other was far more controversial. It even created a front-page headline story in one Sunday newspaper, reading 'Amazing UFO Death Riddle!'. The evidence was so circumstantial that I refused to be associated with that particular story. Sensationalism of that kind helps nobody. Nevertheless facts *are* facts.

Briefly, a Polish mine worker from the village of Tingley, near Wakefield, vanished in broad daylight on 6 June 1980. He had gone to buy some potatoes from a corner shop and was never seen alive again. Despite a massive search and protracted inquest nobody ever came up with a clue as to where he was or why he had vanished. His body was discovered, amid a downpour, on the afternoon of 11 June, on top of a greasy pile of coal in a yard beside Todmorden railway station. This town, thirty miles from his home, was one that (so far as anybody knew) the miner had never visited.

The man had died from a heart attack, aggravating a slight condition he did have. There were suggestions that it might have been brought on by fear. His neck and shoulders also had a large burn (origin unknown) which had been treated by some ointment that nobody recognised. No hospital or doctor in the adjacent counties had treated the man for this condition. However, the coroner was certain the burn had not led to death and was at least twenty-four hours old.

This is clearly a mystery, made more poignant by the fact that the man's wife was disabled and confined to a wheelchair. Everyone agreed that her husband was devoted to her and would not willingly leave. So what turned it into a UFO death riddle? There were three things.

Certain suggestions had been made during the fruitless police investigations that it seemed as if the man had been put on the coal tip *from* the air. His name was also very interesting – Zigmund Adamski. Uncommon in Britain (although not in Poland) it happens to be that of the most famous and original man to claim that he had been taken for rides in 'spaceships' back in the early 1950s. However, the real twist of fate came when the police officer called onto the scene when the body was discovered (PC Alan Godfrey) was the subject of a UFO abduction about half a mile from where Adamski was found (on Burnley Road), approximately five months later.

You have already seen details of the Godfrey story (page 69) and it is unquestionably one of the strangest and most persuasive tales in British UFO history. Its coincidental link with this puzzling death is bizarre, but can we say more than that?

Godfrey himself never regarded the Adamski death to be UFO-related. However, it has to be said that his police car was stopped by a mysterious force and radiation of some sort was emitted to dry the road surface beneath the UFO.

I am also concerned about the degree of pressure that Alan Godfrey received from the West Yorkshire police force. They may have had honest motives to suppress the media sensationalism, but their entreaties to their police officer not to discuss the Adamski death, then not to talk about his UFO story, and finally to disassociate himself from all contact with investigators, ultimately reached ludicrous proportions.

This is not the place to tell the full story of the aftermath of the Alan Godfrey case. It is long, disturbing and of great concern to anyone who values freedom of speech. Suffice it to say that he is no longer a police officer, and not as a matter of choice. On the other hand the investigation team (led by lawyer Harry Harris) took him to several prominent psychiatrists, and nobody considered the policeman to be anything other than honest, truthful and sane.

A second time-loss and car-stop case (involving a truck) has turned up in recent months. Peter Hough and myself travelled to Burnley to investigate the story. It took place on Burnley Road, about two miles further out of Todmorden and several months before the Adamski body was found. It involved several illness symptoms on the witness.

For three major events to occur in the same year in such a small geographical area seems remarkable. Even more remarkable is the story uncovered by the West Yorkshire UFO Research Group and colleagues at the Wigan Aerial Phenomena Investigation Team. This concerns a woman who at 11 pm one night heard 'a great noise, not unlike that of great water surges' above her house in Todmorden. She and her husband went out and saw nothing. The sound died away. Just as they were turning to go back indoors they were confronted by a 'green and red mass of glowing energy' that was practically sitting on top of their roof. It then rose in a vertical and silent fashion, pouring down light onto them. The house glowed red beneath it.

What is most important about this case is the date. It appears to have been 10 June 1980, just thirteen hours before Adamski's body was found very nearby. The coroner had placed his death as somewhere between the time of this UFO encounter and the discovery by the coal merchant's son. Another coincidence?

I shall conclude with one more baffling case, this time from another continent. In this example the death is merely assumed as nobody has ever seen the victim again!

Frederick Valentich, aged 20, was pilot of his own Cessna 182 light plane (VH—DSJ). He took off from Moorabbin Airport, Melbourne, Australia at

6.19 pm on the evening of 21 October 1978. His destination was King Island, across the short Bass Strait, north of Tasmania. He was due to collect some crayfish for colleagues at the Air Training Corps, where he served as an instructor. Although he was inexperienced at night flying, the weather was fine and calm and the route was a direct short hop which would easily allow him to return home by 10 pm for a family reunion.

Valentich flew uneventfully along the twilight shores until he crossed Cape Otway lighthouse at 7 pm. It would take him another 30 minutes to reach King Island. At 7.06 pm the conversation with Melbourne control (which was tape-recorded) entered a strange phase.

'Is there any traffic in my area, below 5000 feet?' he asked.

'Negative – no known traffic,' came the reply from controller Steve Robey.

'Sierra Juliet', the blue and white Cessna, then found itself face to face with a UFO. Thirty seconds after the above exchange Valentich reported that he saw 'four bright, it seems to me like, landing lights', and nearly one minute later, that 'the aircraft has just passed over me at least a thousand feet above.'

Valentich then asked Robey to check military activity. He was certain that something was above him, and, after a period of 'open microphone' (where Valentich appeared to be about to talk but then stopped himself), he explained, 'it's approaching now from due east, towards me . . . it seems to me that he's playing some sort of game. He's flying over me, two, three times at speeds I could not identify.'

You are probably already recognising the similarities with previous mid-air encounters earlier in the book, but three and a half minutes into this perplexing transmission the pilot confirmed, 'It's not an aircraft, it is . . .'. There then came more open microphone and a query from Robey. Valentich responded, 'As it's flying past it's a long shape . . . cannot identify more than it has such speed . . . It's before me right now, Melbourne.' Then, after a further question by Robey, 'It seems like it's stationary. What I'm doing right now is orbiting and the thing is just orbiting on top of me also. It's got a green light and sort of metallic like. It's all shiny on the outside.'

Only two more minutes of conversation were to follow. The object approached again, Valentich explained that his engine was 'rough-idling' and 'coughing', but he was going to continue to King Island. Then he cut in, 'Ah – Melbourne – that strange aircraft is hovering on top of me again . . . It's hovering and it's not an aircraft.'

'Delta Sierra Juliet,' Robey acknowledged.

Then a confused man came back with his final words, putting his call sign first which only a terrified pilot would do. 'Delta Sierra Juliet, Melbourne,' he said. Then came 17 seconds of open microphone punctuated by a strange metallic pinging noise in two bursts.

Sixteen minutes later the Cessna failed to land at King Island and continued not to respond to Robey's calls. A huge search was launched, but no trace of the plane or its pilot has ever been found.

According to investigator Bill Chalker, Robey said of his conversation with Valentich, 'I think at first he was a little concerned about the other aircraft flying around him, and of course I had to assume that it was another aircraft until it developed and became a little mysterious. Towards the end I think he was definitely concerned for his safety. I considered that he would have had to have been a good actor to have put it all together the way he did.'

The story found its way into the press, because the ground-to-air conversations were heard by many people. In addition, that same weekend had been the focus of a major wave of UFO sightings! At 6.43 pm (a quarter of an hour before Valentich flew over) a man in a boat off Cape Otway was taking photographs of the setting sun with an automatic camera. Two show what might be an object climbing up out of the sea in the same direction as the Cessna was about to fly!

Over the years there have been dozens of suggestions as to what might have occurred. These range from a crash after flying upside down and seeing his own plane reflected in the sea (although this would not be possible for the length of time the taped conversation records), through attacks by drug smugglers, to a faked suicide using the UFO story as a cover to escape. Of course, there are also those who say he was kidnapped by aliens.

Guido Valentich, the young man's father, has continued the fight for truth and secured a copy of the tape-recording only after enquiries ceased in 1982 and other copies were supposedly destroyed. He kindly made this available to Dr Richard Haines, a scientist specialising in UFO/aircraft encounters. Haines subjected the weird pinging sound to analysis but could only say that it was not the microphone switch and had 'no discernible patterns in time or frequency'.

Unless, or until, someone finds the Cessna in thirty fathoms of the Bass Strait, or possibly Frederick Valentich turns up alive somewhere with a full explanation, this will remain one of the great aviation mysteries of the century. Possibly a hoax. Possibly an accidental death. Possibly the most disturbing UFO abduction of them all.

This is one of the few UFO reports in which all factors investigated, geometric, psychological, and physical appear to be consistent with the assertion that an extraordinary flying object, silvery, metallic, disc-shaped, tens of metres in diameter and evidently artificial, flew within sight of two witnesses.

(Dr William K. Hartmann, in his final conclusion to his detailed analysis of Case Number 46, the McMinnville, Oregon, photographs, in the 1969 Colorado University report.)

Assuming UFOs are real, then there should be pictures of them. Of course, these things appear unexpectedly, can cause trauma and shock in witnesses and are often visible for very brief periods of time. All these factors conspire against a big stack of convincing photographs, as does the fact that most camera systems cannot cope with something that comes out mainly at night and is perhaps a small light against a sea of dark.

There are quite a number of photographs in this book, taken from the albums of UFO groups around the world. Nobody has counted exactly how many exist, but there are certainly a few thousand. From my own experience, examining about a hundred British snapshots and several clips of movie film, the vast majority do *not* show UFOs at all. There are outright fabrications (since it is fun to try to fool people with a photograph). Many 'UFOs' are simply film or processing faults and correspond with no object seen in the sky when the picture was taken. Several are mistaken identity (since if stars or aircraft can fool the eye they can deceive the camera lens too). Another large group are what we have to call 'insufficient data', because we just do not have enough information to judge one way or another. If a witness fails to provide a negative for scientific analysis (from which it is usually possible to make accurate judgements) then the case must be discounted.

In the end I found only a small handful of pictures that *might* be of UFOs. On a global scale there are probably not many more than one or two hundred worth getting excited about.

This total, just three or four cases a year around the world, is hardly auspicious; but it provides enough scope to tantalise us. Obviously I cannot describe all the potentially genuine examples, and some may still be unknown by UFO researchers as cases often come to light years after they have happened. Witnesses also sometimes claim that they took pictures, but these were removed by the authorities. We cannot know if this is true. A few of the interesting pictures are included elsewhere in this book, plus some of the more doubtful offerings, but here are descriptions of six of the best.

11 May 1950, McMinnville, Oregon, USA

The first impressive UFO pictures were taken by Mr and Mrs Paul Trent, a farming couple who saw a disc with a turret on top cross their land early one evening. They were able to take two clear shots of it, provide the negatives and include foreground and background detail that would help the analyst. The fact that they moved slightly between taking the pictures (as the object was going out of sight behind a wall) gave another useful piece of data.

The witnesses seem not to have recognised the significance of what they had on film. That it was some kind of military aircraft was their assumption. It was left undeveloped in the camera until the roll was used up. Then they only showed the results to a few friends. It finally reached the local press through the devices of someone at the local bank. Eventually it made national headlines in *Life* magazine, but even then the Trents were so uninterested in making money out of what they had achieved that they never claimed the negatives back.

Over the years several investigations have tried to prove the pictures to be fake. Since they so clearly show an unconventional disc-shaped UFO this is the only real alternative to pronouncing them as positive proof. No study has been able to expose a hoax. In 1969 the Colorado University project found these two pictures the most important they studied. The analysis report by Dr William K. Hartmann was a virtual statement that a real artificially designed UFO had flown over the Trents' farm (see quote at the start of this chapter). It was large and about 1.3 km from the camera, he said.

Dr Bruce Maccabee, the US Navy physicist, reached a similar conclusion. A computer-enhancement analysis of the pictures was conducted by William Spaulding and this was able to demonstrate, with reasonable certainty, that the object was *not* a model suspended by thread – the only viable hoax method. No serious objections have stood up against the case. On present evidence, unless the Trents built a full-scale working model of a UFO, test-flew it once, took a couple of pictures and subsequently never used either their photographic expertise or brilliance at aero-engineering, then they saw and photographed a genuine UFO.

16 January 1958, Trinidade Island, Brazilian South Atlantic

Four extraordinary pictures were taken from a ship (the *Almirante Saldanha*), moored off a desolate rocky island hundreds of miles from the coast of Brazil. It was part of a scientific mission with a US navy crew and photographer Almiro Barauna.

At 12.15 pm Barauna and 47 members of the crew saw an object, like two plates back to back, fly in from the sea, circle the peak on the island and whizz off back out to sea. It was in view a little under two minutes (as the automatic sequence of the photographs demonstrates). The object's speed prevented the rest of the crew getting on deck fast enough to witness the UFO.

The negatives were processed immediately on board, by order of the captain – a Brazilian naval officer. As soon as the ship docked back in Brazil a few days later they were taken for study by the government. A messenger and file were even sent direct to the President once the importance of the results had been grasped. Barauna allowed all of this without the least complaint, something no trickster would have been happy with.

The photographs show in great detail the flight of the object, surrounded by a fuzzy outline. This is not due to speed or distance. Witnesses said the UFO was surrounded by a greenish vapour, and it is quite possible that this is caused by the electrostatic field which the object generates that attracts small particles of dust. We have seen this feature in car stop cases (e.g. Nelson, March 1977). Most importantly we have recently learned that during the time when Barauna took his photographs aboard the *Almirante Saldanha* the ship had lost electrical power!

Interviewed a quarter of a century after the case first came to light the cameraman still insisted the pictures were real when questioned by psychologist Dr Leo Sprinkle. However, the Brazilian navy only ever gave a very guarded public announcement. 'The photographs do not constitute sufficient proof,' it said enigmatically. None of the naval witnesses have ever been allowed to speak openly about the matter.

In May 1957 a draughtsman up on a hill near Bolton in Lancashire had a close encounter with a very similar object. This totally unpublicised story on my archives demonstrates the connections between cases that can be found if you look. He drew it as two pie dishes back to back, but saw it close enough to observe a line of square windows on top. It was surrounded by a greenish/red haze that shimmered and as it passed by he felt the hairs on the back of his neck and head rise up as if attracted by an electric field. He also felt a tingling sensation.

I am sure that scientists faced with such similar reports, with so many consistent features demonstrating an electrostatic field, would regard them as prime evidence for a real phenomenon – if that phenomenon was anything other than UFOs. It is time we stopped pretending. The reality of these objects is now established beyond doubt. What they are and how they operate are things these sceptical scientists should now start telling us.

11 January 1973, Cuddington, Buckinghamshire, England

The cases described so far are daylight black-and-white still pictures. Modern photography affords the hope of even better results, including the present case – twenty seconds of colour movie film.

The cameraman was a building surveyor called Peter Day, driving from his home at Thame to a nearby business meeting. On the road to Aylesbury at just after 9 am he saw an orange light in the north, moving eastwards. It travelled more or less parallel with him for some moments until he found a convenient place to stop, wind down his window and project the loaded movie camera that he always takes along to surveying appointments towards the object. He succeeded in filming the orange blob as it pulsated and passed behind distant trees before disappearing suddenly (in a single frame of film).

Peter Day kept his appointment at 9.30 am, and called at the local newspaper office in Thame on his way home. He was surprised to discover that they already knew about the UFO. A yard full of children at a school near Long Crendon (north of where he had been) all saw the orange object making its silent passage. They had reported it to the teaching staff, who seeing their sincerity had called the paper to ask if they knew what it was. One of the teachers, driving to school near Ickford, had also seen the object 'like a giant beachball in the sky'. The three different positions of these witness groups, all seeing the same silent object, offers many clues about it. For a filmed object to be independently observed is almost unprecedented.

The local press carried the story, Peter Day showed his film to an excited school (at the head teacher's request) and a rather inadequate local UFO group investigation resulted. Astronomer Peter Warrington and I discovered the case only four years afterwards and began detailed studies. We arranged for the Kodak laboratories in Hemel Hempstead to examine the film. Their tests proved it to be genuine and they suggested it might be unique in the sense that it showed a 'fireball'. Kodak then assisted in bringing together a who's who of famous atmospheric scientists to look at the film and decide whether it might be the first bona-fide record of ball lightning. Sadly they concluded it was not, but they had no idea what it *did* record! 'I don't think you should be ashamed of calling it a UFO,' one said. 'That's what it is.'

This scientific seminar is something no other UFO case has ever generated in the UK, but it was only possible thanks to Kodak and the fact that the scientists (from various universities and research institutes such as

Harwell) were out of the public eye. We were not interested in headlines, only answers.

We also had it viewed by a Ministry of Defence munitions expert. His only idea was an experimental orange searchlight on top of a helicopter. We checked into this but the solution proved a dead end. The experiment had not been in operation as early as January 1973.

However, there was one other lead that Peter Day himself had pointed us to. On the same morning in 1973 an F-111 jet from the USAF base at Upper Heyford had crashed in flames at North Crawley, Buckinghamshire, about 30 miles north of where the sightings had been made. Day believed that the crash had occurred *before* 9 am, a fact he had allegedly discovered from Upper Heyford themselves. He had called the base, suggesting that he might have movie film of the stricken jet and that this could be very useful in their analysis of the accident. After discussions the base concluded the film could *not* be of the aircraft and did not want it.

In late 1983 a new BUFORA investigation, co-ordinated by a team of investigators in Swindon, began research into this possibility. They discovered that the F-111 had crashed at 9.45 am. However, my own enquiries have revealed the plane was flying in circles for 40 minutes with steering difficulties. So it seems that it *was* in the air at the time the film was taken.

Of course, the film does *not* show the F-111 in flames. If so, then the crash would have happened much sooner than it did. Does it show, however, the F-111 using afterburners to try to use up fuel as quickly as possible? The Swindon team concluded not. They argued that the witnesses got the time wrong and they saw the jet in flames nearer to 9.45. This, I am certain, is impossible; not just because of the time of Day's appointment, but also because the school timetable made it inconceivable for these children (and the teacher) to be outside much later than 9.05 am.

Peter Day is certain he did not film an aircraft, and points out that F-111s are a very common sight over Oxfordshire, even using afterburners. In addition they are very noisy, and no witnesses heard any sound. You can only see the afterburner from the rear, which does not fit the facts, and under the most intense magnification (of what is a film taken in broad daylight, remember) there is no sign of any structure behind the orange ball of light.

We have very little information on why the F-111 crashed. Doubtless there are those who might see the reason for this failure to publish data being one that implies a guilty secret. The pilot ejected safely and the plane caused no damage (crashing in a field). However, it does seem extraordinary that two highly unusual events (an aircrash and a UFO) should both occur around the same place at the same time. Either they are one and the same thing, or else the aircraft accident had something to do with the presence of the UFO.

17 October 1973, Falkville, Alabama, USA

Although there are plenty of pictures of UFOs, there are few which show occupants, and *none* that show alien entities in the vicinity of their 'craft'. Cynics would doubtless point out how difficult they would be to fake. This is certainly a problem for anyone who believes that UFOs are piloted vehicles from somewhere.

Aside from the contactee photographs (always so bad that nobody takes them seriously) I know of seven UFO entity pictures. Two show a small figure in the hands of unknown security men. We know next to nothing about the origin of one of these photographs, and the other is a proven April Fool's joke, using an unfortunate monkey. Another photograph is of a supposedly dead alien burnt beyond recognition in his crashed UFO. The hoaxer in this case overlooked the fact that the snap contains a pair of spectacles and rather terrestrial electric wiring – because it is a gruesome image of a USAF pilot killed in a plane crash.

There *are* three photographs that show a landed UFO and alien. One, from Italy in 1952, has a deformed entity and snow so grainy it is rather hard *not* to believe this is a table-top model. An American shot taken by a small boy in 1967 is said to have been admitted as a hoax, using a doll and a hard-boiled egg. It certainly looks like that to me! Finally, a recent British case concerns a witness in Cumbria trying desperately hard to get someone to arrange a meeting with Margaret Thatcher. He first gained notoriety after a UFO contact story that got publicity in the Sunday press (despite all investigation attempts proving that the case was a hoax). Even his sister does not believe the story! The witness now says the aliens have returned for tourist snaps to be taken and he has tried to sell these to the highest bidder, including myself. After seeing one I quickly declined the offer as it would be of very little use. Most people asked me why it looked so much like a toy soldier stuck in a lump of plasticine.

This leaves only one case I am fairly certain *is* genuine, at least in the sense that the photographer is not a trickster. Nevertheless it is possible that he was hoaxed.

Jeff Greenhaw, aged 23, was chief of police at Falkville. In October 1973 there was a major wave in the USA (six days earlier two fishermen at Pascagoula, Mississippi, had claimed an alien contact and received massive publicity, and the Ohio helicopter incident occurred the day after Greenhaw took his pictures).

A woman had called the station to report a UFO landing and Greenhaw set off to investigate. He found nothing in the field that had been indicated. On his way back a tall figure appeared in the headlight beams. It was wearing an all-over silvery suit with head encased in a helmet. The entity did not respond to Greenhaw's attempts to communicate. Using the loaded camera in his patrol car (for accidents and scenes of crimes) he took four

162

photographs (two at a range of only ten feet!). The figure then turned around and fled. It ran side to side 'robot-like', but was fast. The police chief jumped back in his car and set off after it, but in his haste ran the patrol vehicle into a ditch and lost the 'alien' in the dark. It was late at night and on an unlit road, and so although the story that the alien outran the patrol car has been circulated this is a rather dubious statement.

The Falkville photographs show very well exactly what Greenhaw says he saw, but this is after all just someone (or something) in a silver suit.

It is hard to shake the feeling that there might have been a vendetta to set up the police chief. UFOs were in the news and perhaps it was thought that Greenhaw would lose credibility if he reported seeing an alien. That suspicion finds support in the pressure Greenhaw did face afterwards (eventually forcing him to leave town). His car engine later blew up mysteriously and his trailer home burnt to the ground.

These photographs seem to be the only ones that *might* show an alien. That they are rather less than conclusive only highlights the real problem caused by the non-existence of this kind of evidence.

22 June 1976, Canary Islands, Spain

The Canary Islands lie off the coast of North Africa in the east Atlantic. Aside from being a popular tourist area as a winter suntrap, they have produced several multiple-witness UFO sightings of late. As these are unusual it does seem curious that so many have occurred in this one area.

One case, from March 1979, involves several sets of photographs taken by different photographers (on more than one of the islands). The spiralling rocket-shaped object that climbed up from the sea exploded into an orange cloud that remained in the sky for an hour. Why the Spanish government insist this case remains unresolved is puzzling, especially as there is a phenomenon that fits very well. Experiments have been carried out, launching clouds of barium vapour into the atmosphere to test the conditions up there. The appearance of these is very similar to the March 1979 Canary Islands case. Surely the Spanish government would know if such a test were being carried out? However, the photographs are certainly pretty.

We face a problem such as this when we look at the other bemusing case. This was given to investigator Juan Benitez when a Spanish Air Force Lieutenant General invited him to his office and 'off the record' handed over a 78-page file containing a full account (including photographs, statements and radar plots). The report analysed all possible explanations and found none to be valid.

At 9.27 pm on 22 June 1976, a navy corvette, the *Atrevida*, was anchored off Punta Lantailla to the east of Fuerteventura. The crew saw a strange

163

phenomenon. Both the captain and ensign officer had signed statements in the file 'leaked' to Benitez. They told of 'a vivid yellowish-blue light moving out from the shore towards our position' which became stationary and 'went out [as] a luminous beam from it began to rotate'. After two minutes 'a vivid great halo of yellowish and bluish light developed', which remained for 40 minutes. A yellow ball divided from this and corkscrewed off into the sky. This had long disappeared to the west before the halo faded away.

The yellow light that had moved off west was seen shortly afterwards from Gran Canaria, another island 85 miles in this direction. The file records 11 witness statements from the north of the island, in particular the doctor from Galdar. This man, Don Francisco Leon, was driving through Las Rosas by taxi with the son of a sick woman who was taking the doctor to see her. They saw 'a perfect sphere – as perfect as though marked out with a compass'. It had a light blue rim but a yellow/white centre. They felt cold. The driver began to tremble. Then the taxi cab's radio faded out, but its engine was not affected. This certainly suggests that there was no local electro-magnetic field, but possibly interference high in the atmosphere.

Meanwhile two figures dressed in red one-piece suits were seen walking about on a platform inside the hovering sphere. A very familiar description 'like a giant soap bubble' was given, and the fact that stars could be seen through the UFO was noted. The taxi driver switched on the spotlight atop his car and the object seemed to respond by climbing into the air! The witnesses said that it was 'surrounded by gas' – a mist or vapour.

Rushing into a house nearby, the three people from the taxi and the family in the building all saw the UFO climb, stop, give out a high-pitched whine and streak off in the direction of Tenerife. The family related that their TV set had gone off when the sphere had first arrived.

Witnesses at Puerto de la Cruz, Tenerife, and an inter-island ferry also reported the sphere, as recounted in the file. This also noted how Spanish military radar had tracked the object, although no details are known.

At Maspalomas, Gran Canaria, one local inhabitant had a fully-loaded camera and took (the file claims) no fewer than 36 colour stills of it! If so, this would almost certainly be a record. Only one of these was released with the file. The local police had reported their existence to the Air Force who had apparently sent the Garda to pick them up! The name of the photographer has not been released.

The one photograph we have is spectacular, showing a very large yellow sphere, exactly as reported. Spindle arms reported from the Las Rosas witnesses are also visible and the size is obvious from the lights of Maspalomas visible in the shot. In view of this, one is left baffled because the entire town should have seen the UFO!

This case is a real puzzle. However 'off the record' the General might have wanted this to be, the Spanish government are evidently endorsing a major multi-witness case involving military witnesses, radar trackings and excellent photographs. It also involves occupants, electromagnetic and physiological effects. There could hardly be a better case.

If true, this story is as amazing as its official release. If false, or an exaggeration of something else, the Spanish government must know it and have perpetrated a deliberate hoax on UFO investigators!

February 1984, Hessdalen, Norway

If you wish to see UFOs *the* place to go is a remote, sparsely-inhabited valley not far from the Arctic circle. In December 1981 locals began to see lights in the sky and below the hill-line during the long alternating periods of 'night' and 'day'. They are often just moving yellow blobs. Sometimes they are pulsing red specks. Other times they hover for long periods. In all respects they are the sort of 'lights in the sky' which form the stock-in-trade of UFO groups everywhere.

Because the area is isolated nobody was taking official interest in them, but a group of Scandinavian UFO investigators (including Leif Havik, Odd Gunner Roed and Erling Strand) toured European UFO meetings to raise funds for 'Project Hessdalen'. This set up a scientific advisory board, comprising Dr J. Allen Hynek (the former USAF astronomical consultant), Professor Harley Rutledge (an American physicist who had studied 'ghost lights' in Missouri) and Paul Devereux, a British teacher who had authored a book (*Earthlights*) concerning a possible geological origin for such things.

Loaded up with hired equipment, some obtained by twisting the arms of universities and defence establishments, a caravan monitor site was set up in the valley, and during January and February 1984 teams waited for results. They had the kind of equipment other groups can only dream about, radar, magnetometers, infra-red detectors, spectrum gratings fitted to cameras, seismographs and even a laser beam projector.

In 1985 they published a report on the results. They logged no fewer than 188 sightings (some of which do appear to have been genuine unknowns). Several were photographed. Others were tracked on radar. There were results on most of the equipment.

The team returned in January 1985, although the money was running out and most of the equipment had to go back. The weather was atrocious and there were very few sightings, but Hynek went out there to endure the hardship which these amazingly dedicated UFO researchers were suffering.

1986 produced only a few sporadic trips and a major fund-raising campaign is underway again. However, the photographs and sightings are just of lights. They may well be natural phenomena (although on eight out of nine occasions that the laser beam was projected at a UFO it *seemed* to respond to it!). The team are divided as to what this means. However, with no aliens, car stops, landings or the truly exciting cases to talk about, it is hard to attract the finance.

Nevertheless, the photographs that have been obtained *are* real. They *do* show UFOs (or UAPs) and prove what can be done when you decide not to sit around waiting for UFOs to come to you but go and try to find them.

Part Four:

THE

UFO

COVER-UP

INTRODUCTION

If there are no UFOs — why all the secrecy?
(American newspaper headline.)

I am trying hard to be objective in this book, whilst aware that I am discussing a subject that normally provokes romantic and imaginative thoughts. I *have* selected cases to present from a much larger sample. You may feel that I have chosen the most sensational ones and have not told you about those that were solved or are far less exciting. However, I make no bones about the fact that most UFO sightings do have explanations, and the phenomenon in general is one that repeats itself.

The truth in these things cuts both ways. Of course, I am concentrating on good, solid *un*explained sightings, but I do not hide the suggestion that some of these might one day be resolved (given a bit of luck or extra information we do not now possess). It seems very improbable that *all* will crumble in this way. Some appear to offer little alternative but UFO reality. The very fact that it is the UFO researchers and not the debunkers who carry out the best identifications is itself important. They work on a shoestring budget, in their spare time, being laughed at by friends, called cranks by the scoffing scientists and made the butt of jokes by the media. Yet still they spend most of their time demolishing evidence for the subject they study.

You can find plenty of IFOs (Identified Flying Objects) in my previous books. Nobody can fairly accuse me of ignoring them. However, all of this does mean that when a serious investigator believes a case to be unresolved the chances are good that it is and will remain so. Do not be bamboozled by the cries of those amateurs who know nothing about UFOs, hardly ever interview witnesses and yet appear on the scene whenever a heavily-promoted case comes around. They are the leeches of the UFO world.

Perhaps you feel that my judgement is harsh. However, I do offer references in many instances. This means you can go direct to the source of most of these cases and check out the facts in detail. My material for this book has been selected not merely on the grounds that it is the most fantastic, but also because it is the best investigated. Yet there are hundreds of other cases equally well researched that there has simply not been room for. This mystery is no minor irritant in today's culture. It is vast and overwhelming.

I could have filled your head with many a wild tale, such as are easy to discover if you purchase the supermarket tabloids or the countless UFO books churned out by journalists or hack writers who think they can spend a few days researching UFOs and come up with the answer. I have spent fifteen years, more than half of them in a professional capacity, and I still do not really know what is going on! Nor, I suspect, does anybody else.

Remember when you read stories of death rays instantly ageing people, herds of cattle teleported from place to place or sexual encounters of the absurd kind that these may be fun to read but probably have as much relevance to the truth about UFOs as the latest episode of *Doctor Who* or *Star Trek*.

What you have here is the real Doctor McCoy!

UFOs might be dangerous atmospheric phenomena, living creatures floating about our skies, alien spaceships, inter-dimensional travellers or visitors from our own future. All these and more have been suggested as answers. In the end there may be a solution we have not even dreamt about, or (quite likely) more than one answer will apply.

Now we must turn to the central issue before us. The world powers are certainly capable of knowing at least as much as your average UFO buff. How could they ignore all this disturbing evidence? Perhaps by now you will share my view that such a thought is inconceivable. They *cannot* have ignored it, but then why do they refuse to come clean? Why play games with the facts and skirt around the issues at each opportunity? The more they run away from this baffling problem the less any reasonable person will find their attitude credible.

If there is no UFO conspiracy the proof of that lies in their own hands. It would be remarkably easy to demonstrate this by frank and honest actions. Instead we have very dishonest actions. That can only be regarded as suspicious. If these things continue to be obscured beneath a cloud of evasions, distortions, debunkings and lame excuses, then I need make no sensational claims about what that means.

It will be fairly obvious to you.

27 AUSTRALIA – LAND OF FREEDOM?

The RAAF are probably as confused and uncertain as many civilian research groups, on what to do about provocative UFO sightings.

(Australian Researcher, Bill Chalker, writing in 1982 after being given access to secret files of the RAAF [Royal Australian Air Force].)

Australia was once a place where prisoners were sent from Britain. Now it is a modern country proud of its open democratic style of government. It has a 'Freedom of Information' act, which the 'mother country' still lacks. Yet even before its introduction in 1982 it made a step towards coming clean on the UFO front.

As everywhere else the southern continent has had its share of dramatic cases. On 26 June 1959 missionary William Gill and about 25 natives of the village of Boainai, Papua New Guinea, had a protracted encounter with a disc-shaped object that hovered above them. A group of humanoid figures were within it and seemed to respond to hand signals and waves. The event came amidst a UFO flap on the island, where western news travels slowly. Dr Donald Menzel 'solved' it as an optical illusion of the planet Venus, with the natives merely agreeing with Father Gill (who had 'god-like' status) as a matter of courtesy. Having had the privilege of talking with the Anglican priest I am certain that he was not guilty of a misperception; besides which, he described seeing Venus elsewhere in the sky – precisely where it was that night!

Then, on the warm summer's day of 19 January 1966 a banana-grower at Tully, Queensland, was driving past a reedy swamp when he heard a hissing noise and saw a 'spaceship' take off from Horseshoe Lagoon. It was a grey oval which rotated 'at a terrific rate' as it climbed upwards. In its wake a circular area of flattened reeds was left. This turned out to be thirty feet wide and subsequently the plant growth died (probably because it was forced *under* the water). The witness said it was obvious 'they had been subjected to some terrific rotary force'. Several other 'saucer nests', as they became nicknamed, were later found in the same location.

At the time the investigators were stumped. Summarising some speculation that it might have been a whirlwind, highly objective investigator Bill Chalker said, 'these explanations seem quite unsatisfactory since the weather was fine and sunny at the time and there was no debris scattered about.' That did seem fair comment, but as evidence for the manner in which UFO researchers never give up and themselves seek answers to puzzling cases, we do appear to have the germ of a solution 20 years later.

We have this because of the discovery of identical 'saucer nests' in Britain. From 1980 onwards flattened circles have been reported in fields of corn or wheat crops at a number of sites in Hampshire, Wiltshire and Sussex. They are now known to have been visible there years before. However, after 1980 a local hype turned them into 'UFO landing traces', although nobody has ever seen a UFO in connection with them. They always appear during periods of warm weather, usually in July (the equivalent of the conditions at Tully during Australia's summer). Since 1983, when the national media have promoted them (and even some international media) hoaxers have jumped onto the bandwagon to 'enhance' the patterns left behind.

Dr Terrence Meaden, a local meteorologist, has been working with UFO investigators on the theory that a new type of whirlwind is responsible. In the case of single circles (which have always existed in southern England and turned up in Queensland) his case seems to me undeniable. A very short-duration rotating vortex of wind settles in one spot defined by exact geographical conditions. Because it is so brief it is unlikely to be seen and does not move, creating the sharp cut-off to the flattened area that has previously made others deny the whirlwind theory.

After years of frustrating attempts to persuade the media that UFOs are *not* the cause of the rings, whatever else might be, BUFORA decided to take action in 1986. Paul Fuller, a geographical statistician from Hampshire, got together with myself and compiled all the data on the affair into a booklet, entitled 'Mystery of the Circles'.

The publication explains Dr Meaden's theories for the single circle patterns and reviews the other ideas for the more complex situations. These include mating habits of wildlife, underground force-fields, helicopter rotor downwash and, of course, the ever-faithful 'giant spaceships' possibility. By putting this into context with the social background to the story it is clear that the hoax theory is the most probable, for all but the single ring sets.

For example, we know that in the summer of 1983 a hoax *was* successfully carried out by the *Daily Mirror*. Fed up at the publicity the *Daily Express* had generated, they paid farmers to set up an identical circle pattern and waited (in vain) for the publicity. When it never came the hoax was admitted in virtual silence. If it could be done once, however, it could be done many times.

The manner in which the circles appear to develop into more complex systems each year suggests that someone is out to attract attention. In September 1986, just before harvesting, a hardy soul even went to the trouble of cutting 'We are not alone' in giant letters astride one of the circles in Hampshire. It is most unlikely this was done by either a whirlwind or an extra-terrestrial stand-up comedian!

The area around Warminster, Wiltshire, where the circles congregate, was very popular during the 1960s as *the* place to go to see UFOs. Reports have dwindled and tourism faded. It might well be in someone's interest to manufacture a mystery to bring people back to this favourite UFO hunting ground. However, there does appear to have been a meteorological phenomenon of some interest present in the first place.

The debate continues to rage each summer in the Fleet Street press and on TV chat shows, but the 'mystery of the circles' I think demonstrates one vital aspect of UFO study. The debunkers did *not* explain this. They waved the whole thing away as a hoax. The serious UFO investigators always knew there would be an answer and went out of their way to help find it. The result was a discovery that was of at least minor interest to science.

The lessons are there for scientists everywhere who find the UFO subject amusing. The last laugh could well be on them!

It was well known in Australia that cases such as the Papua, New Guinea and Tully, Queensland, 'landings' had been investigated by official sources. The intelligence branch of the RAAF use the term UAS (Unusual Aerial Sightings) for some reason and summary reports giving brief facts and figures were published regularly between 1960 and 1977. Then they ceased, without explanation. However, many of these UAS 'solutions' mentioned in the summaries seemed doubtful when the case was one that chanced to be known. Many other cases were quite unknown and so could not be judged. What was needed was access to the secret files themselves.

On 6 August 1980 the Director of Public Relations at the Department of Defence wrote to industrial chemist and UFO investigator Bill Chalker. As co-ordinator of field investigations Chalker had inquired about the cessation of the summary and reports and the possibility of direct access. He was told that RAAF policy was now to assess UFOs only as a 'service to the general public' and that this policy change in 1978 precluded summaries, presumably for cost reasons. However, files were 'still retained for record purposes and are available to whoever seeks access . . .'

Chalker soon discovered that this did *not* mean you could go along and see them. It meant that you should ask for a specific case and if the officer processing your request had enough time to try and find it then you might get sent a copy. So within a year Chalker had persuaded the Public Relations office to consider giving him permission to study all the files, on the understanding that this was to be a unique move and that he alone would represent Australian ufology. They quite understandably did not wish to be swamped with requests from enthusiasts and journalists when they had no resources to handle such an onslaught.

So, between 11 and 15 January 1982, Bill Chalker visited Canberra, was given use of a desk, free access to a photocopier and (unbelievably) handed all but one of the RAAF UFO 'files' to do with as he wished.

That missing 'file' was one filled with policy decisions, and its restriction was justified. He was quite fairly asked to sign a waiver protecting the confidence of witnesses in cases where they had requested this. He was also told that some files could not be located, in particular all those before 1975. This was rather disappointing, preventing any information being obtained about both the cases just discussed, for example. However, Chalker does say that these officials were very fair and honest with him and seemed to do all they could to assist in file location.

What did he find in the files? There were two types. One contained letter exchanges on famous cases. The other was related to actual UFO sightings. The sighting reports comprise RAAF standard forms, investigation unit comments, evaluating officers' conclusions, associated memos, telexes and communications with government bureaux during the course of investigations, and all the other trappings of a moderately competent examination of the case; at least up to the calibre of the Project Blue Book files compiled by the US Air Force.

All told, Chalker was given seven inquiry folders and eleven sighting dossiers filled with cases. Squadron Leader Ian Frame, the RAAF liaison officer assigned to data compilation, told the UFO researcher that he must understand 'The RAAF examines UASs primarily for their defence context. If occurrences have no obvious import we have very few resources available for checks other than initial cursory examination.'

It ultimately transpired that the eighteen files he had been shown were only about *one-third* of the sum total potentially available. Frame could not find the others. The rest presumably relate to the period 1955 to 1975, the first year being when UFO study officially began in the RAAF. It will certainly be fascinating to know if the Maralinga case, for instance, is somewhere in there.

It was possible to compile a set of data for the 21 years between 1960 and 1980. A total of 1258 cases were logged with 102 (about 8 per cent) rated unexplained. Six years (1960, 1961, 1962, 1963, 1967 and 1968) had not a single unknown in them! At the opposite extreme one-quarter of the 1978 and one-third of the 1979 cases were listed 'unidentified'. Perhaps there was good reason why no summary for 1978 was released!

After 1964 (a major wave year when most of the world was in Vallée's 'dark ages') only 25 cases were recorded in 1977 (the biggest-ever yearly total in Northern Europe). This clearly shows how the UFO phenomenon migrates around the world and is never totally inactive everywhere.

Of the once secret cases that *could* be followed up, Bill Chalker found some with rather doubtful explanations attached. On 4 November 1976, for example, ground observers and two air crew saw a strange set of green and red lights behave in spectacular fashion. Ground radar at Brisbane and a weather radar at Eagle Farm both tracked what seems to have been the target. Despite the radar operators and air crew all disputing the evaluation, it was 'guessed' that the radar picked up a mirage of a boat and the witnesses saw Venus.

Chalker was quick to point out that he saw no evidence of a cover-up by the RAAF. Their role was clearly minimal and what they had to do they did adequately well. However, high-calibre puzzling cases were entering the archives and still are. So they seem to require better methodology, which the investigator is proposing.

We do not know if these better cases also found their way to another agency doing more in-depth scientific research. That occurred in the USA and there is little reason to think the Australian government would ignore the potential of some cases. However, let us not quibble over that. The RAAF at least showed courage and integrity in sharing their data with a responsible researcher, without hiding the best cases (at least so far as one can judge). That they well knew the dangers of keeping UFO files secret is shown by one of their own internal minutes which says, 'We only foster the incorrect (but nevertheless widely held) belief that we have much vital information to hide.'

It depends on what you call 'vital'. Certainly there is no evidence that the RAAF have crashed UFOs locked away or know absolutely what these objects are. Such things may or may not exist elsewhere. They certainly have provocative cases which do no good gathering dust in their filing cabinets. In a free society it can only be wise to make these available for study by those who can and wi do something with them.

There are many other countri s that could take heed of this suggestion.

When you read and analyse these files, which total almost 300 folio pages, it becomes definitely and categorically clear that UFOs exist and, quite evidently, are a matter of deepest concern to the governments of the planet.
(Juan Benitez, writing in 1979 about the official Spanish files 'leaked' to him.)

Since 1976 remarkable things have been occurring in Italy and Spain. Apart from Britain and France (to be considered separately) they are the principal European nations known to have studied UFOs.

On 2 January 1975 a major flap of UFOs was taking place around the Pennine Hills in England. It was one of my first ever field investigations. Greater Manchester police were chasing lights across the moors in the dead of night. There were all the usual features of the close encounter. Meanwhile, quite unknown to all of us, a thousand miles away in Spain even odder things were happening. The Spanish Air Force target practice range at Las Bardenos Reales had been invaded!

The story filtered out into the local press saying that a UFO had 'landed on the firing range. A few minutes later the device took off.' It was also alleged that 'several of the senior military officers at Las Bardenos base have arrived in Zaragoza to report to the headquarters of this Air Force Zone concerning the incident'. In addition a 'judge' had been appointed by the authorities to review the case, whose findings would be 'conveyed to the Air Ministry who, if they deem it fitting, will issue a statement about it.'

As soon as this news came out a flat denial was issued. The UFO did not exist. There had been an optical illusion caused by a ring around the moon: end of story and, as is so often the case, end of the brief press interest in the matter. It never even made the national level, let alone the international news wires.

This kind of swift stifling of promising cases occurs everywhere, not just in Spain. Pere Redon, a Spanish UFO expert, bemoaned it by commenting that they only ever got 'secrecy and denials, with attempts being made to nullify, by means of a smoke-screen, all knowledge of what really happened.'

Well, yes, a UFO investigator would say that, wouldn't he? That sort of response from the majority of the public is precisely what the authorities count on; but it happens in Britain. I have seen it in operation.

The Las Bardenos case would, like all the others, have vanished into a bureaucratic black hole. Indeed, one enterprising local paper had tracked down a witness to the UFO (sorry, moon halo) only to be told he did not exist either! However, they found this non-existent person, a Lieutenant Campos. He gruffly refused to speak about the matter saying it was *'sub judice'* – a rather peculiar status for the moon!

However, you will recall that Juan Benitez, Spanish UFO writer, was called to Madrid on 20 October 1976 and handed ('off the record') that dossier of Spanish government files by a prominent military source. The Canary Islands photo cases were amongst them. So was the landing by a moon halo at Las Bardenos.

It turns out, according to statements and evaluations, that a sergeant on duty at the base received a call from another office (perhaps Lieutenant Campos), advising that several men in the observation towers that encircle the range had seen something. Could the sergeant go and check it out? He climbed a small hill which gave a good view over the base, and to his astonishment saw an object like an upturned basin sitting on the ground. It had white and amber lights on the side and bright lights on the top and bottom. It seemed to be the size of a truck.

After some minutes it began to rise upwards in total silence and climbed away to the north. Then it changed course north-east and cruised out of view. It was going up at a steep angle. Several of the men in the lookout towers had a superb view as it rose to their eye level and then departed. It projected a 'searchlight' onto the ground as it moved away.

This is quite some feat for a ring around the moon, as you have probably gathered. The file predictably offers no such solution. It merely shows how daft theories are used to squelch prime UFO cases in their immediate aftermath when media attention would be catastrophic. The authorities are playing for time to try to figure out what is going on.

Within three weeks of Benitez being invited to Madrid the Talavera Air Force Base 'entity shooting' (see Chapter 18) took place. In late 1978 Benitez was asked back and given more files. His publication of the others in UFO literature must have pleased the Spanish government. He now has extensive dossiers on fourteen separate events, mostly involving military bases, high-calibre witnesses (from Air Force Commanding Generals down to mere Brigadiers and ship captains!). Many include radar trackings, photographs and jet intercepts. All have occurred in the past ten years.

If such a volume of official testimony exists in Spain, think what must be available on British or American cases. What would the dossier on Rendlesham Forest be like?!

Clearly this opening of files marked a dramatic change in policy. It matches the frank admissions accompanying cases such as the 1979 and 1980 aerial encounters, when the Transport Minister publicly stated that UFOs were real. Although this may be known in Spain, you almost certainly did not know of it.

The situation in Italy seems to have run in parallel. The Italian UFO Centre, CUN, have been given quite liberal co-operation in investigations, something that would have been unthinkable until very recently.

Files have been released to CUN, although this was suspended when 'in the interests of fairness' the Italian government had sent copies to another group that had asked for them. It turned out to comprise just two schoolboys, and when they revealed what had happened there was great press merriment at the use of children as UFO advisers! However, more interestingly, cases that might once have been hidden have found their way into the open.

An example occurred at 3 am on the morning of 1 July 1977, when the NATO base at Aviano near the Yugoslavian border had a close encounter. There are many comparisons with the Bentwaters affair over three years later. The Aviano case was also 'leaked' out in a most uncharacteristic manner.

Antonio Chiumiento summarised CUN's discoveries in 1984 and explains how they were first approached by an Italian Air Force NCO who told the whole story in exchange for anonymity. He even gave names of others involved (including a USAF man called James Blake, who supposedly first alerted the base). Since then they have obtained corroboration from Benito Manfré, a nightwatchman in an adjacent village, who saw the whole incident from his home a mile from the base perimeter.

Manfré told how his barking dog first brought him out. He noticed that the Aviano base was in total darkness, something he had never experienced before. Then his attention was drawn to 'a mass of stationary light low down over a certain spot of the base'. This turned out to be the high-security section known as 'Victor Alert'. His wife refused to come out as she was sleepy. Strange lights were of no interest to her.

After several minutes the object began to climb away. About ten seconds after its departure all the base lights came back on. Manfré was too excited to go back to bed so he watched as a great deal of military activity went on behind the fence. American military police were particularly in evidence.

There was no publicity but CUN succeeded in collecting many local rumours and slotting a jigsaw puzzle together. This is very similar to what Brenda Butler, Dot Street and I had to do in and around Bentwaters and Rendlesham Forest.

The story of the NCO matched perfectly. James Blake, the American, had allegedly seen something over 'Victor Alert' and called security. Special hangars in this part of the base housed aircraft under secure conditions. Anything breaching that location was a potential threat. However, the airfield electricity had gone dead.

The base was being prepared for a major parade involving much top brass a couple of days later, so the alert for possible saboteurs was taken very seriously. Security troops rushed to the scene and were deployed about 150 feet from the still hovering object. It was at 300 feet, directly above one of the secret hangars and spinning like a top. Basically disc-shaped, it had a dome and flashing lights. It also gave off a humming noise 'like the sound of a swarm of bees in flight'. The whole of 'Victor Alert' was lit up.

It was there for nearly an hour before it took off. The base radar operator had been got out of bed to switch the system on. Power returned when the UFO left and the object was picked up as it flew away. NATO headquarters in Brussels were immediately contacted. A few days later all the men present were told that an answer had been discovered. The UFO had been moonlight reflected off some low clouds.

How many of them bought this explanation is unclear, but the fact that so few have talked must be noted. CUN found only two small problems with the solution. There were no low clouds and the moon was setting in a different part of the sky!

No official data on this case has ever been released, which is not exactly surprising, but the fact that we know about it certainly is. The way in which it appears to have been leaked suggests, as similar events elsewhere also suggest, that some bureaucratic leviathan is stirring.

Let us hope so.

29 FRANCE – AN OPEN SECRET?

Amongst these aerial phenomena – these visual phenomena (I won't call them more than that) – which are gathered together under the label UFO – it is certain that there are things which we do not understand and which today are relatively unexplained. I shall even say that it is irrefutable that there are currently things which are unexplained or explained badly.

(Interview broadcast to the nation by French Radio, February 1974. The speaker was the government's Minister of Defence, M. Robert Galley.)

It is no accident that in *Close Encounters of the Third Kind* the scientist in charge of the UFO project is a Frenchman played by actor François Truffaut. On the one hand he is meant to be Dr Jacques Vallée. On the other he reflects the important fact that France is the only nation in the western world which has a government-funded team of scientists behaving in almost exactly the same way as those in the movie!

That a major world power, at the forefront of much research (including pioneering flight earlier this century) pumps money on a regular basis into the UFO mystery is surely the best answer anyone can give to the sceptic. In these money-conscious times this would just not happen, unless the project had succeeded and was continuing to succeed. It may not be inconsequential that France, whilst tied to NATO on one level, is a very independent country which does not follow the American lead in the same way as the majority of western Europe (including Britain) appear to do.

It seems that we can directly trace the change in French attitudes to Dr Claude Poher, an astronomer who was head of the 'Systems and Projects' division of CNES, the French state-operated space centre based at Toulouse. This is similar to NASA and is gaining in esteem with the growing reputation of its Ariane launch rocket and the terrible problems faced by the US Shuttle.

Poher met Dr J. Allen Hynek in 1969 and read the Colorado University report that lead to the closure of Blue Book. He was unhappy with the methodology and could not see how the many positive statements about individual cases corresponded with the denial of any real UFO phenomenon. So he began his own project and, in view of his position, was able to accrue cases from excellent sources.

He published an analysis of his work in the UFO literature between 1973 and 1975, thus keeping it out of the public eye. There were comparisons between sightings and geomagnetic disturbances (he was one of the first scientists to seek such a link). With Vallée he conducted a mammoth search for 'patterns in UFO observations' and found clear indications that a consistent phenomenon, certainly amenable to the scientific method, was present.

Poher's work appears to have impressed his government. This can be judged by an event on 21 February 1974, undoubtedly one of the most momentous in UFO history. Again, you will not have heard about it. Inexplicably it failed to generate any press attention in Britain. It was literally the equivalent of a British or American minister such as Michael Heseltine or Caspar Weinberger, whilst still in office, broadcasting to the nation the news that UFOs exist, are being studied by the correct authorities and remain utterly perplexing.

The man who made this historic speech was Robert Galley, then the French Minister of Defence. His broadcast came on France-Inter, and I am grateful to UFO researcher Claude Maugé for obtaining a copy of the original version of the transcript, as he felt that the English translation based on the work of Gordon Creighton takes a few minor liberties. I think this is a better account of what Galley said.

He began with an honest statement, 'I am sincerely convinced that we must have a very open mind about these phenomena.' After admitting that cases *do* remain without an answer, he spoke of radar-visual encounters involving French pilots. 'There remains a small residue. These cases are unexplained. Similar phenomena do occur abroad.'

Galley agreed that it would be premature to draw too many conclusions, but noted that the French police and airborne Gendarmerie were working with Dr Poher on government orders to channel cases through to the space centre in Toulouse. He expressed concern that if the public saw this material they might become disturbed by its calibre. . . . 'The accumulation of the information is actually rather perturbing.'

According to Gordon Creighton, President Pompidou, known to have been a personal friend of the defence minister, reproved him for spilling the beans. I suspect he felt like many other leaders that what the public do not know they cannot worry about, especially if we can offer them no real assurance that *we* know what is going on or can do anything about it. The quote from Pompidou supposedly was, 'Don't you think we have enough "muck" on our hands without bringing in these UFOs?'

However, mistake or not, there was no turning back. The co-operation between the French government, Poher and the CNES was soon put on a formal basis. In May 1977, as the European wave was at its height, a special team was established under the astronomer's leadership. It was based at the space centre and called GEPAN (Study Group into Unidentified Aerospace Phenomena).

Initially Poher and one administrator worked full-time, but there was part-time allocation from no less than fifteen scientific staff at universities and laboratories with government aid. The case investigations were to be carried out by the French special police on an official basis. As the procedures became refined these dossiers ranked with the best any amateur group could hope to achieve. It was decided not to keep this a secret, but neither to go out of their way to talk to the media: a sort of open secret.

Of course, all this was happening in the period 1976–78, exactly as the Spanish and Italian governments were becoming more liberal about issuing UFO data and as the Spielberg movie was being released.

Possibly Poher was too close to the UFO community for some people's liking. Whatever the reason, after establishing the team he left to sail around the world and made no further impression on the scene. At least I have not been able to trace any more writings by him on the subject of UFOs.

In a February 1979 GEPAN document, obtained from Toulouse, the results of the first eighteen months are cited and set out policy and plans. It is easy to see that the first results were astonishing. One-fifth of the cases deemed worthy of study remained unexplained. More importantly, the better the quality of the report (according to ratings systems they adopted) the *less* likely it was to have a solution. This turned on its head all evidence the debunkers use for shooting down the unknowns: that they are unknown because we lack information. Given more data then they would not be. The GEPAN experiment was suggesting that there were real cases that could *not* be explained, however much information was available.

It is apparent that Galley's use of the term 'perturbing' was valid. If this kind of information became widely known it would virtually establish the reality of UFOs. An annual review board (called a 'scientific council') studied the GEPAN work and made recommendations. There would be governmental influence in this, of course. Seeing these results it made a very firm decision. For 1978, 354 filtered cases had been studied. Over half of them were 'close encounters' (the Gendarmerie never even bothered with lights in the sky!). There was no definite answer for 59 per cent of them! Not surprisingly GEPAN reported that these 'pose a real question', and the council advised 'great vigilance regarding the distribution and publication of these studies and results'.

Here we see in microcosm what probably happened in the USA thirty years before. The original idea to be 'open' was quickly superseded when the awesome nature of the UFO data was understood. Then the policy became one of taking great care about what was said. This probably explains why you have not read about GEPAN in your newspapers and its dramatic work has not featured in magazines such as *New Scientist*.

Dr Alain Esterle took over from Poher to head GEPAN. He did not write articles for UFO journals. However, Dr Pierre Guerin, an astronomer associated with the team, has expressed his view that the French government is wrestling with the terrible consequence that aliens do control the UFO phenomenon, and possibly all life on earth. As he says, how do you tell the world that without creating chaos?

Esterle visited Britain in May 1981, when he attended an International UFO Congress. He did not address the meeting and few realised who he was. However, in a nearby café he told some of us that the work of GEPAN was proving the alien reality of UFOs.

In February 1983 I went to France to collect some technical notes which GEPAN publish on a regular but small-scale basis. They are not sold in shops and only a few mimeographed copies are distributed. You have to know they exist and where to get them. In any case, after issuing about twenty, they seem to have ceased from 1984 onwards. These 'technical notes' are the size of small books and filled with photographs, graphs, analysis results and data on individual cases. One of the last published in 1983 was on the Trans-en-Provence landing, which you have already read about (see page 146).

The same weekend that I was in France, the *Sunday Times* broke years of silence on GEPAN with a semi-humorous article entitled, 'Flying Saucers Sought No More'. This alleged that the French UFO team was being closed as an economy measure by the Mitterand government, because it had achieved nothing. That statement is absurd to anyone who has read the GEPAN reports and results, and has never been retracted to my knowledge.

You will not be too surprised to learn that the *Sunday Times* was 'premature' and that GEPAN was *not* axed. It was reorganised and went even further underground (the Trans-en-Provence case must have been truly disturbing). An optical engineer, Jean Velasco, took over as head, and although he has written a few pieces for the UFO literature the public profile of GEPAN is much lower than it was before his time.

I have recently been in correspondence with Dr Richard Niemtzow, a US Air Force Major who has conducted detailed research ('off the record') into the possible radiation effects created by UFOs. He has consulted on Cash/Landrum enquiries (see page 147) for the US government and serves GEPAN. Dr Jacques Vallée tells me that they both attended a 1985 seminar in Paris at which more funds were granted to GEPAN. The *Sunday Times* did not report that, of course!

Official and highly significant UFO research goes on not 20 miles across the English Channel. Anyone who doubts the importance of UFOs should ponder the implications of that. For if France has done it, and continues to, it is hard to imagine that they are out on a limb.

30 USSR – A SECRET OPENING?

Soviet scientists took the subject seriously and accepted that there were occasional well-documented sightings for which they could find no plausible explanation. (Scientist Anatoly Logunov and cosmonaut Pavel Popovich) avoided comment on the possibility that some cases might involve spaceships from another world, and said only that it was necessary to improve research methods.

(*Chicago Tribune*, interview with leaders of the new Soviet UFO project, 30 May 1984.)

The Soviet Union is one of the least likely places we might expect UFOs to be taken seriously. Indeed, for a long time it maintained the illusion (if that is what it was) that good Communists should not fall for such absurd Capitalist superstition and propaganda. American documents released under Freedom of Information show that, after satisfying themselves that the UFOs were not Russian, the next step was for the security agencies to monitor sightings that were going on in that country.

The first real information came from a visit paid by Dr Jacques Vallée to the Soviet Academy of Sciences in Moscow. This was in 1967 and we knew that they were getting interested in UFOs because (like the Chinese science library, the House of Commons and House of Lords libraries and other similar sources) they have been long-time subscribers to the UFO journal, *Flying Saucer Review*.

Vallée discovered that a group was being set up by two people. One was an Air Force Major General called Stolyarov. The other was Professor Felix Zigel, a Cosmologist at the Moscow Institute of Aviation and the man who trained the Soviet astronauts. This was a powerful double-act and they were, according to Zigel, promised the 15,000 cases the Kremlin already had on their archives! So they set their operation up and went back for the cases, whereupon they were told a very firm 'Nyet! This is too big a matter and you are too small.'

However, the two men were given permission to make a TV appearance and appeal for sightings. On 10 November 1967 they said, 'UFOs are a very serious subject which we must study fully . . .'. In 1968 Zigel published a book on UFOs, presumably based on these reports.

Something funny obviously went on around this time. A British journalist has recalled that he was in Moscow when the UFO group was launched by Stolyarov and Zigel. He went to the office but there was nobody in. He returned the next day, as suggested, and the office was no longer there. Nobody had even (officially) heard of its existence! Perhaps Zigel was shown the Kremlin archives in return for his silence.

Zigel became an enigma in the years that followed. When Ostrander and Schroeder visited the Soviet Union for a book on research into strange phenomena they were given free access to everyone, except a solitary scientist – Zigel! Then he began to act as an obvious puppet for the Kremlin. Some of UFO debunker James Oberg's best work has been in exposing major Soviet UFO sightings, such as an event in September 1977 (identified as the launch of Cosmos 955) and another in June 1980 (which was certainly the launch of Cosmos 1188). There is no doubt that the UFO nature of these spectacular events was deliberately fostered by the Soviet Union. Whilst the west clearly knew that they were rockets taking off from the secret site of Plesetsk, the Russian people do not even know the site exists! Of course, Zigel does. Yet he chose to speak volubly about aliens and UFOs in connection with these events and *was* allowed to talk to two American journalists, Gris and Dick, writing a new book about unusual research in the USSR. They did no checking and promoted the Zigel fairytale about 'spaceships over Moscow'. Ironically, in this case, that is exactly what they were!

Several Soviet UFO researchers have concluded that Zigel is a government mole and have suggested that he is responsible for stopping them forming private UFO research groups. Nikita Schnee, scientific secretary to a Moscow research institute, is one who was present when a UFO meeting was raided by the KGB. Another ufologist, Juri Lina, even had to set up a fake marriage to a Finnish ufologist to escape the country and speak out against the oppression of any private UFO views.

Another scientist who is allowed to conduct research is Vladimir Sanarov, at the Institute of Clinical and Experimental Medicine in Novosibirsk. Here they are alleged to carry out mind-control research. From the time when I began to write actively on UFOs in the mid-1970s I began to get many postcards from this man. He also wrote to others, I understand. His requests were 'modest', merely asking for copies of virtually everything I produced: my books, etc, and the work of others. Some of the people he was interested in were associated with behavioural science. The serious after-effects of UFOs also figured prominently. He explained that the kind of research could not be freely obtained in the USSR. However, I was advised by an expert I consulted that he would only be sending these frequent requests if he had the blessing of his government. I took no action, and after several years and many more cards, they stopped coming.

In 1981 he began to contact Harry Harris, a Manchester lawyer who had just become interested in UFOs. Where Sanarov learned of his involvement (or indeed had access to knowledge about my work if he did not see it) was never clear. Harris knew nothing of my previous communications from Novosibirsk and was willing to help with information. Sanarov then sent him a stack of cards to post on to other people in Britain (some who were scientists with no known UFO connections). We both then became very suspicious!

Harry Harris and I had a mutual contact, a very senior police officer, and without our knowledge he informed the Special Branch! They visited Harris, examined the documents and initiated an enquiry. On 7 May 1982, Harris had a letter from the MoD which said, 'We can see nothing to suggest that (Sanarov's) motives are suspicious.' However, it added, 'we also do consider there is unlikely to be any advantage to you, and certainly not to the MoD, in allowing the correspondence to continue . . . it would be in everyone's interest for it to be properly but firmly concluded.'

In other words, they did not think Harry was being used as a post-box for spies (an idea suggested by Special Branch); but – cease the correspondence. Harry Harris did, and neither he nor I have heard from Sanarov again.

I *hope* the doctor is sincere. This may all have an innocent explanation, but we have enough problems investigating UFOs without playing James Bond! In any case other ufologists, clearly impressed by having a Soviet doctor on their masthead, have co-operated with the man from Novosibirsk. I wonder if the MoD are monitoring that!

The Russian UFO story is certainly an odd one, but in the past three years it has taken a new turn. According to Reuters in early 1983 a Soviet source explained, 'The existence of UFOs should not be ruled out.' This 'official' source (as it came from the Soviet press it *must* have been official!) had added that a 'fighter plane had a brush with a mystery object two years ago . . . a fiery ball, 16 feet in diameter, had damaged [the] Soviet plane.' Scientists had studied this and 'at first assumed that the phenomenon was ball lightning, but the damage to the plane did not tally with this'. All of this meant 'there were still many unexplained phenomena behind various "flying saucer" reports'. The source urged scientists to 'collect and collate as much information as possible on the subject'.

It was more than a year before we learnt more of this new initiative. The next story came from the Soviet paper *Trud* and was published in summary by several major western sources (e.g. the London *Times* and *Chicago Tribune*). It came on 30 May 1984 and explained that 'a commission to investigate UFOs' had been created under the direction of 'Pavel Popovich, a former cosmonaut' (presumably trained by Felix Zigel!). Popovich and Anatoly Logunov ('a vice-president of the Academy of Sciences') were both quoted as making very positive statements on UFOs and appealing for cases.

Several sightings are known to have precipitated this study, including the usual spheres and lights. One of the most dramatic had happened on 27 March 1983 when a 'steel grey cigar about the size of an airliner but without wings or tailfin' invaded top secret airspace above Gorky – the city where dissidents are held. Air Traffic controllers at the airport not only saw it but picked it up on radar at 3000 feet and drifting by at 125 mph. It was in view for 40 minutes. It failed to respond to radio messages, but no action was taken against it. This is all very interesting, because six months later a similar thing occurred over Sakhalin Island. A radar target was tracked and an interceptor *was* sent up. It blasted the UFO out of the sky. As the whole world knows, that 'UFO' was a Korean Airlines jumbo jet full of civilian passengers, who were all killed.

We do not know if the two events are connected; but the Americans forgave the Soviets mighty quickly for what at first sight appears a terrible crime against humanity. Was the fatal intercept by the controllers at Komchatkha more understandable in the context of what had just taken place over Gorky?

The Popovich 'Commission on Abnormal Atmospheric Phenomena' took the Gorky case very seriously. 'The witnesses were trained aircraft experts who could be relied on to give an accurate and dispassionate account of what they saw.'

As you have seen from Chapter 20 there was renewed activity and more investigation during 1985. I am quite sure the Popovich commission is still going strong. Meanwhile the group's vice-chairman, Dr Nikolai Zheltukhin, said in January 1985, that 'a systematic study of sightings of UFOs observed over the territory of the USSR' was underway. 'The material we have already is quite considerable, so we do have something to work on.'

Every country in the world could echo that statement.

31 UNITED KINGDOM –
NO DEFENCE SIGNIFICANCE?

What does all this stuff about flying saucers amount to? What can it mean? What is the truth?

(Sir Winston Churchill, writing to the Secretary of State for Air on 28 July 1952.)

Sir Winston Churchill asked his first parliamentary question about UFOs in 1913! Britain was then jittery with war nerves and strange lights seen over the east coast were considered to be German 'Zeppelins'. They were not. Nobody ever found out what they were. It was then almost forty years before Churchill got interested in UFOs again.

The 1955 cabinet papers were released in the usual way (following the expiry of the 'thirty-year rule' on public documents in 1986). These show how Prime Minister Churchill had become concerned in the wake of the Washington DC invasion of July 1952. He had written to Lord Cherwell and received a reply from the Secretary of State dated 9 August 1952. This explained how all UFOs had been shown to be misperceptions, illusions and hoaxes, that the Americans had so concluded in 1948, and that nothing had happened to change the views of the RAF.

If you look back over the early years of UFO history elsewhere in this book you might question how the British Air Ministry could so mislead its Prime Minister, but the reply did say that UFOs had been 'the subject of a full intelligence study in 1951'. The Yorkshire UFO Society, who have been hot on the trail of such a dossier, which they already suspected to exist, have found further proof in an exchange of letters during March 1955 between MP Duncan Sandys and Antony Montague Brown, DFC. This refers to 'an article from the Air Ministry Secret Intelligence Summary about UFOs'. However, as I do not suppose you will be astonished to learn, the MoD claim to have no knowledge about this, and it was not released in 1982 as the 'thirty-year rule' implies it should have been.

Ralph Noyes, then a civil servant in the Air Ministry, was privy to cabinet level discussions at this time and told how enquiries were made in the USA to discover the conclusions of the Washington DC events. Of course, the CIA panel was also being convened at this time. This matches what Ruppelt said in his 1956 book about RAF Intelligence officers asking questions of Blue Book and the Pentagon, and the 'Operation Main Brace' sightings in September 1952 (just six weeks after the reply to Churchill) having ensured that the British government became interested in taking UFOs very seriously.

All of this forms a definite pattern. The Townsend-Withers mid-air encounter out of RAF Boscombe Down came immediately in the wake of these events and he was informed of an MoD UFO investigation team. So a project in the UK must have been set in motion around late 1952. It is hard to imagine the Lord Cherwell letter to Churchill being all that was said on the matter, but that is all the cabinet papers contend.

Noyes also says that shock waves went down the corridors of Whitehall in August 1956 when the major sightings, radar trackings and intercepts by an RAF Venom took place above the NATO bases of Bentwaters and Lakenheath in Suffolk. The possibility that gun camera film was taken must be considered. Of course, we do not have it. Indeed we have *no* gun camera film from British cases, although Noyes (when he later had access to the MoD UFO archives) insists there *was* such film there.

The August 1956 events were never publicly admitted, and we discovered them by a fluke when an airman told the Colorado University project late in their two-year study. He assumed the scientists knew about it, since the US government had supposedly given all the best cases to them. The US government had apparently 'forgotten' this one, which involved both RAF and USAF personnel in the air and on the ground.

Eventually the Colorado 'staff' concluded on the case that 'the probability that at least one genuine UFO was involved appears to be fairly high'. Its radar expert, Gordon Thayer, added in his own conclusions, 'this is the most puzzling and unusual case in the radar-visual files. The apparently rational, intelligent behaviour of the UFO suggests a mechanical device of unknown origin as the most probable explanation of this sighting.'

That one case alone ought to have been enough for the Colorado team to recommend a major UFO study. In fact it was one of many similarly unexplained. Yet the project ordered the decrease of activity that lead to the closure of Blue Book.

Thayer said, in a 1980 update on the case, 'There is simply no way that any known sort of anomalous propogation effect could account for this. In fact, any explanation even remotely conceivable seems to demand the presence of some physical object in the air over Lakenheath on that August night in 1956,' and he was a sceptic! The case has been re-investigated by other scientists (e.g. atmospheric physicist Dr James McDonald). Much new information has come to light, including the discovery of the Squadron Leader (Freddie Wimbledon) who vectored the jet onto the radar target and ground observers at Ely who saw the jet and the UFO.

However, the British public were not told about this case. The MoD claim that the file on it was routinely destroyed in 1961. All my efforts to get straight answers out of them about it met a brick wall (usually no answers at all rather than denial). Fate and the Rendlesham Forest case took me to Whitehall in August 1983 and I grasped the opportunity of asking Pam Titchmarsh (of the secretarial department DS-8, which handled UFO data) why she had not answered two letters about the case. She admitted that the MoD had them, but they knew nothing about the Lakenheath events. 'You tell us about such cases, we don't know of them,' she seriously asked me to believe.

Faced with such a policy it is hard to know how we might puncture holes in the British wall of secrecy. The experience of Clive Ponting, taken to the Old Bailey (and acquitted) is instructive. The MoD perceived a breach in the Officials Secrets Act when he told a serving MP that there had been a cover-up regarding the sinking of the Argentinian battleship *General Belgrano* during the Falklands War of 1982. Ponting felt the country had a right to know that Parliament was being deceived. The ship had been sailing away from the Fleet when it was attacked, with huge loss of life. Apparently the court agreed with him.

Ponting was under-secretary in charge of the MoD division DS-5, concerned with naval intelligence. This puts into context the role of Ralph Noyes, whose statements about MoD UFO actions we have already met. In the early 1970s Noyes had the exactly equivalent rank as head of DS-8, the department handling RAF matters and (for obvious reasons) UFOs.

Since his strange appearance on the scene in the wake of the Rendlesham Forest publicity of October 1983, Noyes had made some extraordinary comments. Many of these were on the record. Some I have on tape. He even attended the press conference in London to endorse the launch of *Sky Crash*, the book Brenda Butler, Dot Street and I wrote about the case. Noyes spoke of situation maps in Whitehall where the best cases were logged and flagged, RAF jet chases, and grave concern over unexplained cases; and he told me, 'We now have evidence – I blush to say about my own Ministry – that they have lied about this. They have covered it up.'

Ralph Noyes said these things even as Ponting was being taken for trial, but he was not prosecuted. One wonders why. In fact, in 1985 he published a very bizarre novel called *A Secret Property* which is built around MoD interest in UFOs. Whilst it claims not to be true in any sense, or based upon any real people or incidents, this is quickly seen to be absurd, when read by anyone who knows the subject. It begins in Rendlesham Forest near a NATO air base called 'Bentbridge' (a combination of Bentwaters and Woodbridge!). The base commander is Colonel Hoyt (not Halt), there is a female Prime Minister with an 'Iron Lady' disposition, and UFO groups and researchers that are transparently real. The 'Maggie Thatcher clone' ends the book by calling these UFO researchers (myself included) to Wembley Stadium in 1990, where she addresses us all and finally admits the truth about UFOs!

For a man trained in bureaucracy and secrecy, Noyes seems to have taken extreme risks at a time of unusual threat to former MoD employees. I am rather tempted to wonder if he knew that he was safe and the book was a part of the 'Education Programme'. Shortly after it was published, Noyes 'retired' to live abroad, ending a very puzzling two-year spell in which he toyed mysteriously with the UFO community.

Since I became a full-time researcher in 1978, I have battled with the MoD to try to persuade them that if they genuinely do have nothing to hide they should make their data openly available. Bill Chalker's success proves it can be done, and that Australia at least sees the sense of the idea. However, both Ralph Noyes and Lord Hill-Norton (Admiral of the Fleet and actually Chief of Staff at the MoD during Noyes' time) believe there *is* something to hide. The conspiracy, Noyes suggests, is one of bafflement. They have no real clue what is going on and prefer not to admit that the UFO phenomenon, is beyond the control of Westminster. All governments desire to be re-elected. A good way to ensure that you are not is to explain that Britain is the subject of a possible invasion by an unknown, evidently far superior, technology.

This makes a lot of sense; but is it an honest position to take? Perhaps, at last, we are being given credit for our intelligence and ability to handle the truth. The 'Education Programme' might be the only way to escape the hole the authorities have dug for themselves by long insisting that UFOs are irrelevant.

In an interview on 10 March 1982, following a House of Lords debate on UFOs, Hill-Norton argued the problems of the cover-up. Why, as such a high-ranking MoD official, did he *not* know if there *is* a conspiracy? 'Let me put it this way,' he said, 'I think I ought to have known. But I certainly did not, and had I known I would not of course be allowed on an interview like this to say so.' He added that for many years the MoD had collated evidence 'which is not available to the public and was not available to me whilst I was in office'. He was now (but had not then been) aware of the CIA and FBI UFO research indicated by Freedom of Information documents, or the French scientific team analyses. So 'what we want to do is to get our own government to tell us the results of an investigation which simply *must* have happened here too.' Quite.

Assuming Hill-Norton is being sincere, and having met him I have no reason to doubt his integrity, we face the question as to exactly what level of 'need to know' there is for the UFO conspiracy. Certainly it would appear pointless arguing with the civil service minions at the MoD. They are no more than filing clerks. The RAF Intelligence officers who do the investigation might have their own files somewhere (e.g. at RAF Farnborough). If so, they are neither admitted to, nor publicly accessible. Talking to the 'shop window' is a thankless task. You almost certainly know far more about UFOs than they do after simply reading this book, but what other choice was open to me?

The MoD have a party line that they give all standard enquirers about UFOs, hoping that it will drive them away. A 20 January 1983 annex to a letter to me best explains this. 'The sole interest of the Ministry of Defence in UFO reports is to establish whether they reveal anything of defence interest (e.g. intruding aircraft). Reports are passed to the appropriate (Intelligence) staff who examine them as part of their normal duties. There is no unit within the Ministry appointed solely for the study of UFOs, and no staff are employed upon the subject on a full-time basis. The Ministry does not deny that there are strange things to see in the sky. It believes, however, that there are adequate material explanations for these . . . It certainly has no evidence that alien spacecraft have landed on this planet.'

However, they continue to go to some lengths to collect UFO reports. Chapter 4 of the Manual of Air Traffic Services, section 3, prints the form required to obtain data on UFOs. The July 1984 version says, 'A controller receiving a report about an unidentified flying object must obtain as much as possible of the information required to complete a report in the format shown below.' There then are fifteen sections, labelled A to P, which include all obvious things (date, time, place etc) plus some less obvious ones (e.g. proximity to reservoirs, dams, power stations etc).

These forms are held by all civil, military and other airports, coastguards and police stations. In conclusion all these people are told where to find a 'list of telephone numbers and locations' in order to report. I understand these are mainly Squadron Leaders at selected RAF bases. One of these is RAF Finningley in Yorkshire, whose base commander Derek Exley confirmed that he held such a role. Aside from sending the report form to the MoD (where it reaches DS-8, or as it is now called Air Staff-2) the manual urges that 'the details are to be telephoned immediately to AIS (Military), LATCC', which is the air traffic control centre at West Drayton near London.

This is an awful lot of fuss over nothing. Especially when you note the total number of reports that are collected each year. You have seen the number of cases the main British civilian group BUFORA receive (page 87). The MoD UFO archives obviously contain a lot of sightings by air crew, military personnel or police officers. Yet they far outweigh what BUFORA is obtaining!

According to an exchange between Viscount Long, representing the MoD, and the Earl of Cork and Orrery (House of Lords, 7 April 1982) a total of 2250 sightings were recorded in the four years after the film *Close Encounters of the Third Kind* (1978 – 1981) (BUFORA equivalent – just 907). Long claimed that none of these are 'classified for security reasons'. Nevertheless, none have been released either.

On 24 October 1983, Conservative MP Sir Patrick Wall asked questions in the House of Commons about the Rendlesham Forest story, which my colleagues and I had just made public. He was told that from January 1981 until the time of his question a further 1400 sightings had been logged, but for all these 'there were no corresponding unexplained radar contacts'. The reply from Armed Forces Minister, John Stanley, who was according to Clive Ponting heavily involved in the *General Belgrano* cover-up, ended with the tongue-in-cheek remark that 'subject to normal security constraints, I am ready to give information about any such reported sightings that are found to be a matter of concern from a defence standpoint, but there have been none to date.'

Clearly, if the government can claim that a landing of an unknown object disgorging radiation, leaving damage in its wake and being chased by airmen half a mile outside a NATO base, has no defence concern, it is likely that anything (whatever it was) would similarly be excluded from release under this ridiculous definition.

On 13 March 1984, Sir Patrick Wall tried again and got more specific figures showing that year by year they were: 1980 – 350; 1981 – 600; 1982 – 250; and 1983 – 390. There is no evidence of a decrease in sighting numbers via these military sources – a highly important piece of information. When added to the previous statements we can see that in the six years between 1978 and 1983 the MoD recorded nearly 3000 UFO sightings from our shores. Even if we take only the 10 per cent they claim (when the last such figure was given to Parliament some years back) then that leaves 300 recent *unexplained* UFO events over Britain in MoD hands.

That ought to be considered of defence significance, by any government with the slightest concern for the protection of this land.

Interestingly, Patrick Wall asked another question at the same time as the above, 'How many unexplained sightings . . . and which of these had been tracked on radar and with what result.' The MoD literally ignored that, which as anyone used to asking specific UFO questions (such as I have) will well know is the route they often take when there is no other way.

Bill Chalker's success in Canberra led me to suggest that I might be given a similar privileged access by the MoD. Bill even kindly endorsed my request, and the MoD confirmed receipt of his letter in writing to me. On 27 October 1982, Peter Watkins of DS-8 said, 'While the UFO reports which we receive remain closed to the public, it is difficult to rebut such speculation [of a cover-up] . . . It is for this reason that we decided several months ago to make the reports generally available. However, largely owing to the intervention of the Falklands crisis [then long over – JR] the necessary preparatory work has not yet been completed. Once we are in a position to start releasing the reports, you will, of course, be informed . . . since it is our intention to publish the UFO reports we have received, it would be inappropriate to give particular individuals privileged access to our records. However, should our plans be subject to further significant delay we will obviously reconsider our position on this point.'

I was so pleased at such a welcome move that I did all I could to avoid media publicity. I could have gone to the press with the story. Instead I did not even show the letter to my UFO colleagues. I wanted nothing to upset the applecart. Some months later I was given a statement I could make public, saying, 'In response to demands for publication of UFO reports Viscount Long said that he saw no objection to these reports being made public. We are therefore studying the best means of publishing this material.'

As a token of good faith I was sent two of these reports! In fact, the word 'report' is a little exaggerated. They were pieces of paper 9 inches by 6 inches which contained very short (often one-word) answers to questions A to K on the standard report form (L, M, N, O and P have always been omitted in MoD releases). There were no names of witnesses, almost no sighting details and rarely any clues as to where the event took place. One did talk of a September 1982 light in the sky at Cwmbran, Wales. The other (from the same month) spoke of a 'cottage loaf shape with bright porthole lights and a pulsating red light beneath'. There were no data relating to possible radar tracks, identification attempts or evaluations of any sort. The least competent UFO spotting club would have thrown these scraps of paper in the bin!

As the weeks drifted by I did decide to request a couple of specific cases, for which I was quite certain these pathetic bits of paper would be the start of the enquiry. They were cases that must have resulted in proper investigations. One was the Rendlesham Forest landing, which in early 1983 remained just a collection of rumours and had no official confirmation. The MoD had ignored all our previous enquiries about it, since our first discovery in January 1981.

Instead of the case I received another unsolicited document about an event in south Wales! This was dated 19 January 1983 and, as before, was a small piece of paper. It merely spoke of a light 'similar to a star or planet, alternating blue and red in colour'. Again, there were no witness names or locations. So there was no hope of following it up. However, more than a year later I worked with BBC Wales on a documentary about UFOs. Through their agency we found two independent sets of witnesses to this case. We know they reported it to sources which channel to the MoD. One was an aircraft engineer from the RAF who was coaching a group of soccer players when a huge triangular object floated up across an RAF base at St Athan, south of Cardiff. The other was a doctor and a woman who was driving him to an appointment. They were at Llandaff, to the north-east. Each group was filmed by camera crews sketching the object with separate BBC artists. Neither had opportunity to talk to the other. The object was extremely unusual, certainly not an aircraft and (as the film proves) unquestionably the same thing in both locations. By no stretch of the imagination could it be termed a light in the sky.

I tried again to get the file on Rendlesham Forest. This time, whilst I did not receive it, on 13 April 1983 the MoD confirmed that 'unusual lights' were seen near Bentwaters for which 'no explanation . . . was ever forthcoming'. At the time this was a major breakthrough in the case. I later had it confirmed (during my August 1983 conversation inside the MoD with the writer of this letter) that she had based it on the unreleased Halt memo (the only thing about the case on MoD files, remember?). I do have to ask why my letter offered such a lukewarm version of the facts that it was bordering on the realms of fabrication. I was told of a few lights. The memo tells of a structured craft, chased through the woods, landing and leaving radiation and physical damage after upsetting local wildlife. If this is what the MoD call an 'unusual light', one shudders to think what would be called a 'close encounter' in their records!

The release of the Halt memo in the USA came two months after the MoD official confirmation that an incident had happened. In August 1983, after visiting Whitehall, the decision was taken by myself and my colleagues that the only hope of getting anywhere on this case was to publicise it for the whole world to see. This led to the October 1983 stories in the *News of the World* (including a front-page banner headline, 'UFO lands in Suffolk − and that's official!'). The prominence afforded the story was due in no small measure to the personal interest shown in it by editor Derek Jameson. Jameson had dinner with Ralph Noyes a few days later. Shortly afterwards he quit Fleet Street. He is now one of the BBC's leading radio presenters, with his own TV show as well. The *News of the World* dropped the story with his departure.

I suspect that all of this publicity had a dramatic effect on the MoD. The Ralph Noyes meeting with Derek Jameson was his first action. It may, or may not, have been coincidental. The Patrick Wall questions in the House caused a few minor headaches. I am sure that I was, at least for a time, a source of concern (and probably surveillance), as were my colleagues.

Whatever the case, the MoD promise about releasing UFO data went out of the window. My letters to them were not even receiving answers any more.

In March 1984, I was so frustrated that when Martin Bailey from the *Observer* came to me with his plan to do an article about the MoD and UFOs I agreed to co-operate. This was a credible paper that might have some influence. I told him the tale of the 'file release' promise and gave him a copy of one of the cases (which I had been given without restrictions). This was the case which gave a location (Cwmbran). With clever on-the-beat journalism the witnesses were traced.

The case turned out to have a lot more interest than the MoD 'form' had suggested. David Mason and his wife did not know that the MoD had a file on them, and rightly asked how their observation of a yellow object over a local hill could have been investigated when neither the police (to whom they reported) or the MoD had spoken with them about it. 'It's Official – there *are* UFOs' was Bailey's calm and reasoned article. Sadly, since writing it, he has declined all further suggestions to follow up the matter.

A few weeks later Andrew Mathewson, new man at DS-8, wrote (24 April 1984) to tell me, 'Since [we] last wrote to you it has been decided not to publish the reports of alleged UFO sightings we_receive.' Why this sudden change of heart? 'We receive hundreds of these reports each year and to prepare them for publication [i.e. censor them – J.R.] would involve a great deal of editorial work, for which we have neither the money nor the staff.' What about reviewing the possibility of giving me privileged access, as they had promised? 'Although they contain no classified papers they are, like all Ministry of Defence files, subject to the Public Records Act.' In other words, as the earliest records they hold are from 1962, come back in 1993 and we will see what we can do!

Of course, the MoD knew all of this in October 1982. Indeed they had cited figures in the House, so knew how many cases they had, and their letter to me implied they had already begun the 'necessary preparatory work', so presumably some data, at least, could be released. This all smelt rather fishy to me, coming in the wake of the Bentwaters publicity.

In 1985 I tried a new approach. Working with Ralph Noyes and a very co-operative Liberal MP, David Alton, we tried to reason it out with Lord Trefgarne, Minister for Defence. I am very grateful to David Alton for his help (Conservative and Labour MPs we also approached had far less time for us!). My original letter, forwarded by Alton, simply explained why it was unacceptable that the MoD would hold no further data on the Rendlesham Forest story. To be sure there were no defence implications somebody must have looked into it!

In reply, Trefgarne gave Alton the usual standard 'no defence significance' waffle, adding (19 March 1985) 'the alleged "UFO sighting" at Rendlesham Forest in December 1980' was supported only by the Halt memo. 'We are satisfied [but how? – J.R.] that the events [it] describes are of no defence significance. I can assure you that there is no question of attempting to cover up any incident or mishap, nor are we attempting in any way to obscure the truth.'

Meanwhile Ralph Noyes tried the old pals act on the MoD. It took him months to get an answer (a factor which he said persuaded him more than any other that the MoD had something to hide – because he had used the tactic himself before!). So both Noyes and I wrote letters and sent them together, through David Alton. He forwarded them to Michael Heseltine.

Ralph Noyes concentrated on one key point. Here was 'an extraordinary report made to the MoD by the deputy commander at the base . . . Unless Lt. Col. Halt was out of his mind, there is clear evidence in his report that British airspace and territory were intruded upon by an unidentified vehicle . . . and that no authority was able to prevent this. If, on the other hand, Halt's report cannot be believed, there is equally clear evidence of a serious misjudgement of events by USAF personnel at an important base on British territory. Either way the case can hardly be without defence significance.'

Do not forget that when these letters were written Halt had been promoted to full commander, and endorsed by the MoD. This hardly suggests they believed his judgement to be questionable.

Funnily enough, the very day our package arrived at the House of Commons, P.M. Hucker at the MoD (at last!) decided to answer Noyes' personal letter. He told the former DS-8 chief, 'No unidentified object was seen on any radar recordings during the period in question', which rather makes you wonder how Hucker knew this, if there are no other documents available on the case! As for UFOs, 'we treat all these reports seriously . . . However, we have never found any reason to believe that, in the defence context, such reports warrant more detailed research.' Why then go to such lengths still to collect them?

David Alton told us he sent the package on 16 May 1985 to both Heseltine and Lord Mayhew. Neither replied. Lord Trefgarne (again) did respond officially on 17 June, merely offering the 'defence implications' statement yet again, concluding, 'In this context the report submitted by Colonel Halt in January 1981 was examined by those in the department responsible for such matters . . . there is nothing I can usefully add.'

When even a serving MP, former head of department at the MoD and an ex-chief of staff all get the same, tired answer using virtually the same few words constantly regurgitated, then you have to be suspicious. Refusal to answer straight questions (like the one Noyes fired in his letter) can only mean they do have something which they are determined *not* to say.

Before starting this book I sent another letter direct to Trefgarne, telling him what I was doing. 'I have absolutely no desire to do or say anything that is harmful to our defences . . . [but] since it is completely impossible to dismiss the reality of UFOs, faced with the evidence, I have to take this as an argument to continue what I perceive to be in the interests of the common people.'

I repeated my plea for access, offered to sign the Official Secrets Act to protect witness confidentiality (if that was all that worried them) and waited. 'If the facts are not of defence concern,' I told him, 'then surely there can be no objection to my examining them. They most definitely are of public concern.'

Receipt was acknowledged. Four months later, as I end my writing, I have still not had any answer.

32   USA – FREEDOM OF INFORMATION?

If 'they' discover you, it is an old but hardly invalid rule of thumb, 'they' are your technological superiors.

(From 'UFO hypotheses and survival questions', NSA report released under Freedom of Information.)

Much of this book has been concerned with the importance of the American government to western thought on UFOs. Here I will simply tie up a few loose ends.

A great deal really does turn upon what did (or did not) happen at Roswell, New Mexico, in July 1947. If, as many sources now allege, proof of a solid UFO 'machine' was captured by the security forces, then this has been successfully hidden for a remarkably long time. The tiny number of people with a 'need to know' might not extend to Prime Ministers and Presidents and certainly not to NATO chiefs of defence staff. Whilst such a conspiracy would make sense of the great UFO cover-up, it would be almost impossible to contain without leaks (and the fact that we know about the possibility indicates that those *have* occurred!).

It is certainly worth noting that two American leaders (Ford in the 1960s and Carter in the 1970s) both made public stances on UFOs before taking office at the White House. Carter even made a specific promise to release UFO evidence. Whilst he did try (rather half-heartedly) to get NASA to launch a new study, and Freedom of Information revelations came in his time, Carter does seem to have gone back on his word. Unless, as it has been alleged, he was persuaded that it was not the correct thing to do.

Why should positive proof of real UFOs be withheld? Perhaps we are still trying to understand how it works (imagine a medieval astrologer and alchemist being given jurisdiction by the king over a nuclear submarine that has been beached on their shores). Yet surely the best way would be to share the search for knowledge with scientists everywhere?

However, if the alien nature of some UFOs is strongly suspected but their exact status remains puzzling, then there could be an even greater motive for secrecy. Possibly the MJ-12 team was created to work on the data fed to them by the public relations 'shop windows'. Perhaps that is the real reason why the MoD still collect UFO stories, even though the people who run the show do not know what is going on backstage.

It is easy to conjure up science-fiction scenarios, but it is a lot harder to justify how or why the cover-up would continue for forty years. Yet the facts seem plain. Cover-up of something (even if only ignorance) there surely must be.

The interest of the various security forces may have been incidental. Any secret project probably went on far beyond the need-to-know of the CIA or FBI. The documents released under Freedom of Information give the impression of various bodies picking up and playing with the UFO mystery, before putting it back down again more puzzled than before. The 1976 CIA memos about surveillance and monitors on 'UFO reporting channels' probably sum up the attitude these agencies have. They do not know what is going on. They guess that something is. So the best policy appears to be to sit, watch and wait.

Of course, our view is incomplete. There are admitted files that have never been released, particularly from the NSA (National Security Agency). The reason for this may at times be quite legitimate. Routine security procedures must quite rightly not be prejudiced. So files might be held back even if in UFO terms they do not contain 'hot' information. However, at times we know this is not the real reason for the denial of a file. The cases where files were at first denied and then released under appeal are perhaps amongst the most illuminating.

In 1985 Ray Boeche made a request for more records on the Rendlesham Forest case. Even if the MoD have none, the US government do! Those he got turned out to be routine telex messages discussing how to answer public questions about the case. One, from Bentwaters to the Pentagon (via the Mildenhall USAF headquarters in Suffolk) was dated 6 November 1984, less than two weeks after the release of our book *Sky Crash*. It told how the USAF were 'using the following statement in response to local queries'. The statement read, 'we are aware of the book and its accusations. It would be inappropriate for us to comment on these speculations. Nor will we be drawn into a discussion about motivations behind the book.' It added that 'the British MoD, failing to find any defence implications, chose not to investigate . . . current USAF policy is that we no longer investigate UFO sightings . . . We have no official interest in what may have happened, especially since the incident did not take place on the installation.'

This is rich in things I could comment on. How do they know the MoD position unless there has been some communication, which the MoD deny? The book is not 'speculation' but contains witness statements, documents and facts, as the base well know. To claim that they can pass the buck because the event did not happen on base is ridiculous, because the

201

security policemen had left on the morning of 27 December 1980 in response to a matter officially reported and with sanctioned permission to enquire into it.

Let us hope that Arab terrorists do not become aware of the claim by both the MoD and US Air Force that a suspected infiltration of the base perimeter at a NATO installation is considered of such minor importance that they would 'choose not to investigate'!

More realistically, let us hope this official response is as ludicrous as it sounds.

On receipt of such files, Boeche was denied seven others. He appealed but received only one. The other six remain secret. The appeal document is a teletype message from a USAF Europe Captain Wiley, dated 17 August 1984 – about the time the Halt tape was released by Colonel Sam Morgan. It is essentially a list of questions from Chuck de Caro, a former USAF intelligence officer who is now working as a journalist with Cable News Network in Washington DC. In December 1984 I spent a most disturbing two days with this man, and I was unhappy about his activities in and around the base. He evidently has a very high security clearance and his interest in the case was rather puzzling.

In the memo de Caro asked Wiley many deep questions about USAF security codings. These seem to be related to nuclear incidents or radiation mishaps. The last few words are peculiar – 'Ziegler says thanks for the Shepherd release' (Major Ziegler/Zickler being the chief of security on base at the time of the incident). Wiley also adds, 'I realise that [this] is long and about UFOs but I believe we need to explain the Bentwaters incident.'

These odd statements or the security codes may be the reason for non-release. As indeed might be the joke which Wiley cracks, by drawing little UFOs in a line across the top with what appears to be an alien standing next to one! 'Is anyone still there?' the first line reads!

We must wonder what the other six papers contain, not to mention any not admitted or traced.

However, for the saga to outdo all soap operas we must turn to the National Security Agency. This is one of the biggest-budget and most secret security agencies in the world. It concentrates on electronic and satellite surveillance. Its interest in UFOs would be significant anyhow, but after initial denials a hundred or so documents were traced. In subsequent Freedom of Information requests to obtain them, almost all were denied. The 'UFO hypotheses and survival questions' file *was* released. This discussed various theories for UFO origin, seeming to favour an extra-terrestrial source (see a quote from it at the start of this chapter).

An appeal was lodged for the missing files. This went to the highest possible court, where a top security cleared judge was disallowed the right to see the files. Instead he was shown a 21-page memo which summarised the reasons for non-release. In hours he made his judgement (it usually takes weeks). The NSA won because, as the judge put it, release of the files 'would seriously jeopardise the work of the agency and the security of the United States . . . public interest and disclosure is far outweighed by the sensitive nature of the material.'

The 21-page memo then became the subject of a new appeal. On 27 April 1982 this was released, in 'sanitised form'. In practice that meant that eleven of the pages were *totally* censored out, and all but four of the rest largely so. Of course, we do not know what lies behind the thick black lines, let alone what the documents themselves contain, but there are fascinating clues in the material we can read.

The opening portions form the bulk of what we can see. The NSA merely explain what the request was, how they searched for papers and what they found. 'A total of two hundred and thirty nine documents were located in NSA files', it tells us. This is many more than originally alleged! One unreleased document is 'an account by a person assigned to NSA of his attendance at a UFO symposium'. This is denied because it has no relevance! Another file is by the unknown author of the 'Survival Questions' paper. This is a seven-page monograph entitled 'UFOs . . .' (the next one-and-a-half lines of the title are missing!). The memo adds, 'In this document the author discusses what he considers to be . . .' (then the next seven lines of text vanish under a sea of black ink!).

As you can see, *these* censorings are apparently not for reasons of NSA procedure but precisely because of the UFO content of the material being denied. That fact is emphasised by the next readable section of the memo which explains why this 'type of candor' is vital. 'Public disclosure of such information, especially when it advances a novel theory, could have the effect of stifling such candor by the risk of diminution of professional standing the employee runs if subsequently found wrong.'

Just what sort of 'novel theory' about UFOs could be *that* risky?

The memo then tells of more material considered irrelevant and therefore not available for release. This discusses 'the ability of the agency employees to deal with unusual phenomena'. The remainder of the memo then itemises messages about UFOs received between 1958 and 1979 through NSA actions, 'intercepted' (presumably from foreign powers). However, virtually all of this section is deleted.

UFO researcher Barry Greenwood lodged a final appeal, suggesting that the dates and countries of origin of these 156 intercepted messages surely were so vague as to offer no threat to security. This was denied, but a few extra words were allowed to peek through the black lines. These used the fascinating term 'surprise material' to describe UFOs.

I trust that you are as surprised by the material on UFOs which you have now read as apparently the National Security Agency were.

CONCLUSIONS

I have chosen not to tell you what UFOs are, nor to bombard you with theories. Instead I have given you a torrent of facts which you must sift and evaluate in your mind. You may dismiss some as exaggeration or fantasy, but can you afford to dismiss them all? If only one of these cases really happened, the consequences are pretty obvious.

My simple aim has been to demonstrate that if we can discover these things with relative ease, then the authorities of this world must have chanced upon them long ago. To imagine them all making stupid errors of misjudgement and washing their hands of this serious matter is unthinkable. The various documents, statements and governmental actions prove that it is also incorrect. The truth about UFOs *is* being hidden – for whatever reason.

It may be that UFOs are alien devices and the powers-that-be see no way to cope. Bluff and bluster might seem a good response when faced with a magical technology. Economic factors might also prevail. An overnight disclosure of some revolutionary power source could have dire consequences for the money markets. Then also ponder the thought that some long-range experiment might be underway. Primitive ape-like creatures could have been stimulated to the threshold of intelligence and observed for many aeons. The apes (i.e. us!) may have been guided by these godly aliens who could even have provoked our moral and cultural development. What if the appearances of Jesus Christ and Mohammed were staged events – aliens in disguise? How do you tell the people of the whole planet, fractured by racial and political divisions, that they are pawns? We do not run the universe. We only think we do.

Alternatively, UFOs might not be alien after all. We considered the prospect of travellers from our future viewing a cataclysmic time in the earth's history. Supposing they have told us of an inevitable future – war, natural disaster, who knows what? Do you warn of something that cannot be avoided?

Of course, not knowing, we tend to think dark thoughts. We speculate about power-hungry administrations out to get the secrets of the UFO before anyone else, in order that they may build bigger and more destructive weapons. Let us hope that these things remain science-fiction. Without truth, however, our minds are bound to turn that way.

It really matters little what UFOs are. Perhaps we simply have no comprehension of the real truth. The cover-up *is* bad, because all uncertainty breeds disquiet. We are owed better than botched official investigations, shows of disbelief or the cowardly face of apathy. If you are happy putting this book down and denying what it means then that is your choice. If you are not, then you must fight to do something about it.

There are signs of a change in the air. The 'Education Programme' could be real. When I first heard tell of it I thought it was a joke. Now I am much less certain. The seed of an idea was planted in my mind during that drink in the House of Commons bar. Perhaps there was more to that casual conversation than I imagined at the time.

The facts can certainly be viewed in a way that makes them seem part of a pattern. Look at some of them.

In 1974 the French Minister of Defence makes an open admission that UFOs are real and initiates a permanent scientific investigation.

In 1976 the Spanish government invites a researcher to Madrid to receive 'off-the-record' confidential UFO files that demonstrate deep interest and tangible evidence involving military witnesses. On 29 June that year, General Carlos Cavero makes a provocative statement to the Spanish people. 'I have for some time held the view that UFOs are extra-terrestrial craft. The position is that it is as difficult for official quarters to admit that something exists as it is for the Church to affirm that this or that is a miracle.' Then he suggests that a world collaboration on UFO research would soon lead to the truth being told.

In 1977 the Freedom of Information act began to bring forth many thousands of pages of American documents proving the reality of UFOs and the level of security agency interest. Security agencies do not get interested in things that do not exist.

In 1978 the Steven Spielberg twenty-million-dollar movie plays around the world. *Close Encounters of the Third Kind* tells the UFO story as it has never been told before – complete, unabridged and realistic. It also, rather interestingly, tries to justify the cover-up; and ends when a civilian takes the one picture of a Rendlesham Forest style military landing that will forever change the world.

In 1980 there are more revelations by European nations and the process of filtering information continues as the UFOs themselves begin to dwindle in number.

As 1981 begins the astonishing Rendlesham Forest landing case is leaked in quite remarkable fashion. During the next three years a catalogue of escalating releases (witness testimony, then memos, then the tape recording, and as I go to press an alleged 'movie film' of the event!)

percolate into the community. The case makes major headlines everywhere. Slowly public opinion is altered.

In 1982 the Australian government invites a leading UFO researcher to view their archives and do what he wishes with them.

In 1983 Spielberg tells the world that aliens (or 'Extra-Terrestrials') are cuddly and friendly. The British government release UFO files for the first time.

In 1984 China announces the funding of a major UFO research centre.

In 1985 the USSR, which has just launched a scientific study of UFOs, reveals details of major close encounters. Back in Britain a former head of the MoD's UFO section produces a novel saying that UFOs are real and there is a cover-up, but the truth will eventually be told.

In 1986 the Brazilian Air Force chase UFOs and set up a major enquiry into what they explain is a serious matter.

All of this could be a coincidence; but it seems to be very strange that after years of silence these voices are all beginning to cry at once. Whispers have a habit of turning into shouts.

I cannot believe that the authorities of all the nations mentioned in this book seriously think that there is nothing to the UFO mystery. Whether they are concealing a little or a great deal, whether they think they understand what is happening or they do not, something *is* going on. That cannot be denied.

The time has come finally to remove this matter from the province of the Hollywood movie and the occult shelves of backstreet bookstores. The time has come to treat the evidence for UFOs with due respect, to debate it as we would debate any other issue subjected to a massive policy of obscuration.

There follows a list of fifty names, picked almost at random from society. These are just a few of the people who have made positive statements about UFOs in the past forty years.

Scientists:
Dr J. Allen Hynek (astronomer), Dr Carl Jung (psychologist), Dr Lincoln La Paz (meteor expert), Dr Bruce Maccabee (optical physicist), Dr James McDonald (atmospheric physicist), Dr Shirley McIver (sociologist), Dr Hermann Oberth (rocket expert), Dr Thornton Page (NASA), Dr Carl Sagan (cosmologist), Dr Robert Sarbacher (Pentagon scientific adviser), Dr Wilbur Smith (engineer), Dr Leo Sprinkle (psychiatrist), Dr Clyde Tombaugh (discoverer of the planet Pluto), Dr Jaques Vallée (computer scientist).

Politicians:
David Alton (Britain, Liberal MP), President Jimmy Carter (USA), Winston Churchill (Britain, Prime Minister), President Gerald Ford (USA), Sir Eric Gairy (Grenada, Prime Minister), M. Robert Galley (France, Minister of Defence), Barry Goldwater (USA, senator), Lord Kimberley (British peer), Octabio Lima (Brazil, Air Minister), Merlyn Rees (Britain, Labour MP), Salvador Teran (Spain, Minister of Transport), Sir Patrick Wall (Britain, Conservative MP).

Entertainers:
Michael Bentine, Kate Bush, Richard Dreyfuss, Jackie Gleason, Derek Jameson, John Lennon, Shirley McLaine, Leonard Nimoy, Bill Roache (Ken Barlow), William Shatner, Steven Spielberg, Jules Verne.

Others:
Sir Francis Chichester, astronaut Gordon Cooper, Air Chief Marshall Lord Dowding, Air Marshall Sir Victor Goddard, Admiral of the Fleet Lord Hill-Norton, William Lear ('Lear Jets'), astronaut James McDivitt, Earl Mountbatten, Ralph Noyes (head of section in MoD handling UFOs), Prince Philip of Great Britain, Edward Ruppelt (head of USAF project handling UFOs), U Thant (Secretary General of the United Nations).

Are you willing to join them in a plea for truth? If so, then write to your local MP or Senator, or whoever, or better still get up a petition, saying that you are not claiming that little green men rule the earth, but merely that something is happening and the public deserve to be told about it. This is not a subject that should be hidden any longer. The truth about UFOs belongs to mankind. It is up to you to make sure that we get it.

LIST OF REFERENCES

Chapter 1
The Riddle of the Flying Saucers, Heard G., Carroll and Nicholson, 1950.
The Coming of the Saucers, Arnold K. & Palmer, R., Boise, 1952.
The Ed Murrow interview with Arnold is reproduced by the Center for UFO Studies in their newsletter dated Feb/Mar 1984.

Chapter 2
The Roswell Incident, Moore, W., & Berlitz, C., Granada, 1980.
William Moore has published several updates on new discoveries available through MUFON, in the USA.
An important debate on 'Crashed UFOs' can be found in the CUFOS publication *International UFO Reporter,* Jul/Aug 1985, involving Dr David Jacobs and Richard Hall.

Chapter 3
The Report on Unidentified Flying Objects, Ruppelt, Edward, pp. 46–56, Ace, 1956.
Project Blue Book, Steiger, B., pp. 43–62, Sphere, 1978.
UFOs Exist, Flammonde, P., pp. 218–248, Ballantine, 1976.
A Mantell Diary, Crain, T. Scott, in *MUFON Journal,* May 1986.
As with all historical events, references to the Ruppelt book indicate his Air Force memoirs about the incident, to Steiger summaries of the actual Blue Book case files, and Flammonde to a review of media reaction to the story.

Chapter 4
This chapter is based on the original Air Force case file.
The Flying Saucers are Real, Keyhoe, D., Fawcett, 1950.

Chapter 5
Scientific Study of UFOs, Condon, Dr E. (Ed), pp. 155–157, Bantam, 1969.
Ruppelt, pp. 207–227.
Steiger, pp. 137–152.

Chapter 6

This chapter is based on first-hand interviews with the witness.

For a censored version of the released Robertson Panel report see Condon, pp. 905–921.

Chapter 7

The BOAC Stratocruiser case is briefly reviewed in Condon, pp. 139–140. Here I also draw upon a detailed first-hand investigation case report by Barry King.

One of the best reviews of early entity sightings can be found in:

The Humanoids, Bowen, C. (Ed), Futura, 1970.

Chapter 8

The Lubbock Lights, Wheeler, J., Award, 1977.

A good summary of his first-hand research into the Levelland cases was published by Don Berliner in the otherwise unreliable *Official UFO*, January 1976.

Chapter 9

The Interrupted Journey, Fuller, J., Souvenir, 1980 (updated with new material).

The O'Brien Commission report is concisely released in Condon, pp. 812–818.

Chapter 10

The Schirmer case (what there is of it) can be found as No. 42 in Condon, pp. 389–391.

The Alan Godfrey story is fully recounted in my book *The Pennine UFO Mystery*, Grafton, 1983.

For a more general review of these abduction type cases see:

Missing Time, Hopkins, B., Merek, 1982.

Chapter 11

This chapter is based on various Freedom of Information Act releases. A general summary of the battle to release these thousands of pieces of paper can be found in:

Clear Intent, Fawcett, L., & Greenwood, B., Prentice-Hall, 1984.

Chapter 12

This chapter is based on first-hand investigation by myself, Brenda Butler, Harry Harris and Dot Street in the UK and Ray Boeche in the USA. See also:

Sky Crash, Butler, Randles & Street, Grafton, 1986.

Chapter 13

This is a report based on personal investigation files, with thanks to Ian Mrzyglod. The cases in the introduction to this section come from official Air Force archives. See also:

In Search of a UFO Stereotype, Dillon, B., & Randles, J., *FSR*, Vol. 28, No. 4, 1983.

Chapter 14

This is a report based on personal investigation files, with thanks to Bill Chalker.

Chapter 15

Humanoids Encountered at La Baleia, Aleixo, Professor H., *FSR*, Vol. 14, No. 6, Vol. 15, No. 1, 1968.

Chapter 16

FSR, Vol. 19, No. 1, 1973, contains some copyrighted photographs of the damage.

The catalogue of physical traces, edited by Ted Phillips, is available from CUFOS.

Chapter 17

A report by Jennie Ziedman appears in *FSR*, Vol. 22, No. 4, 1976. She is also the author of *Helicopter Encounter over Ohio*, the fully detailed file available from CUFOS.

Chapter 18

A report by Benitez on the Talavera case appears in *FSR*, Vol. 23, No. 5, 1978.

Vanquelef's updated account of the tape-recording appears in *FSR*, Vol. 30, No. 6, 1985.

A full summary of the Dakelia, Cyprus, case can be found in my book *UFO Reality*, pp. 116–118, Hale, 1983.

Chapter 19

Apart from my personal correspondence with radar controller, John Cordy, this chapter can be illuminated by referring to Foggarty's reply to debunkers in *FSR*, Vol. 26, No. 2, 1980; Maccabee's own summary under 'Wellington' in *The UFO Encyclopedia*, Story, R. (Ed), NEL, 1980, and the pilot's own accounts in *The Kaikoura UFOs*, Hodder & Stoughton, 1981.

Chapter 20

This chapter is based on translations of the original Soviet versions of the case.

Chapter 21

Several of these cases are based on personal investigation files, with thanks to Mike Sacks and Peter Warrington. Benitez reports on the Spanish cases in *FSR*, Vol. 25, No. 5, 1979, and Vol. 26, No. 6, 1981. As I go to press Dr Willy Smith has just produced an update report on the 1986 Brazilian sightings in *International UFO Reporter*, Jul/Aug 1986. It still looks to be promising.

Chapter 22

Oberg publishes much of his negative reasoning against the McDivitt case in *MUFON Journals*, Jan and Feb 1986.

Chapter 23

The British cases are based on personal investigation files, with thanks to Brian Grimshaw and Peter Hough. The best source for the Loch Raven dam encounter is: *Challenge to Science*, Vallée, Dr J., pp. 191–198, Spearman, 1967.
There are two catalogues of 'vehicle interference' cases, from BUFORA and CUFOS.

Chapter 24

The British cases are based on personal investigation files. Velasco is quoted at some length on the Trans-en-Provence case in *International UFO Reporter*, Mar/Apr 1985.

Chapter 25

The British cases are based on personal investigation files, with thanks to Norman Collinson, Harry Harris, Peter Hough and Mike Sacks.
The Valentich disappearance is reviewed days after it occurred, by Chalker in *FSR*, Vol. 24, No. 5, 1979, and in much more depth later in *FSR*, Vol. 30, No. 2, 1984. The wave which surrounded the episode is recounted in detail by Paul Norman in *FSR*, Vol. 31, No. 2, 1986.

Chapter 26

McMinnville, 1950 – Condon Case No. 46, pp. 396–407, Maccabee, in Story (Ed), pp. 223–226.
Trinidade Island, 1958 – Review and interview by Dr Willy Smith, *International UFO Reporter*, Jul/Aug 1983.
Cuddington, 1973 – based on the 100-pp BUFORA case file. See also my book *UFO Reality*, Hale, 1983, for more detail.

Falkville, 1973 – see *Beyond Earth*, Blum, J. & R., Corgi, 1974.

Canary Islands, 1976 – see *Photographs of the Unknown*, Rickard & Kelly, NEL 1980, and FSR, Vol. 23, No. 3, 1977.

Hessdalen, 1984 – see Project Hessdalen technical report No. 1, Strand, E. (Ed). Dr J. Allen Hynek reviews his 1985 visit to the site in *International UFO Reporter*, Mar/Apr 1985.

Chapter 27

'UFOs and the Royal Australian Air Force', in *UFORAN* (Australia), Vol. 3, Nos. 2, 3, 4, 1983, Chalker, W.

Mystery of the Circles, Fuller, J., and Randles, J., BUFORA 1986.

Chapter 28

The Spanish document releases are reviewed in *FSR*, Vol. 24, No. 5, 1979 and Vol. 25, No. 2, 1979.

A. Chiumento reports on the Italian incidents in *FSR*, Vol. 30, No. 2, 1984.

Chapter 29

Poher's geomagnetic anomaly research was published in *FSR*, Vol. 20, No. 1, 1974. His search for patterns in sightings with Dr Jacques Vallée is in *FSR*, Vol. 21, Nos. 3 and 4, 1975. There is a mildly inaccurate translation of the full Galley transcript, along with other data from the France-Inter radio broadcasts, in the book (translated by Gordon Creighton) *The Crack in the Universe*, Bourrett, J., Spearman, 1978.

Chapter 30

A good account of some of the strifes of Soviet UFO investigators can be found in Creighton's articles on USSR ufology in *FSR*, Vol. 27, Nos. 3 and 4, 1981.

Chapter 31

Much of this chapter is based on my own research and files. However, I would like to mention Tim Good, the Yorkshire UFO Society (and their magazine *Quest*) who have also done a lot of work to uncover British UFO secrecy.

A Secret Property, Noyes, R., Quartet, 1985.

Chapter 32

This chapter would not have been possible without the hard work of Ray Boeche and others at MUFON and the movement CAUS (Citizens Against UFO Secrecy) which has masterminded the release of thousands of documents under Freedom of Information.

USEFUL ADDRESSES

If you have had a personal experience of UFOs and wish to report this to an organisation who can investigate (in full confidence if so desired) contact Jenny Randles, c/o 8 Whitethroat Walk, Birchwood, Warrington, Cheshire, England WA3 6PQ.

Groups and magazines mentioned in the text can be contacted as follows:

Americas
CAUS (Citizens Against UFO Secrecy), 471 Goose Lane, Coventry, Connecticut 06238, USA.
CUFOS (Center for UFO Studies) *(International UFO Reporter)*, 1955 Johns Drive, Glenview, Illinois 60025, USA.
MUFON (Mutual UFO Network), Box 12434, San Antonio, Texas 78212, USA.

Australasia
UFO Research Australia, PO Box 229, Prospect, South Australia 5082.

Europe
GEPAN (France), c/o C.N.E.S., 18 avenue Edouard Belin, Toulouse 31055, France.
Project Hessdalen (Scandinavia), PO Box 14, Duken N-3133, Norway.

UK
BUFORA (British UFO Research Association), 16 South Way, Burgess Hill, Sussex RH15 9ST.
FSR (Flying Saucer Review), FSR Publications, Snodland, Kent ME6 5HJ.
MAGONIA Magazine, 5 James Terrace, Mortlake Churchyard, London SW14 8HB.

MUFORA (Manchester UFO Research Association) *(Northern UFO News)*, 6 Silsden Avenue, Lowton, Lancashire WA3 1EN.
QUEST Magazine, 68 Buller Crescent, Leeds, West Yorkshire LS9 6LJ.
WYUFORG (West Yorkshire UFO Research Group) *(UFO Brigantia)*, 19 Bellmount Gardens, Bramley, West Yorkshire LS13 2ND.

Those seeking copies of old, probably long out-of-date books mentioned in the text, could try specialist UFO booksellers:
Arcturus Books, 263 N. Ballston Avenue, Scotia, New York 12302, USA.
Specialist Knowledge, 30 South Row, London SE3 0RY.

If a reply is expected an S.A.E. should be sent in all cases.

They HAVE landed
SAY UFOLOGISTS, CLAIMING A BIG COVER-UP

'Green cloud' stirs Soviet UFO dispute

Suffolk UFO posed no threat, MPs told

MoD quiet on UFO

1,400 UFOs reported in 3 years

Russians see light on UFOs

DEPARTMENT OF THE AIR FORCE
IN AIR... A... A... A... A... A... A... A...
AFO BEN WAT ERS

BM P... 10   CD   13 Jan 81
AJ IN 01

SUBJECT: Unexplained Lights

TO: RAF/CC

1. Early in the morning of 27 Dec 80 (approximately 0300L), two USAF
security police patrolmen saw unusual lights outside the back gate at
RAF Woodbridge. Thinking an aircraft might have crashed or been forced
down, they called for permission to go outside the gate to investigate.
The on-duty flight chief responded and allowed three patrolmen to proceed on foot. The individuals reported seeing a strange glowing object
in the forest. The object was described as being metalic in appearance
and triangular in shape, approximately two to three meters across the
base and approximately two meters high. It illuminated the entire forest
with a white light. The object itself had a pulsing red light on top and
a bank(s) of blue lights underneath. The object was hovering or on legs.
As the patrolmen approached the object, it maneuvered through the trees
and disappeared. At this time the animals on a nearby farm went into a
frenzy. The object was briefly sighted approximately an hour later near
the back gate.

2. The next day, three depressions 1 1/2" deep and 7" in diameter were
found where the object had been sighted on the ground. The following
night (29 Dec 80) the area was checked for radiation. Beta/gamma readings
of 0.1 milliroentgens were recorded with peak readings in the three depressions and near the center of the triangle formed by the depressions.
A nearby tree had moderate (.05-.07) readings on the side of the tree
toward the depressions.

3. Later in the night a red sun-like light was seen through the trees.
It moved about and pulsed. At one point it appeared to throw off glowing
particles and then broke into five separate white objects and then disappeared. Immediately thereafter, three star-like objects were noticed
in the sky, two objects to the north and one to the south, all of which
were about 10° off the horizon. The objects moved rapidly in sharp angular
movements and displayed red, green and blue lights. The objects to the
north appeared to be elliptical through an 8-12 power lens. They then
turned to full circles. The objects to the north remained in the sky for
an hour or more. The object to the south was visible for two or three
hours and beamed down a stream of light from time to time. Numerous individuals, including the undersigned, witnessed the activities in paragraphs
2 and 3.

CHARLES I. HALT, Lt Col, USAF
Deputy Base Commander

216

PARLIAMENTARY UNDER-SECRETARY OF STATE
FOR THE ARMED FORCES

D/US of S(AF)/DGT 5173   19 March 1985

Dear Mr Alton,

Thank you for your letter of 21 February with the enclosed
from Ms Jenny Randles of Birchwood, Warrington.

I should first of all point out that the sole interest of the
Ministry of Defence in reported sightings of Unidentified Flying
Objects (UFOs) is to establish whether they have any bearing on the
defence of the country.

There is no organisation in the Ministry of Defence appointed
solely for the purpose of studying UFOs, and no staff are employed on
the subject full time. The reports we receive are referred to the
staff in the Department who are responsible for the air defence of
the United Kingdom, and they examine the reports as part of their
normal duties. Unless there are defence implications we do not
attempt to identify sightings and we cannot inform observers of the
probable identity of the object seen. The Department could not
justify the expenditure of public funds on investigations which go
beyond the pure defence interests.

The only information we have on the alleged "UFO sighting" at
Rendlesham Forest in December 1980 is the report by Colonel Charles
Halt, of the United States Air Force, which Ms Randles mentions in
her letter. We are satisfied that the events described are of no
defence significance. I can assure you that there is no question of
attempting to cover up any incident or mishap, nor are we attempting
in any way to obscure the truth.

I am also enclosing with this copies of 2 Parliamentary
Questions, one of which is that put down by Sir Patrick Wall and
which Ms Randles also mentions.

Yours sincerely,

Lord Trefgarne

David Alton Esq MP

217

- Colonel's top secret report tells the facts
- Mystery craft in exploding wall of colour
- Animals flee from strange glowing object

UFO LANDS IN SUFFOLK

And that's OFFICIAL

A UFO has landed in Britain—and that staggering fact has been officially confirmed.

Despite a massive cover-up, News of the World investigators have proof that the mysterious craft came to earth in a red ball of light at 3 a.m. on December 27, 1980.

It happened in a pine forest called Tangham Wood just half a mile from the United States Air Force base at RAF Woodbridge, in Suffolk.

Two weeks ago the staggering facts in this story were in official reports. Late one night three beings in silver dress suits boarded the craft.

Farm lands and forest animals ran berserk as the spacecraft, a sloping silver disc about 20ft across lit base, silently glided to land in a blinding explosion of lights.

About 300 military and civilian personnel, British and American, witnessed the astounding event. The airmen said the visitors appeared to be expected.

Two nights later a series of fast-moving objects beaming powerful lights earthward were spotted

NEWS WORLD INVESTIGATES

By KEITH BEABEY

over the base by a number of airmen.

It sounds like aliens coming to earth in the film Close Encounters, but the PROOF that an Unidentified Flying Object landed in Britain is irrefutable.

The key witness is Lt. Colonel Charles I. Halt, deputy commander of the USAF 81st Tactical Fighter Wing stationed alongside the British at Woodbridge.

With the help of UFO experts in Britain and the US we have obtained a copy of his official report on the incident, part of which is reproduced on the right.

On official USAF notepaper and headed "Unexplained Lights," Colonel Halt wrote:

PULSING

Thinking an aircraft might have crashed or been forced down they called for permission to go outside the base to go investigate.

The on-duty flight chief allowed three patrolmen to proceed on foot.

The individuals reported seeing a strange glowing object in the forest.

The object was described as being metallic in appearance and triangular in shape, approximately two or three metres across the base and approximately

two metres high. It illuminated the entire forest with a white light.

The object itself had a pulsing red light on top and a bank of blue lights underneath. The object was hovering or on legs. As the patrolmen approached the object it manoeuvred through the trees and disappeared.

At this time the animals on a nearby farm went into a frenzy.

The object was sighted approximately an hour later near the back gate.

The next day three depressions one and a half inches deep and seven inches in diameter were found where the object had been sighted on the ground.

The following night, the colonel reported, the area was checked for radiation and readings were found in the depressions and at a tree.

His report goes on:

Later in the night a red sun-blue light was seen through the trees. It moved about and pulsed. At one point it appeared to throw off glowing particles and then broke into five separate white objects and disappeared.

Immediately thereafter three star-like objects were noted in the sky two objects in the north and one to the south all of which were clearly in degrees of the horizon.

The objects moved rapidly in sharp angular movements and displayed green and blue lights. The objects to the north

TRUTH

appeared elliptical through an 8-10 power lens.

They then turned to full circles. The objects in the sky for no more than an hour. The object to the south was visible for two or three hours and beamed down a stream of light from time to time.

Numerous people, including himself, witnessed these events, Colonel Halt concluded.

Last week he declined to say anything further when we called on him at the base.

"This is a very delicate situation," he said.

"I have been told very clearly that I could jeopardise my career if I talk to you about it."

It was this report and the report Colonel Halt made to his superiors that brought advice from the RAF base commander, Squadron Leader Donald Moreland, who told me:

"The Colonel sat in my office and was a very worried man.

"The first I knew of these events was when he came to me and related what he had seen. I know Col Halt well and respect him and I fully believe he was telling me the truth.

"Whatever it was it was able to perform feats in the air which no known aircraft is capable of doing. I put the events the Colonel related to me down to inexplicable phenomena.

The Colonel's report confirms the strange events in the forest that night, but lacks the conclusive detail given to us by Art Wallace, a USAF security Policeman, then back in America as a private.

He was sent to the site in a number of military vehicles from hostile

EVIDENCE

DETAIL from Lt. Col Charles Halt's confidential report about the sighting of "unexplained lights" and a strange glowing object that lit up the forest

NO HOAX: Brig. Gen. Williams

NO HOAX SAYS THE AIR CHIEF

THERE has been no hoax, says the man who was in charge of the USAF base at Woodbridge when the UFO came down.

The Wing Commander, now Brigadier General Gordon Williams, said back home in America: "I recall Lt Colonel Halt's report.

"I don't know exactly what happened. It is all blarney. He is not a man who would hoax the British Ministry of Defence — the American Air Force Department."

Despite official silence News of a World reporters discovered that the UFO was tracked on radar by RAF Watton, 50 miles from where it landed.

Radar technicians reported "tracing unidentified blips."

They followed its progress across the east coast until it disappeared off the screen.

USAF intelligence officers later checked the types of radio installations in the area.

SILVER

"But others did. They said there were three, wearing silver suits.

Art Wallace — have changed his name for security reasons tells his story on Page 3 said:

"One theory is that the craft was a military space vehicle returning to earth from a top secret mission but that would hardly explain why Colonel Halt knew nothing of it.

"Last we could see in some strange bluey-white glow, who lives in a cottage nearby.

"Something happened to cause the craft to go back then came down and then we didn't see it come out.

"It was all very strange."

Bestwaters that night and described what he saw—

"We looked up in the sky and saw a red ball of light coming towards us from over the trees.

"There was no noise, no sound at all. We were all mesmerised. All at a sudden the red ball exploded. The place was filled with an explosion of colours, all kinds of colours.

"We were momentarily blinded and when the colours died down there was a machine.

Art said there were beings in the craft, but he could not say what was at the wrong side.

VEHICLE

LOOKING like a giant tortoise, this is airman Art Wallace's drawing of what he saw when the pulsating craft come to earth in the Suffolk countryside

INDEX

219